# Managing Projects
# in Organizations

J. Davidson Frame

# Managing Projects in Organizations

## How to Make the Best Use of Time, Techniques, and People

*Third Edition*

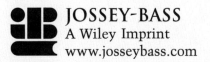

JOSSEY-BASS
A Wiley Imprint
www.josseybass.com

Published by Jossey-Bass
A Wiley Imprint
989 Market Street, San Francisco, CA 94103-1741   www.josseybass.com

Jossey-Bass books and products are available through most bookstores. To contact Jossey-Bass directly call our Customer Care Department within the U.S. at 800-956-7739, outside the U.S. at 317-572-3986, or fax 317-572-4002.

Jossey-Bass also publishes its books in a variety of electronic formats. Some content that appears in print may not be available in electronic books.

**Library of Congress Cataloging-in-Publication Data**

Frame, J. Davidson.
   Managing projects in organizations : how to make the best use of time, techniques, and people / by J. Davidson Frame.—3rd ed.
       p. cm.
Includes bibliographical references and index.
      ISBN 0-7879-6831-5 (alk. paper)
   1. Project management.    I. Title.
      HD69.P75F72   2003
      658.4'04—dc21

                                                                2003014283

Printed in the United States of America
THIRD EDITION
*HB Printing*   10  9  8  7  6  5  4  3  2  1

The Jossey-Bass

Business & Management Series

# Contents

*To Deborah and Sally*

# —ᵥᵥᵥ— Preface

The first edition of *Managing Projects in Organizations* was published in 1987. Its entry into the marketplace at that time was propitious, because it coincided with a surging worldwide interest in project management. From the beginning, book sales were respectable. Quite a few colleges and universities adopted it for use in introductory courses in project management, and training departments in organizations such as AT&T, Fannie Mae, and Freddie Mac distributed it to employees who were studying project management topics.

The second edition was published in 1995. Although the fundamental premises of project management had not changed since the book first came out, new developments in the business arena altered the business environment sufficiently that the book's contents needed to be adjusted to reflect the new conditions. For example, the explosive growth of Total Quality Management in the late 1980s and early 1990s put customers at center stage of all business activity. My copious references to "end users" in the first edition seemed too limiting in the new environment. In the second edition, I broadened my approach to address the concerns of all customers, not just end users.

Time marches on, and it became necessary to issue this newest edition of *Managing Projects in Organizations*. Of particular note has been the growing influence of the Project Management Institute (PMI) as the world's standard-setting body in project management. In 1996 and again in 2000, PMI made revisions to its *A Guide to the Project Management Body of Knowledge*, known best by its acronym, *PMBOK* (PMI, 1996, 2000). In these revisions, PMI took major steps toward updating world standards on project management practice. For example, over the years, there has been substantial confusion about how work breakdown structures (WBSs) should be developed. One approach was to focus on product-oriented WBSs and the other on task-oriented WBSs. PMI finally resolved this issue in 2001 when it published *PMI Practice Standard for Work Breakdown Structures*

(PMI, 2001) and suggested that WBSs could contain both product and task elements.

Another example: Many business enterprises were reluctant to adopt the important earned-value approach to integrated cost and schedule control because they saw this method as too arcane. It originated in the military and employed unfriendly terminology that was difficult to comprehend. Beginning in the mid-1990s and continuing through today, the earned-value community has made some changes to earned-value processes and vocabulary to make this method more accessible to ordinary businesses.

This third edition of *Managing Projects in Organizations* has been updated to accommodate changes in the business environment and project management practices that have arisen since 1995. In addition to the changes already noted, the book has new material on establishing a project office, managing project portfolios, and managing virtual teams.

## INTENDED AUDIENCE

Let the reader beware! *Managing Projects in Organizations* is designed to be an *introduction* to project management. It is written to provide readers with a fairly quick and painless overview of key issues. I recently received a copy of a project management textbook by a prominent author. It is more than one thousand pages long! I suspect that novices would take one look at this book and conclude that project management is an arcane discipline best left to engineers with plenty of technical training. In my opinion, that conclusion would be incorrect.

This book is written for information age workers searching for a way to get a handle on the projects they have been assigned to run. I am talking here about office workers, educators, information systems managers, R&D personnel, lawyers, writers, budgeters, and the vast number of other people whose work causes them to manipulate information rather than tangible things. It is likely that these individuals have drifted into positions of responsibility as a natural outgrowth of their routine activities. By showing some degree of initiative and organizational ability in carrying out their daily tasks, they find one day that they have been given responsibility for carrying out a project.

# PROJECT MANAGEMENT AS THE ACCIDENTAL PROFESSION

Project management has been called the accidental profession. It is accidental in at least two senses. First, until quite recently, it has not been a profession that people have consciously chosen to pursue. No child answers the question, "What do you want to be when you grow up?" with the answer, "Why, a project manager, of course!" People typically become project managers after stumbling onto project management responsibilities.

Project management is an accidental profession in a second sense as well: knowledge of how to run projects often is not acquired through systematic inquiry but is gained in a hit-or-miss fashion. Having received little or no formal preparation for their jobs, typical project managers set out to reinvent the fundamental precepts of project management. Frequently, their trial-and-error efforts result in costly mistakes. If novice project managers are good at their jobs, they chalk up these mistakes to experience and avoid them in the future. After five to ten years of this process, the novice (if he or she has survived this long) graduates to the status of seasoned professional.

Great strides have been made in recent years to reduce the level of accident in our projects. Beginning in the late 1980s, key decision makers in organizations began to realize that the project management approach could offer them significant help in achieving results in chaotic times. To diminish the level of accident in managing projects, organizations began requiring their employees to learn project management skills more systematically.

Today, many companies are working diligently to improve their project management competencies. Interestingly, this new commitment to project management excellence is occurring in a wide array of industries. Some are traditional project-focused industries, such as construction, aerospace, and defense. But most of the commitment seems to be coming from nontraditional information age industries, such as telecommunications, computer systems, banking, insurance, and pharmaceuticals.

Commitment to upgrading project management skills is not solely a North American concern. East Asian, European, Middle Eastern, and Latin American organizations are now putting their employees through project management training programs and encouraging them to become certified Project Management Professionals through the certification program of the Project Management Institute.

## MY EXPERIENCES

I have worked with information age projects all my adult life. As an undergraduate and graduate student, I was immersed in information-based projects for homework assignments, computer programming, term papers, and finally my doctoral dissertation. In industry, I was a full-time project manager for seven years, running about twenty-five archetypical information age projects. Most of them involved the design of scientific research evaluation systems, software development, office automation, and the writing of technical reports. Like 99 percent of my colleagues, I learned project management on the job. In 1979, I left industry for academia, and since then I have been teaching graduate courses on project management.

Since 1983, I have also been conducting seminars on the management of information age projects. About thirty thousand experienced project managers have taken these seminars. My family refers to them as my road show, since they are held in different cities throughout the world. I first took my road show abroad in the summer of 1985, when I carried it to China, where I frequently return with my project management courses. I have also delivered seminars in Hong Kong, Singapore, Taiwan, Thailand, Australia, Argentina, Brazil, Korea, France, Germany, Great Britain, Spain, Finland, Poland, South Africa, and Canada. It is comforting to see that Murphy's Law is as alive abroad as in the United States.

## CONTENTS OF THE BOOK

My experiences as both a practicing project manager and a teacher have led me to conclude that what information age project professionals want and need is a practical and flexible approach to managing their projects. This book is designed to give them such an approach. It recognizes that many of the commonly employed tools used on traditional projects are of limited utility to information age knowledge workers. It shows how the traditional tools, with some modification, can be usefully employed on these projects. It also offers insights into new tools that are emerging and are ideally suited for application on information age projects. Readers interested in a more advanced treatment of project management might want to investigate my recently published work, *The New Project Management* (2002).

The Introduction to *Managing Projects in Organizations* provides a broad overview of what project management is about. It defines terms and describes the stages of the project life cycle. I focus special attention on two key lessons that the book emphasizes: avoiding pitfalls and making things happen.

Part One, encompassing the first three chapters, addresses the overall project context, encompassing people, teams, and the organization. The first two chapters examine projects in their organizational context. Chapter One examines how organizational issues can lead to project success or failure. One of the principal organizational realities that project managers face is lack of authority to control directly the resources necessary for carrying out a project. Another is the central importance of politics in projects. The first chapter offers strategies for coping with these and other realities.

Chapter Two shows how project managers can improve their managerial efficacy by paying more attention to the people involved in projects. The most difficult aspect of project management is the management of human resources. When managers develop a knack for dealing with project staff, bosses, vendors, and fellow managers who control needed resources, they increase immeasurably the likelihood of project success.

The relationship between team structure and effective project management is the topic of Chapter Three. A major goal of good project managers is to fashion effective teams in environments that are inherently inimical to team building. This chapter offers pointers on how managers can improve the chances of a project's success by selecting a team structure that strengthens team efficiency. Special attention is directed to four team structures that seem particularly effective in projects: isomorphic, specialty, egoless, and surgical teams.

Part One thus focuses on projects from the perspective of organizational issues. Part Two, consisting of Chapters Four and Five, casts light on the interrelated topics of needs and requirements analysis. Although everyone acknowledges that cost and schedule overruns are bad, a little reflection suggests that a more serious failing is providing customers with deliverables that are underused, misused, or not used at all. If we define project failure in this way, then it becomes clear that an enormous fraction of the projects undertaken are in some sense failures.

Why are so many project deliverables not well used? Often because customer needs have not been met or the requirements are poorly specified. Chapter Four offers ways to improve identification of customer needs (for example, by building a needs hierarchy), and Chapter Five provides suggestions on defining requirements more effectively (for example, by employing the application prototyping methodology).

Part Three looks at a third pitfall in the management of projects, poor planning and control, and then ties together the many components of project management. Chapter Six describes the standard tools used for enhancing planning and control—for example, work breakdown structures, Gantt charts, precedence diagram method networks, resource loading charts, and resource spreadsheets. Chapter Seven discusses special planning and control topics that are not usually covered in conventional project management texts: planning and control of multiple-project portfolios, very large projects, projects that are carried out under contract, and projects carried out by virtual teams. Planning and control tools that are infrequently discussed—such as the earned-value approach, gap analysis, and the schedule milestone review technique—are also investigated here. Finally, this chapter addresses what became a hot topic in the late 1990s and continues to be important today: how to establish and maintain a project office. Chapter Eight then brings together the different pieces into a cohesive whole.

Good tools make the job of project manager easier, but the tools by themselves will not ensure success—or even mediocre performance. Going beyond a mere litany of project management techniques, this book offers an overall methodology for dealing with information age projects. It emphasizes seeing projects in their organizational context and stresses doing things right at the earliest stages to minimize the inevitable grief of having to do them over again later.

When projects are carried out nicely and chaos is converted into order, project managers justifiably feel as high as kites, denizens of a heaven of sorts that is reserved for the supercompetent. When projects go wrong, they can be like hell on earth. I hope that this book will help project managers affix the wings that will enable them to reach the heights. But as experienced project managers, we are always looking over our shoulders, always aware of the ever-present law of Murphy. Let's aim for the heights ... but remember Icarus, remember Lucifer.

# ACKNOWLEDGMENTS

Writing books is a solitary undertaking, but every now and then, the solitude is punctuated with significant inputs from the outside. Without doubt, the greatest stimulus to my writing comes from my students in academic and corporate classrooms. They apprise me of the latest developments in their organizations, enabling me to gain early insights into issues that enterprises are facing and solutions they are implementing to deal with the issues. They also keep me on my toes as I test new ideas on them. If my ideas are without merit, they let me know, so I find myself continually humbled in the classroom.

Special thanks go to my editor at Jossey-Bass, Kathe Sweeney, who served as a sounding board for my ideas. Finally, thanks to my immediate family, Yanping, Katy, and Lele, who put up with me cheerfully when I get grouchy at the writing table.

*Arlington, Virginia*                                      J. Davidson Frame
*July 2003*

# The Author

*J. Davidson Frame* is academic dean at the University of Management and Technology (UMT), where he runs graduate programs in project management. Prior to joining the UMT faculty in 1998, he was on the faculty of the George Washington University. In that capacity, he established the university's project management program and served as chairman of the Management Science Department and director of the Program on Science, Technology, and Innovation. Since 1990, he has also served as director of the Project Management Certification Program and director of Educational Services at the Project Management Institute. Before entering academia in 1979, he was vice president of Computer Horizons and manager of its Washington, D.C., office. While there, he managed more than two dozen information age projects. Since 1983, he has conducted project management and risk management seminars throughout the United States and abroad. About thirty thousand professionals have attended these seminars.

Frame earned his B.A. at the College of Wooster and his M.A. and Ph.D. in international relations at the American University, focusing primarily on econometrics and economic development. He has written more than forty articles and seven books, including *The New Project Management* (second edition, Jossey-Bass, 2002), *Project Management Competence* (Jossey-Bass, 1999), and *Managing Risk in Organizations* (Jossey-Bass, 2003).

# Managing Projects
# in Organizations

# Understanding the Process of Managing Projects

eople have been undertaking projects since the earliest days of organized human activity. The hunting parties of our prehistoric forebears were projects, for example; they were temporary undertakings directed at the goal of obtaining meat for the community. Large, complex projects have also been with us for a long time. The pyramids, the Great Wall of China, and Hadrian's Wall were projects that, in their time, were of roughly the same dimensions as the Manhattan Project to build an atomic bomb or the Apollo Project to send humans to the moon.

All of us are constantly undertaking projects in our day-to-day lives. Some common examples are preparing for a picnic, repairing a leaky faucet, fixing up the house for Aunt Telia's visit, and writing a term paper for a class. Projects are an integral part of our lives. Typically, we carry out these projects in a haphazard way. We finally get around to fixing the faucet when we can no longer tolerate the din of dripping water, and we begin writing our term paper the day before it is due. We tell a subordinate in an offhand manner to develop a marketing plan, and we are upset with him when the completed plan

1

in no way looks like what we envisioned. We are given money to investigate the physical properties of a new polymer, but we run out of cash before we are even half finished.

We are surrounded by projects, we work on them daily, but rarely do we consciously strive to get a grip on them—to *manage* them. Although people have been carrying out projects for millennia, project management as a unique management form is a recent development. To a large degree, it was a by-product of the major projects of World War II, the best known being the Manhattan Project. A conscious attempt was made to coordinate its enormous budget, schedule, and resource complexity as efficiently as possible. The Manhattan Project moved project management from the realm of the accidental to the domain—at least ideally—of the carefully contrived.

Beginning in the 1990s, project management became a hot management approach. As the U.S. economy entered a postindustrial phase, American managers discovered that many of the management guidelines established for a manufacturing economy no longer served them well in an information economy. In a manufacturing environment, emphasis is placed on predictability and repetitive activities, and to a large extent, management is concerned with standardization and rationalization of production processes. With an information economy, uniqueness of events has replaced repetition. Information itself is dynamic and ever changing. Flexibility is the watchword of the new order, and project management is a key to this flexibility.

## WHAT IS A PROJECT?

We use the term *project* frequently in our daily conversations. A husband, for example, tells his wife, "My main project for this weekend is to straighten out the garage." Going hunting, building pyramids, fixing faucets, and preparing for a picnic share certain features that make them projects:

- They are goal oriented.
- They involve the coordinated undertaking of interrelated activities.
- They are of finite duration, with beginnings and ends.
- They are all, to a degree, unique.

In general, these four characteristics distinguish projects from other undertakings. Each of these characteristics has important implications, so we should examine them closely.

## Goal Orientation

Projects are directed at achieving specific results—that is, they are goal oriented. These goals drive the project, and all planning and implementation efforts are undertaken so as to achieve them.

Projects are permeated with goals from top to bottom. The principal goal of a computer software project may be to develop a sophisticated database management system. An intermediate goal will be to test the evolving system to free it from bugs, and a lower-level goal will be to identify days when project staff are available to attend progress meetings.

The fact that projects are goal oriented carries with it enormous implications for their management. For one thing, it suggests that an important feature of managing projects is to identify relevant goals, starting at the highest level and then working down to the grassroots. It also suggests that a project can be viewed as the pursuit of carefully chosen goals and that progress on the project entails achieving ever higher levels of goals, until finally we have attained the ultimate goal.

Fortunately for those of us concerned with managing projects, a whole methodology has been developed over the past few decades to help us in setting and achieving goals, Management by Objectives (MBO), and its development occurred independently of the growth of project management. A solid grasp of the basic principles of MBO can make a project manager's life easier.

At its heart, MBO is concerned with two things: establishing clear objectives (or goals or requirements or milestones) and making sure that they are achievable. The need for clear objectives cannot be overstated. An objective lacks clarity if, when shown to five people, it is interpreted in multiple ways. Ideally, if an objective is clear, you can show it to five people who, after reviewing it, hold a single view about its meaning.

The best way to make an objective clear is to state it in such a way that it can be verified. This can be done by building in measures in the statement of objectives. Consider, for example, a coach's objective that her star swimmer "swim the pool as fast as possible." That objective is filled with ambiguity. How fast is "as fast as possible"? Which pool should the swimmer swim? What stroke is to be employed? By when should the swimmer be able to achieve the objective? The objective can be strengthened considerably if it is stated as follows: "To be able to swim, by March 15, four laps of the twenty-five-meter pool, using the freestyle stroke, in sixty or fewer seconds." There is still some ambiguity in this objective (Should the pool be filled with water?), but it clarifies the coach's intent quite nicely.

Nevertheless, a clear goal is not enough. It must also be achievable. The coach's goal becomes unachievable, for example, if she changes it to require the swimmer to do the four laps in ten or fewer seconds.

MBO's solution to establishing realistic goals is to have both the people who want the work done and the people who are to do the work develop the goals jointly. Realism is introduced because the people who will do the work have a good sense of what it takes to accomplish a particular job. In addition, this process of goal setting ensures some measure of commitment on all sides. The need for commitment is dramatized at the end of the goal-setting exercise by having both managers and workers sign an MBO "contract," in which management expresses its commitment to supporting the work effort and workers demonstrate their willingness to do the work.

*develop goals jointly

Four decades of experience with MBO suggest a number of pitfalls that must be avoided if it is to be implemented effectively. One common problem is that people get bogged down negotiating objectives. They may spend more time defining what the objectives should be than actually doing their work. Practitioners of MBO must be vigilant in reducing the bureaucratic tendencies of goal setters. Another common problem is that during the negotiation of objectives, management subtly imposes its will on the workers, so that the resulting objectives do not truly reflect the workers' concerns. In this case, MBO can be seen to be a threatening exercise and might be resisted by the workforce.

*can descend into bureaucracy

## Coordinated Undertaking of Interrelated Activities

Projects are inherently complex. They entail carrying out multiple activities that are related to each other in both obvious and subtle ways. Some tasks cannot be executed until other tasks have been completed, some must be carried out in parallel, and so on. Should the tasks get out of sync with each other, the whole project may be jeopardized.

If we reflect on this characteristic of projects, we realize that a project is a system—that is, a whole made up of interrelated parts. Once again, the project manager is in luck: management specialists over the past few decades have developed sophisticated methodologies for dealing with systems. These methodologies taken together are called *systems analysis*. The project manager who has a grasp of the basic principles of systems analysis can use that knowledge to great effect in running projects.

Today, the systems analytical perspective is experiencing a revival in management circles. This revived interest is reflected in the enormous influence exercised by Peter Senge's book *The Fifth Discipline* (1990), which suggests that the systems perspective is important if we are to manage work efforts effectively in a complex world.


## Limited Duration

Projects are undertaken in a finite period of time (although project managers facing schedule slippages may feel they endure an eternity). They are temporary. They have reasonably well-defined beginnings and ends. When the basic project goals are achieved, the project ends. A large part of the project effort is dedicated to ensuring that the project is completed at the appointed time. To do this, schedules are created showing when tasks should begin and end.

Contrast this to typical production runs for successful manufactured products. The product is cranked out indefinitely, depending on how much demand there is for it. When demand disappears, the production run ceases. Production runs are not projects.

While recognizing that projects have defined end dates, we should be aware that the project team's responsibilities extend beyond the handover of the deliverable. To ensure customer satisfaction with their work, the team members should design and build deliverables that are operable and maintainable after they have been delivered. They should also do everything possible to bring about a smooth transition during the handover. From customers' perspectives, the deliverable does not have much value unless they can use it, and the easier it is to do this, the happier they will be.

## Uniqueness

Projects are, to a degree, nonrecurring, one-of-a-kind undertakings, although the extent of uniqueness varies considerably from project to project. If you are an engineer building the fiftieth identical ranch-style unit in a housing tract, the extent of uniqueness is quite low. The basic elements of this house are identical to those in the forty-nine other houses you have built. The principal sources of uniqueness may lie in the special soil conditions surrounding the house, the requirement to install a new model boiler for the first time, the need to work with a new team of carpenters, and so forth.

If, in contrast, you are designing the operating system of a new-generation computer, you are clearly working on a highly unique effort. You are doing something that has not been done before. Because experience offers you little precise guidance on what you can expect in your project, it is filled with risk and uncertainty.

# WHAT IS PROJECT MANAGEMENT?

If you ask seasoned project professionals to describe their most fundamental objective in carrying out a project, you are likely to hear the following response: "To get the job done!" This is the project professional's universal credo. If given a few moments to reflect further on their efforts, they will probably amplify their response: "My most basic objective is to get the job done—on time, within budget, and according to specifications."

These three items are so commonly identified by project professionals as important parameters in the project management process that they have been given a name: the *triple constraint.* They constitute the focal point of the project professional's attention and energy. Project management entails carrying out a project as effectively as possible in respect to the constraints of time, money (and the resources it buys), and specifications.

Over the years, an array of tools has been developed to help project managers to cope with the triple constraint. To deal with the time constraint, project professionals establish deadlines and work with schedules. Some fairly sophisticated computer-assisted scheduling tools—such as PERT/CPM (Program Evaluation and Review Technique/Critical Path Method), GERT (Graphical Evaluation and Review Technique), and VERT (Venture Evaluation and

*constraints —*
*money,*
*time, resources*

Review Technique)—are available to help them manage the time dimension more effectively.

Money constraints are handled with budgets. First, estimates are made as to what the project tasks will cost. Once the project is under way, the budget is monitored to see whether costs are getting out of hand. Money buys resources, and project managers have developed several tools for managing human and material resources—for example, resource loading charts, resource Gantt charts, and linear responsibility charts.

Of the three basic constraints, the most difficult to manage is specifications. Specifications describe what the product of the project effort should look like and what it should do. For example, if we are building a boat, one specification we might have to address is that the boat be 5.23 meters long. If we are designing a purchase order system, we might have to wrestle with a specification that only three days of training are necessary for the people who will use it.

The problem with specifications is that they are notoriously difficult to establish and monitor. For example, it is not enough to have specifications that define a technically masterful product; they must be geared to satisfying customers as well, even if this results in suboptimization of technical performance. We will look at this issue in some detail later in this book (Chapters Four and Five). For the moment, let it be noted that project professionals have been struggling mightily to come up with techniques for developing and monitoring specifications, and they have achieved some notable successes.

## THE PROJECT LIFE CYCLE

Projects have beginnings, middle periods, and endings. This may seem self-evident, but it is not trivial if you are concerned with the management of projects, since where you are in the project life cycle will have a strong bearing on what you should be doing and what options are open to you.

There are many different ways to view the project life cycle. One of the most common has the life cycle broken into four broad phases: project conception, planning, implementation, and termination. In the information sciences, one often-used approach cycle focuses on these six phases: needs recognition, requirements definition, system design, implementation, testing, and maintenance.

*models of project life cycles*

Figure I.1 provides a graphical approach to the project life cycle. It shows that during their lifetimes, projects consume varying levels of

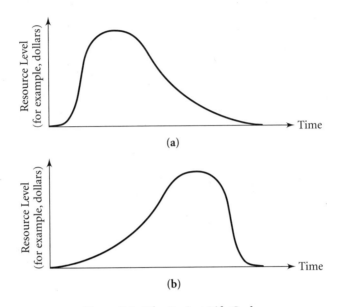

Figure I.1.  The Project Life Cycle.

resources (for example, money, people, materials). In Figure I.1a, the project gears up quickly and then slowly winds down. This could illustrate a typical market research project, where there is a lot of front-end activity such as gathering consumer data through questionnaires and interviews. Once the data are gathered, resource consumption drops off gradually as data are analyzed and findings are written up. In Figure I.1b, there is a gradual buildup of activity until the project peaks and then a rapid end. This often occurs with scientific research projects, where substantial time may be devoted to establishing research hypotheses, designing an experiment, setting up equipment, and so forth. Project activity reaches a peak when the experiment is actually carried out and the resulting data are observed.

Regardless of the specific approach to the life cycle, the main point to bear in mind is that projects are dynamic, continuously evolving organisms.

One approach that usefully illustrates the chief features of the life cycle disaggregates the cycle into six functions that are addressed during the course of a project: project selection, planning, implementation, control, evaluation, and termination. This approach is illustrated in Figure I.2. Let's briefly examine each of the six functions.

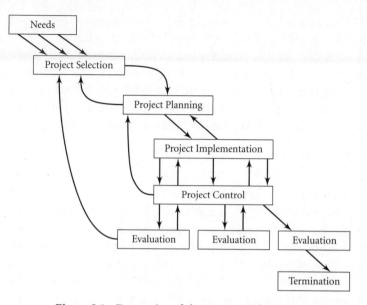

Figure I.2. Dynamics of the Project Life Cycle.

## Project Selection

Projects arise out of needs. The whole project management process begins when someone has a need to be fulfilled. The need may be to reduce the number of forms that patients have to fill out in a hospital admissions procedure, or to develop antisatellite weapons, or to throw a party for Katy's fifth birthday.

Unfortunately, we live in a world of resource scarcity, and we cannot develop projects to address all of our needs. Choices have to be made. With project selection, we make our choices. We select some projects and reject others. Decisions are made on the basis of the resources available to us, how many different needs must be addressed, the cost of fulfilling those needs, and the relative importance of satisfying one set of needs and ignoring others.

Project selection decisions are enormously important, because they make a commitment to the future. They tie up resources, sometimes for just a few days but sometimes for years. They have what economists refer to as *opportunity costs:* by selecting project A and not project B, we are giving up the benefits that project B could have provided.

The project selection process might be triggered by a number of possible factors. For example, the stimulus for the project might come from the external environment in the form of a request for proposal or invitation for bid. In this case, potential clients are soliciting bids to build something or offer some kind of service. Our concern here is whether it is worth our time to respond to the solicitation. Or the stimulus might come internally from management or a task force charged with reengineering corporate processes. Here we have to decide whether we have the resources, will, and capability to pursue a given project.

## Planning

The plan is a road map of how to get from one point to another. Planning is carried out for the duration of a project. At the outset, we typically have an informal *pre*plan—a rough idea of what the project would entail should we support it. These preplans can take different forms. For example, a *proposal* is a preplan of sorts, since it lays out a road map for the project. Similarly, *feasibility studies, business cases,* and *competitive analyses* are preplans of sorts. All of these tools play a role in selecting projects by providing decision makers with an idea of what the project will entail and what its benefits are. The project selection decision is based on these preplans to a large extent.

Once we have decided to support a project, formal detailed planning commences. Project milestones are identified, and tasks and their interdependencies are laid out. A plethora of tools exists to assist the project manager in devising the formal project plan: work breakdown structures, Gantt charts, network diagrams, resource allocation charts, resource loading charts, responsibility charts, cumulative cost distributions, and so forth.

As the project is carried out, the plan may undergo continual modification, reflecting encounters with and responses to unanticipated circumstances. Project plans are rarely static statements of how things should be done; instead, they are dynamic instruments, allowing project staff to manage change in an orderly fashion. In fact, all plans are guesses to some extent. Good plans are good guesses; bad plans are bad guesses. The point is that even with good plans, variance from the plan will occur when the plan comes up against the real world.

## Implementation

Once a formal plan has been devised, we are ready to carry out the project. Military personnel like to call this process *project execution,* but this term has an air of finality about it that may make the typical project manager a little nervous. When you have your head on the block, as many project managers do, you don't want to hear any talk about execution! So I use the term *implementation* here.

In a sense, implementation lies at the heart of a project: it entails doing the things that need to be done, as spelled out in the project plan, in order to produce something to meet the users' needs. Precisely how the project is implemented is dependent on its specific nature. In a construction project, foundations are poured, scaffolding is erected, and so on. In a drug development project, new compounds are tested in a laboratory and then clinically tested. In a market research project, customer attitudes are measured by means of questionnaires and interviews.

## Control

As the project is being implemented, project managers continuously monitor progress. They look at what has been done to date, and they look at the plan; then they determine whether there are major discrepancies between the two. In project management, these discrepancies are called *variances.*

One absolute certainty in project management is that there will be variances. We have not yet mastered forecasting to the point where we have a precise idea of what the future holds, and so long as the future is clouded with uncertainty, project plans will be imperfect. Never forget that the plan is a guess. In controlling a project, then, the question is not, "Do we have variances?" Rather, it is, "Are the variances that we have acceptably small?"

The acceptable levels of variance should be determined at the outset of the project. In a typical construction project, acceptable levels are low, because the building contractor has a good deal of experience in building houses and knows what it takes to do the job. In addition, houses are usually built on a fixed-price basis (that is, the contractors agree ahead of time to sell their services for a given price). If cost variances are too great and they incur major cost overruns, building contractors will lose money on their projects. Consequently, there is great incentive to keep variances low.

In a speculative research project, acceptable variances may be quite high—say, in the range of 20 percent. Because research usually entails substantial uncertainty, the research plan is necessarily crude. We have only the roughest idea of how things will turn out, so we must be willing to accept wide divergences from our initial expectations.

*↓ management*
*by exception -*
*opposite of micromanagement*

This process of establishing tolerable ranges of variance is called *management by exception*. It is the polar opposite of micromanagement. With micromanagement, managers fret over all variances. With management by exception, only variances that appear exceptionally large or otherwise peculiar become matters of concern.

The collection and examination of data on a project's progress lie at the center of the control process. Given this information, project managers have various courses of action they can pursue. For example, if their schedule is slipping unacceptably, they may decide to speed up a number of critical tasks by devoting more resources to them. If they find that for one series of tasks, their staff has spent 40 percent less budget than planned, they will want to investigate this variance, because the underspending suggests that work is not being done or that corners are being cut.

## Evaluation

Throughout its life, a typical project undergoes a variety of evaluations. Examples include technical evaluations such as preliminary design reviews and critical design reviews, personnel appraisals, MBO reviews, audits, and postmortems.

*need evaluation*

Like control, evaluation serves an important feedback function. There are, however, a number of significant differences between evaluation and control:

- Control entails continuous monitoring of project progress, whereas evaluation involves taking stock only periodically.

- Control focuses on the details of what is occurring in the project, whereas evaluation is more concerned with the big picture.

- Control activities are the responsibility of the project manager, whereas evaluations are typically carried out by an individual or group not directly working on the project (so as to maintain objectivity).

These practical distinctions between evaluation and control suggest the following nonrigorous definition of evaluation: evaluation is an objective, periodic stock taking to determine the status of a project in relation to its specified goals.

Evaluations occur in midproject and also at the end of the project. Clearly, the basic role of evaluation is different in these two instances. With midproject evaluation, we can use the results of our findings to affect the future course of the project. In fact, the consequences of midproject evaluation can be dramatic: a premature termination of the project, a reassessment of project goals, or a restructuring of the project plan. A summary of the process and major consequences of midproject evaluation is provided in Figure I.3.

End-of-project evaluation obviously will not have an impact on the future course of the project because the project is now concluded. The fundamental role of evaluation at the end of a project is to offer an exercise in lessons learned. By applying these lessons to other projects, we can beneficially learn from both our mistakes and our successes.

Unfortunately, evaluations are often only marginally effective, because they are perceived to be threatening by those who are being evaluated. In fact, threat is built into evaluation since evaluative efforts are designed to surface problems. The point of the problem focus should not be to identify troublemakers who should be punished but to identify problems while they are still small and manageable, before they grow into monsters that wreak havoc on our best efforts.

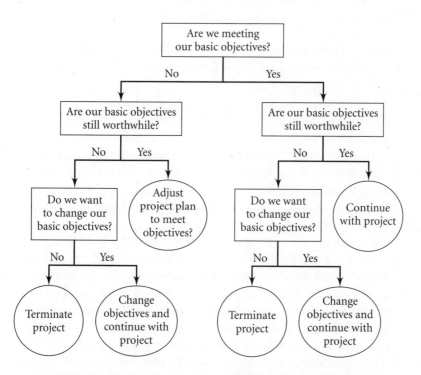

**Figure I.3. Major Consequences of Midproject Evaluation.**

*evaluation feels threatening*

The people being evaluated often have a number of questions that they fear to raise: Who chose the evaluators? Are they competent? What are their marching orders? Are they familiar with the environment in which the project is being carried out? Who will get the evaluators up to speed? For evaluations to be effective, the level of threat inherent in them must be reduced to as great an extent as possible.

## Termination

Projects ultimately come to an end. Sometimes this end is abrupt and premature, as when a project is killed early. The hope, however, is that the project will meet a more natural ending. In any event, when projects end, the project manager's responsibilities continue with assorted wrapping-up duties. The precise nature of these duties is dependent on the character of the project. If equipment was used, this equipment should be accounted for and possibly reassigned to new uses. Similarly, project staff members should be given their new assignments. On contracted projects, a determination must be made as to whether the project deliverables satisfy the contract. Final reports may have to be written. Users should be contacted to determine their satisfaction with the deliverables. And so on.

*tedious wrap-up work*

One big problem in regard to termination is that at this point in the project life cycle, most of the interesting work has been done, and few—if any—engaging challenges remain. In fact, wrap-up work is generally tedious: documentation is rampant (systems documentation, training material, user manuals, budgets), and dozens of annoying problems inevitably arise as a project is being closed out. It is tempting for project staff to drift away in search of more challenging assignments. Consequently, loose ends often are not tied up, leading to postproject problems. For example, equipment may not be assigned to new uses, close-out documentation may not be documented, and final tests on the system may be forgotten.

And then there is the question of maintenance. After a system has been designed and implemented, it must be maintained. Maintenance can take several forms: it may involve debugging problems inherent in the system, making so-called enhancements to the system, integrating the system with other systems, and periodically testing the system to determine whether it is still performing the way it should. Systems maintenance is very important. It is generally acknowledged that the great bulk of the life cycle cost of computer systems is devoted to maintenance.

Although I believe that maintenance is crucially important, I do not include it in the project life cycle for a good reason. Projects are efforts that occur within a finite period of time and have clearly defined beginnings and ends. Maintenance, in contrast, is ongoing and of an indefinite duration. A specific act of maintenance—for example, revision of corporate purchasing guidelines—may be viewed as a project, but it is a separate and distinct undertaking from the initial project that produced the original guidelines.

## PROJECT MANAGEMENT IN THE INFORMATION AGE

Project management has traditionally been carried out in the construction, architecture, and engineering professions, where there has been a need to get a firm handle on large, complex undertakings. Most of the tools used in project management evolved in an environment where men and women build things—and fairly large things at that.

In the past two or three decades, we have been dramatically propelled into an age where people are working less with tangible things and more with intangible information. This is reflected in statistics that show that some four-fifths of the American working population is engaged in service sector jobs, many of which involve the manipulation of information (U.S. Bureau of the Census, 2001).

Because knowledge workers function heavily in the realm of the intangible, the character of their projects is fundamentally different from what one finds in, say, the construction industry. For example, it is often difficult to define precisely what they are supposed to do and how they are to go about doing it. Consequently, many of the project management tools developed for working with tangibles are of marginal use to them.

The archetypical information age project involves computer software development. Systems architects, analysts, programmers, integrators, and testers collaborate to produce instructions that they hope will cause electronic devices to perform miracles. Software development has become very important in our information age economy and will continue to grow in importance. It is interesting to note that software workers over the past one to two decades have created their own approaches to the management of software projects, largely independent of the traditional project management approaches. For example, the well-known structured techniques (structured design, structured programming, structured walkthroughs) owe little debt to traditional project management thinking.

In this book, I take special note of the management requirements of information age projects. These are projects carried out by office workers, educators, information systems managers, R&D personnel, marketers, financial analysts, lawyers, writers, budgeters, and other people whose work causes them to manipulate information rather than tangible things.

My perception is that the fastest-growing area of project management lies in the information area. Although traditional projects in the construction and defense arenas continue to thrive, the real growth is occurring in such areas as finance, marketing, pharmaceuticals, and information systems. This book makes liberal use of cases and examples of information-based projects. I also offer examples from the construction and defense industries, even though this is not an engineering project management book. I typically use these examples to illustrate the contrast between the classical, well-structured project environment and the amorphous, free-flow environment facing today's information age workers.

## KEY LESSONS TO LEARN

A project professional is something like the driver of a car, its windshield spattered with an opaque layer of mud, who is trying to negotiate the vehicle down a steep, twisting road filled with potholes and littered with broken shards of glass, boulders, and patches of treacherous ice. It is a hazardous undertaking.

This book can be viewed as a travel guide written to help project managers negotiate their difficult journey. It is in part a road map, designed to guide project professionals over the twists and turns of the contorted course. A special feature of this road map is that it points out the more salient obstacles that project professionals are likely to encounter on the way. It is also a repair guide, giving project professionals pointers on preventive maintenance (so that they can avoid serious breakdowns), and showing them how to make minor repairs when needed.

Managing projects is difficult. The environment in which projects are carried out is complex. Common wisdom has it that the only certainty governing project performance is Murphy's Law: if something can go wrong, it will go wrong. The inherent difficulty of managing projects is exacerbated by the fact that people typically stumble into project management responsibilities with no systematic training, giving rise to the observation that project management is the accidental profession.

While it is naive to suppose that managing projects can be made easy, it needn't be as difficult as many project managers make it. Effective project management can be learned. There are two fundamental lessons to be mastered, and the primary goal of this book is to convey these two lessons to readers. One is how to identify and avoid some of the common pitfalls encountered in managing projects. With this knowledge, the project professional can avoid the more obvious potholes and obstacles. The second lesson is how to organize and carry out the project for success—how to make things happen. It is not enough simply to avoid problems. The effective project professional must also actively guide the project forward in the most effective manner possible.

## Lesson 1: Avoiding Pitfalls

Things *will* go wrong on projects. Of this you can be sure. Perfectionists running their first project will be plagued with disappointment, for despite their best efforts at planning and controlling project activities, they will find that things never go precisely as expected. If they are hell bent on sticking with their original plan because they believe it is perfect, they will face serious troubles. *must be adaptable*

Project professionals must recognize that problems *will* arise in spite of their best efforts. Much of their effort will be directed to minimizing the negative consequences of these unanticipated problems. Projects are filled with pitfalls, and as we shall see in the following chapters, many are not of the project professional's making. Nevertheless, project professionals must deal with them. If they cannot do so effectively, their projects will fail in some sense: they may face unmanageable budget overruns, damaging schedule slippages, reductions in the quality of the product they are developing, or worse. Effective project professionals must anticipate the pitfalls they will encounter and then figure out ways to avoid them.

There are many ways in which projects can go awry. Generally, though, there are three principal sources of project failure:

- Organizational factors
- Poorly identified customer needs and inadequately specified project requirements
- Poor planning and control

Let's look more closely at each of these factors.

**ORGANIZATIONAL FACTORS.**  It has been said that from an aerodynamic standpoint, the bumblebee should not be able to fly. When we look at the organizational setting in which projects are carried out, we might similarly be tempted to say that it should be impossible to undertake projects effectively.

Most project professionals are aware that many of the problems they face are tied to organizational issues. That is, they sense that arbitrary work rules, micromanagement from the top ranks of the hierarchy, the inability to get the right people for the job, haphazard budgeting, and so forth make a tough job a lot tougher than necessary.

What is interesting is that these project professionals seem to believe that the organizational problems they face are unique to their particular organization. They harbor the notion that things are better outside their particular environment. They do not realize that many of the organizational problems they face are ubiquitous. *These problems are the norm:* the very nature of project management ensures that they will arise.

To illustrate this, consider one common characteristic of project management: project professionals rarely have direct control over much of anything. They are given responsibility to carry out the project (that is, heads will roll if things go wrong), but little or no authority over how things are done.

Let us look for a moment at a project manager responsible for carrying out an office relocation project for a company that will be moving to larger quarters in a newly constructed building in a different city. Who will make up her staff? She may be given a full-time assistant for the duration of the project. Chances are, however, that this assistant will be on temporary loan to her. When the project ends, the assistant will return to regular duties elsewhere in the organization. This project manager may work with an architect for several weeks in order to design the layout of the new facilities, but again, the architect is not her employee. She will also work with an interior decorator who will help her select appropriate furnishings for the new location, with a moving company, with building maintenance personnel, with higher levels of management in her company, and so forth.

For the most part, this is the way things have to be, since it would not be cost-effective to have an architect, interior decorator, and moving company worker permanently assigned to the project. Because of these circumstances, the project manager has little direct authority to impose her will on the individuals working on the project, even though they are vital to its success. If the project is to succeed, it will largely be a consequence of her ability to coordinate and influence the relevant project actors and their willingness to cooperate with her.

The organizational factors discussed here require certain qualities in effective project professionals. These managers should first of all be aware of the limitations of the job: as project professionals, they are essentially coordinators and influencers, not bosses in the conventional sense. They should also have a high frustration quotient, because things will constantly be going awry despite their best efforts to keep them on track.

We have examined only one organizational source of project failure: the divorce of responsibility and authority. There are many additional organizational sources of problems that we examine in Chapters One, Two, and Three. Explicit recognition of these problems and why they arise should greatly help project managers in doing their jobs. If nothing else, it should make them aware that they are not alone in the problems they face and that a number of these problems are not of their making but are organizationally induced. With this knowledge, they can spend less time tilting against organizational windmills and more time working on things over which they have some influence.

INABILITY TO IDENTIFY CUSTOMER NEEDS AND SPECIFY REQUIREMENTS ADEQUATELY. Too often, what customers need is not what they get. This is illustrated in a popular cartoon found on the bulletin boards of many federal workers in Washington, D.C. It shows six pictures of a tree with all sorts of complex and useless paraphernalia hanging from it. Each picture has a different label, such as, "What the planning officer suggested," "What government approved," and "What purchasing ordered." The final picture is of a tree with a child's tire swing hanging from a branch, and it is labeled, "What was actually required."

A project that produces something that is not used or is grossly underused is a failure, even though a product may have been developed on time and within budget. Sadly, this is a common occurrence. The final deliverable does not really address the customers' needs, or it meets with customer resistance, so the customer does not employ it. What the customers need (or want) is not what they get.

There are various reasons that this happens. The deliverable may have been generated in a top-down fashion and therefore reflects top management's view of the customers' needs, as opposed to their actual needs. Or the deliverable may reflect the system designer's opinion of what is best for the customers (that is, the "expert" opinion) without regard for customer sensibilities. Or problems may stem from the fact that the customers do not know what it is they really need.

Frequently, major problems in this vein arise well before the termination of the project. During a midproject review, the customers and the project staff are sometimes at loggerheads because they hold different interpretations of what the project specifications mean. At other times, the project staff find themselves bombarded with customer requests to change different features, with devilish consequences for the project schedule and costs. And so on, and so on.

What we face here are problems that arise out of inadequate definition of customer needs, poorly written project specifications, and midproject changes in these specifications. Inevitably, such problems contribute to cost and schedule overruns. If the deliverable is never used, what results is total project failure. In its projects, the Department of Defense is almost overwhelmed with such problems. We regularly read stories in newspapers about the development of costly weapons systems that don't do the job they were intended to do or about hideous cost overruns and schedule slippages. In reading these stories, we typically attribute the problems to corrupt practices by defense contractors and general government ineptitude. In fact, the major culprits behind these project failures are poor needs recognition and inadequate definition of requirements.

Customer needs and project requirements are issues that all project managers must deal with and are a major source of project failure. Many failures could be avoided if project managers were more sensitive to needs and requirements. In Chapters Four and Five, a number of simple techniques will be offered for defining and monitoring needs and requirements effectively.

POOR PLANNING AND CONTROL.  A poorly planned project will likely run into trouble. Good planning is a necessary, though not sufficient, condition for project success. Similarly, good project controls are important. They allow us to determine whether our plan is being carried out properly, and with this knowledge, we can make the necessary adjustments to our project to keep it on track. A project with poor controls is a project that is out of control.

The importance of planning and control to project success is widely recognized. Planning and control topics constitute the bulk of the project management literature. The tools with which project management is so closely associated—Gantt charts, PERT/CPM charts, resource loading charts—are planning and control instruments.

There is good reason for this attention to planning and control. First, planning and control are palpable activities of honest-to-goodness substance. We plan and control budgets, and because budgets are denominated in dollars, we can measure what we want against what we are actually getting. Similarly, planning and control of schedules permit us to work with another measurable commodity: time. We can measure to ten decimal places the precise time when an activity should commence, and we can measure with equal precision how far off schedule we are. Planning and control also focus on human and material resource allocations, which also are measurable. Because planning and control are amenable to measurement, we can easily develop and use tools to help us in our planning and control efforts.

A second reason for the attention directed at planning and control is that they are so often carried out inadequately. It is common to have budget overruns because no one planned for given contingencies or schedule overruns because no one was keeping track of whether tasks were being completed in a timely fashion.

Of the three principal sources of project failure I have identified here, planning and control are the easiest to deal with because good planning and control practices can be readily conveyed to project managers and staff. Organizations or individual project managers can establish routine planning and control protocols, which, when implemented, will eliminate some of the more egregious planning and control oversights. Planning and control procedures can be computerized and take advantage of the explosive growth of inexpensive, commercially available budgeting, scheduling, and resource allocation software.

Not all planning and control issues have been resolved. One question that frequently arises is, "How much planning and control should we undertake?" This question underscores a number of trade-offs associated with planning and control. For example, we can have overplanning and overcontrol that stifle creativity and reasonable project modifications. On the one hand, we may harm a project by excessive planning and control; on the other hand, the project may fail owing to a lack of plans and tracking mechanisms.

Chapters Six and Seven address frequently encountered planning and control problems and offer techniques for dealing with them.

## Lesson 2: Making Things Happen

Several years ago, after I had finished a planning and control presentation before a group of corporate project managers, one of the attendees approached me in the parking lot. He told me that he had found my presentation interesting, but he had not learned anything new. He already knew about the techniques I described, he said, and in fact, he religiously employed them in his projects. He also offered that he was pretty good at circumventing some of the more obvious project management pitfalls. However, despite the fact that he was pushing the right buttons and pulling the right levers, his project performance was lackluster; he feared that he would soon be removed from project management responsibilities if things did not improve. "Why," he asked, "can't I seem to make things happen in my projects?"

I spent only a few minutes with the fellow—just enough time to deduce that he wasn't very articulate, was clumsy in his human interaction, and was excessively didactic. Though he made an effort to ask me my opinion of what his problem was, he was not really interested in hearing my views; he interrupted or contradicted me every time I uttered five words. No doubt he *was* following the book in how he ran his projects. If my experience with him was at all typical of his dealings with people, however, there was no great mystery about why he was not effective in getting work done.

The effective project professional has mastered the important lesson of avoiding pitfalls. However, this is not enough. To be truly effective, the project professional must also be able to guide the project forward proactively in the best manner possible—to make things happen.

This is easier said than done. To a large extent, project guidance has something to do with leadership and all that it implies. A large body of literature has been written on leadership, some of it scientific but most of it anecdotal and inspirational. It also has something to do with the concept of entrepreneurship, since the chief trait of an entrepreneur is the ability to make things happen. To muddy the waters further, it also has something to do with politics, where politics is defined as *the ability to influence others.* Because project managers have little direct control over anything, to get things done they must be effective in influencing others to do their bidding—that is, they must be good politicians.

# PART ONE

# The Project Context

## People, Teams, and the Organization

# CHAPTER ONE

# Operating Within the Realities of Organizational Life

S everal years ago, I was sitting in a hotel lobby with four experienced project managers, idling away the time by swapping stories about project management experiences. One manager made a remark that clearly struck a responsive chord in the others: "I spend a lot of time fantasizing about how much I could get done on my projects if one day my company and its budget officers and upper-level managers and purchasing agents and lawyers all went *poof!*—evaporated into the stratosphere." His three colleagues vigorously nodded their heads in approval. If this comment were made before an audience of one thousand project managers, I think that you would find most of them nodding their heads in approval also. There is a strong consensus among project managers that projects would be better undertaken outside the usual organizational environments.

It is easy to sympathize with this view. However, it is unrealistic. Projects occur in organizations. To design and manage projects out of their organizational context is similar to designing machinery for a frictionless world. In both cases, we have something that looks good on paper but will not work very well in the real world.

Chapters One, Two, and Three look at project management from an organizational perspective. They show that to study projects out of the context of their organizational setting is a fruitless undertaking.

In this chapter, we focus on organizational realities and how to work effectively *with* them, as opposed to struggling *against* them. As an introduction to these realities, consider the hypothetical case of Jerry Wallenstein and his first hands-on encounter with project management and organizational realities. The experiences Jerry faces are common to inexperienced project professionals, This case, which follows Jerry from the first to the last day of his project, shows that things can easily get out of hand even when project staff do their best.

### THE EDUCATION OF JERRY

Jerry was delighted when he was made manager of a project to explore the possibility of integrating his company's purchase order processes into the supply chain management (SCM) system his company, Globus Enterprises, was developing. The SCM project was the largest that Globus had ever implemented. The order processing subproject was one component of the larger SCM project.

Once developed, the SCM system would enable Globus to establish seamless connections with its vendors. Although Globus already incorporated computers in its order processing system, the bulk of transactions entailed manual interventions. This caused the order fulfillment function to operate slowly and led to errors because the manual interventions were error prone. With the new SCM system, customers would enter orders using the Internet. Once captured by the SCM system, the orders would be processed entirely by the computer.

This project provided Jerry with his first real management experience. He had received his M.B.A. degree directly after finishing college and then was hired right out of business school by Globus Enterprises, where he spent two years as special assistant to Max Weiner, vice president of operations. The job gave him plenty of exposure to high-level decision making, but was somewhat frustrating because he was a spectator in the decision-making process, not a performer. Now, with the order processing subproject, he could do something tangible and have real responsibilities.

Jerry put together a list titled "Things to Do." At the very top of the list was the item "Assemble Project Staff." He approached his boss, Max, and asked how big a staff he would have and who would be on it. "Use anyone you need," Max responded. "The important thing is to give me a report on your findings within a month. Your preliminary investigation will give us an idea of how we should go about computerizing the order processing function at Globus, and we need that information in time for our next quarterly executive meeting."

Jerry determined that to do a good job on his project, he needed the following people: a secretary, an assistant, a logistics expert, an Internet expert, an accountant, and a representative from each of the company's five divisions. He reckoned that he, the secretary, and an assistant would be the only full-time workers on the project. Nonetheless, the other members of the project team would have to make a fairly substantial commitment to the project if it was to be completed in a month; each would have to dedicate about 25 percent of his or her time to the project.

According to Jerry's plan, the five divisional representatives would each write a section of the study, detailing the impacts of the order processing system on their operations and defining whatever order processing needs they have. His assistant would write the technical portions of the report. Jerry's chief function would be to coordinate the efforts of the others and to integrate all the pieces into a cohesive whole.

As Jerry started to put his team together, he immediately ran into trouble: he was unable to get a secretary assigned full time to the project. Because his division was in the midst of a reorganization, all secretarial staff were already overcommitted. When Jerry went to Max with his problem, Max nodded sympathetically and told him that he would just have to make do with whomever was available on a given day.

Jerry's luck in obtaining a full-time assistant was a little better—or so it seemed at first. After spending half a day trying to find someone who was free to work on the project, he came across the name of Bob Roulette, who worked in the contracts and procurement department. Bob, it was reported, was two months from retirement, so his workload was being reduced. A one-month assignment would dovetail nicely with the plans to ease him into retirement.

The easiest team member to recruit was the Internet specialist. Jerry approached the information resource management chief (IRM is located in the information technology division) and told him of his need for an Internet expert. The IRM chief immediately assigned Margaret Block to help Jerry with Internet matters. Unfortunately, the company had little practical experience with e-commerce systems, so Jerry was told that he would have to go to an outside consultant for the e-commerce expertise he might need.

Jerry met with varying degrees of success in recruiting representatives from the different divisions. He had a good reception from the finance division; the vice president of finance, Mary Garrett, announced that it was about time Globus Enterprises entered into the twenty-first century and said she would be glad to assign someone from her office to help Jerry on the project. In contrast, his reception at the information technology (IT) division could not have been cooler. His request for assistance from the division's vice president, Sam Ruff, was met with an uncomfortably long silence. Finally, Sam said, "I don't fully understand why you and Max are playing the lead role on something like this. Building an order processing system is basically an information technology chore and should be left to the IT experts. As it turns out, I've had a couple of our people looking into the matter of automating the order processing system for several months." He dismissed Jerry without promising cooperation and said something vague about having to "look into things personally."

Jerry was unnerved by his encounter with the IT vice president. Until now, all of his experiences at Globus had been quite friendly. He was still brooding about his meeting with Sam when he was accosted outside his office by Bob Roulette, his new assistant on the project.

"Listen, Jerry," Bob said. "As you know, I'll be retiring in just under two months. I'd like to help you on this project of yours, but let me say that I really don't know anything about computers or order processing. To tell you the truth, I hate computers and think order processing is horridly dull. Frankly, I think somebody did both of us a dirty trick putting me on this project. I'll gladly work with you, but don't expect too much from me."

All these things happened by the third day of the project, a Thursday. To get the project moving quickly, Jerry tried to arrange a kickoff meeting of all project staff for nine o'clock the following Monday morning. Sam Ruff's office (IT) still had not assigned a representative, so it would not be represented at the meeting. The finance division representative said he thought it was a great idea to get moving so quickly, but unfortunately he would be out of town throughout the week. The other project staff members said that they would attend the meeting, but they sounded less than eager. The only individual who sounded interested in the meeting was Margaret Block, the Internet expert. Jerry wasn't sure what he would do about getting an e-commerce expert. He would talk to Max Weiner about it next week.

Jerry spent all day Friday, Saturday, and Sunday preparing for the meeting. He put together a five-page preliminary position paper, identified milestones the team members would have to meet, created guidelines for the activities to be undertaken, and read several journal articles on Internet technology. On Monday, at nine o'clock, Jerry arrived at the conference room and found it empty. By nine-thirty, only two other project team members had shown up. Conspicuously absent were his assistant, Bob Roulette, and Margaret Block.

When a much-discouraged Jerry returned to his office, he found a message asking him to call Margaret. He called her. She apologized for missing the meeting and explained that her boss in the information resource management department (part of the IT division) had told her that he was pulling her off the project. She wasn't sure why.

At one-thirty, Max Weiner called Jerry into his office to tell him that he was putting the order processing automation project on hold. "All hell's broken loose," he explained. "Sam went to the big guy and complained that you and I, a couple of amateurs, were running amok, doing things we had no business doing. Sorry, Jerry. You win some and lose some. Next time we'll do better, right?"

"Sure," said Jerry in a daze. He didn't really understand what all this meant. All he could think of was that someone had told the company CEO that he, Jerry, was some kind of amateur. Jerry wondered about his future at Globus.

## ORGANIZATIONAL REALITY: THE DIVORCE OF RESPONSIBILITY AND AUTHORITY

Although most of our first experiences with project management are—I hope—not as traumatic as Jerry's, his experiences at Globus illustrate a number of traits common to the great majority of projects. One of the most obvious is that Jerry was given responsibility for getting the job done, but he had very little authority to see to it that his decisions were implemented. This was reflected in his problems in recruiting project team members and evidenced in the fact that he could exercise only marginal control over Bob Roulette, his assistant and the only other full-time team member.

This feature of Jerry's story—the divorce of responsibility and authority—is the rule in project management. Project professionals have little authority to carry out their work. They have little or no direct control over the people and things that make the difference between project success and failure. Their staff generally are on temporary loan to them. The people who make decisions on whether these staff members get promoted, get a pay raise, or get tuition paid for graduate course work—that is, their true bosses, and thus the people who really count—work elsewhere. Similarly, the material resources they need on their projects—work stations, mass spectrometers, bulldozers—are usually controlled by others and must be borrowed.

"Well, then," an observer of this plight might say, "it seems that this problem can be easily addressed. Let's give the project professional authority over all resources—material and human—employed on the project." This is easier said than done and, in most cases, bad management. It is not an accident that project professionals have so little direct control over anything. It stems from the very nature of projects, as well as organizational requirements that resources be not squandered but used efficiently. To see this, we need merely reflect on several features of the basic definition of projects that was posited in the Introduction. Consider the following:

• *Projects are temporary.* Projects occur in a finite period of time: minutes, hours, days, weeks, months, or years. Jerry's project was supposed to last one month. Generally, the organization in which they are carried out existed before their beginning and endures after their end. For that reason, it is often difficult on economic grounds to justify assigning staff and material resources to the project on a full-time basis.

• *Projects are unique.* Projects are one-of-a-kind undertakings. At Globus Enterprises, feasibility studies of order processing systems are not a daily occurrence. Projects are structured to address momentary needs.

• *Projects are systems.* Projects are composed of different pieces linked together in intricate ways. People with specialized skills often work on the individual pieces. On the order processing automation project, the team was structured in such a way that most of the members would bring their own specialized skills to the project (for example, knowledge of the Internet, knowledge of the workings of the finance division, typing skills). Often, though, the skills are so specialized that they are employed only briefly. It is not at all uncommon to have the composition of the project team continually changing as the project progresses through its life cycle. The person who can be usefully employed full time on a project is the exception rather than the rule.

*requires stuff & resources to be borrowed but not permanent*

The very nature of projects requires that human and material resources be borrowed rather than permanently assigned to the undertaking. As long as project professionals are dealing with borrowed resources, they have limited control over them. This reality overwhelmed Jerry in the one week that he was "managing" his project. The narrative is full of instances in which he is incapable of getting people to do what he needs to have done. He cannot get a secretary assigned full time to his project. His full-time assistant makes it clear that he is just treading water until his retirement, and he doesn't even show up for the important kickoff meeting. Jerry finds a cooperative and competent colleague in Margaret Block, the Internet expert, but owing to the political dynamics of the situation, she is pulled off the project by her boss. Because Globus does not have an e-commerce expert, Jerry will have to obtain the necessary expertise from an outside consultant, over whom he may or may not be able to exercise some degree of control.

From Jerry's perspective, the problem is that *he is not the boss,* although he is project manager of the order processing automation feasibility study. It would be understandable if, after spending hours mulling over his first project debacle, he had concluded that he could have been successful on the project if only Max Weiner had made him a boss—someone who could exercise clear and unambiguous authority over the resources he needed to employ in his work. While understandable, this would be a naive conclusion. It would suggest that Jerry did not learn much from his unpleasant project experience. To be boss, he would have to possess control over the career development of all the personnel working on the project—in view of the nature of his small project, highly impractical.

One final word on Jerry's unfortunate adventure: a substantial share of his problems is rooted in his inexperience. For example, he does nothing to strengthen his authority. Rather than go out on his own in dealing with people in other departments at Globus, he should have worked through his vice president, Max Weiner. He could have drafted a memo, signed by Max, that explained the purpose of his inquiries. In this way, he would not look like a loose cannon. It is particularly bothersome that Jerry dealt directly with vice presidents in the company. For all the talk we hear of flattened organizations, business entities remain hierarchical and do not countenance junior employees' initiating important meetings with senior managers in other departments. It really is not surprising that the information technology vice president saw Jerry's actions as an infringement on his territory.

## NURTURING AUTHORITY

If project professionals lack authority and this presents a problem for them, why don't they create and nurture it? Successful project professionals do exactly that. They emphasize their strengths and use these strengths to build a base of authority.

Authority is the capacity to get people to take us seriously and to do our bidding. In the old days, kings had authority based on their power, which was embodied in their troops. When the powerful king issued a command, wise citizens listened and obeyed. A doctor's authority lies in a knowledge of medicine that allows him or her to heal patients. People certainly take their doctors seriously; they generally follow the regime suggested and swallow the pills prescribed without questioning the wisdom of such behavior.

One of the most common authoritarian characters in our everyday lives is the police officer, an individual whose very survival in some communities depends on the ability to project an image of authority. In fact, when a community is in the throes of lawlessness and rioting, we often ascribe this situation to "a breakdown of authority."

Advertising specialists recognize that an important consequence of authority is that people do the bidding of those who possess it. Thus, we find sober men and women in medical garb—looking every bit like everyone's image of the family physician—hawking all manner of medication on television, from allergy medicine to analgesics.

If project professionals want people to take them seriously and to do their bidding, they have to create and nurture a base of authority. Here we look at five kinds of authority that they can focus on. The first three are all derived from the specific organizational circumstances in which they arise: formal, purse string, and bureaucratic. They are rooted in the specific organizational setting in which project professionals find themselves. The two other kinds of authority, technical and charismatic, are personal. They are intrinsically tied to the project professional's personality and achievements.

## Formal Authority

All project professionals possess some degree of formal authority to carry out their work. This formal authority is automatically conferred on them as soon as they are appointed to the project. The appointment itself suggests that an organization's leaders have confidence that a particular individual can carry out a project, and this further suggests that he or she has backing from above, no matter how tenuous.

If the formal authority that project professionals possess is no more than a vague sense that someone has confidence in their abilities, that authority will not be very helpful in getting others to do their bidding. If, in contrast, the corporate CEO makes a big show of appointing the project professional and makes it clear to everyone that the new appointee has the CEO's fullest backing, people in the organization will be readier to take note of the project professional's wishes. In this instance, the formal authority can be translated into real operational authority. The project professional has acquired *borrowed* authority.

Most project professionals do not receive the kind of clear-cut upper management backing that will make whatever formal authority they have very meaningful. Usually, the little formal authority they have is not enough to offset other forces that keep them from exercising direct control over people and material resources.

Preferences for and dependence on formal authority are common among inexperienced, insecure, and unimaginative project professionals. What they find most appealing about it is that authority is conferred on them; they don't have to work at developing it. Unfortunately for them, the authority they derive in this way is often more apparent than real.

## Purse-String Authority

If project professionals have some budgetary discretion and use it effectively, they can exercise authority of the purse strings. Clearly, this kind of authority is effective only in dealing with individuals who are affected by a project professional's budgetary actions. It is particularly useful in dealing with outside vendors and contractors, whose livelihood depends on payment for goods and services delivered.

The power of purse-string authority can lie in both the offering of a carrot and the wielding of a stick. Promises of future business or the payment of an incentive bonus for work done ahead of schedule may encourage outside vendors and contractors to do a good job. Threats of withholding payment for poor work may stimulate lackadaisical vendors to improve their performance; however, by the time it becomes obvious that a stick is necessary, poor schedule, cost, or quality performance may have already seriously jeopardized the project.

A problem that project professionals face is that typically they do not have much control over budgets. However, if they use their imagination, they may still be able to employ purse-string authority through their control of nonmonetary resources. For example, they have some measure of control over people's time: they can determine who gets the good assignments and who gets the dog work. They may also determine who gets the new equipment or occupies the most desirable office space.

### Bureaucratic Authority

History is filled with examples of individuals who attained power in their organizations through the quiet mastery of bureaucratic skills. This is summarized in a comment made by Lyndon Johnson, one of the most effective American politicians of the twentieth century: "Learn how the system works so that you can work the system." The colorless Joseph Stalin is a case in point. In vivid contrast to Lenin's charisma-based authority, Stalin's authority lay in his capacity to manipulate the Communist party and government bureaucracies to do his bidding. He focused on the smallest details of personnel assignments and was a master of organization charts.

To project professionals with good bureaucratic skills, the organization is not an obstacle. In fact, knowledge of the organization and the rules that make it tick is a positive blessing. Bureaucratic managers do not struggle against the organizational current; rather, they go with the flow. Their authority is based precisely on an understanding of the importance of filling out the paperwork properly, meeting seemingly arbitrary due dates for project status reports, and knowing the details of the organization's procurement procedures.

### Technical Authority

Technical workers typically have a high degree of respect for technical competence. Often they judge the value of other workers according to their technical capabilities. In a laboratory environment, for example, a researcher may hold a fellow scientist in low esteem because he or she "hasn't published anything worth a damn in five years."

The emphasis that technical workers place on technical capabilities often causes them to resent management's authority over them. I have heard many researchers in laboratories complain about working for bosses who "aren't all that sharp technically." One scientist I know quit his job on this account and set up his own company, vowing that he'd never again work for someone who wasn't smarter than he. For an employee who measures a person's worth according to whether he or she understands quantum mechanics, working for a boss who never went beyond first-year calculus may be a bitter pill to swallow.

In our society, we tend to have a high regard for people of technical or intellectual accomplishment. Consider the public's adoration of past men and women of great intellectual accomplishment, such as Thomas Edison, Marie Curie, and Albert Einstein. On a more mundane level, we are in awe of the wizards of our own organizations: the people who can program computer code ten times faster than the norm, or who are masters of the intricacies of the tax code, or who have managed to secure two patents annually over the past fifteen years. When these people speak, we listen. If they make a request of us, it is an honor to oblige them.

Project professionals who possess technical authority can use this authority to great effect. They can get people to do their bidding not because they control salaries or prospects for promotion but simply because people respect their technical competence.

Lack of technical competence may preclude an individual from managing technical projects. On projects that require the project professional to carry out technical tasks—a common arrangement in, for example, small software development projects—this is understandable. But frequently a technical background is required of project professionals even when they do not carry out technical duties. In part, the rationale here is that only a technically trained individual can appreciate the technical nature of the problems faced by the project staff. Perhaps more significant is the feeling that nontechnical managers lack credibility with the project staff and will not be taken seriously by them. That is, nontechnical managers lack the technical *authority* to manage the project.

## Charismatic Authority

Project professionals who possess charismatic authority are able to get others to listen to them and do their bidding through the force of their personality. The principal appeal of such authority is that it is "portable"; it can be carried from project to project and from organization to organization. If properly developed, it can be employed by the project professional to gain some influence over the many actors in the project environment who can make the difference between project success and failure.

Charismatic authority is rooted in a number of different traits. The charismatic manager often possesses a sense of mission, has a good sense of humor, is empathetic to staff needs, is enthusiastic, and is self-confident. The charismatic manager is a *leader*.

## The Importance of Multiple Forms of Authority

It should be clear by now that project professionals who do not possess formal or purse-string or bureaucratic or technical or charismatic authority are in trouble. Actually, if they possess only one of these forms of authority, they probably are still in trouble. For example, if a project professional has only charismatic authority, staff may initially enjoy his management style but ultimately may perceive him as all form and no substance. If his bureaucratic skills are not well honed, he may miss crucial deadlines for filling out nuisance forms. And so on.

In general, project professionals should develop and nurture at least two forms of authority; three is even better. The importance of authority is that it gives project professionals some leverage over the many other actors in the project environment. Without such leverage, project professionals are not really in control of their project.

## THE FULL PROJECT ENVIRONMENT

Jerry's dismal experience has given us only a small glimpse of the project environment. It is something like looking through a keyhole into a room. With some effort, we are able to discern a chair here and a lamp there, but at best we have only a vague idea of the full layout of the room.

A view of the full project environment reveals a situation that, from a management point of view, is extremely complex. Figure 1.1 portrays the full project environment from a Ptolemaic point of view: the

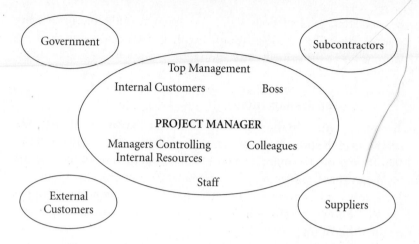

Figure 1.1. The Project Manager's Operating Environment.

project manager stands at the center of things. Of course, this is a distorted view. In truth, project managers must cope with a Copernican reality: like the earth, they are but a small speck off in a corner of their galaxy.

A survey of this figure confronts us with a couple of interesting facts. First, the sheer number of actors that project managers must deal with ensures that they will have a complex job guiding their project through its life cycle; problems with any of these actors can derail the project. For example, suppliers who are late in delivering crucial parts may blow the project schedule. To compound the problem, project managers generally have little or no direct control over any of these actors.

The figure also shows that project managers often have to deal with the environment external to the organization, as well as with the internal environment. What we have here is a complex management milieu—certainly more complex than what a manager in a retail store or a manufacturing environment faces.

In dealing with human relations on projects, books and courses usually focus on project managers' relationships with their staff. These relationships certainly are important and warrant close scrutiny. It should be noted, however, that relations with the other actors identified in Figure 1.1 are also important, because problems with any one of them can jeopardize the project. On a more positive note, it might be added that good relations with any of them can aid project managers tremendously. Let us look in some depth at these actors and their relationships to the project professional.

## Top Management

Top management in the organization may or may not be directly involved with the project. Large projects are highly visible, and it is likely that their project managers will have direct interaction with top management. IBM's launching of the personal computer in the 1980s and Steve Jobs's ongoing support of new-generation computers at Apple are well-known examples of projects that receive constant top management scrutiny.

Obviously, managing a high-visibility project has both advantages and drawbacks. On the plus side, the highly visible project is more likely to have top management support, which means that it will be easier to recruit the best staff to carry out the project and acquire needed material resources. This visibility can also significantly boost the project manager's professional standing within the organization.

On the minus side, any failure will be quite dramatic and visible to all. Furthermore, if the project is a large and expensive one (and highly visible projects usually are), the cost of failure will be more substantial than for a smaller, less visible project.

Another negative feature of highly visible projects is that top management may find the temptation to meddle in them irresistible, leading to micromanagement. Micromanagement by top management puts project managers in an awkward position. It takes strong, self-confident, and brave project managers to resist the intense second guessing of their efforts by the organization's top brass.

With low-visibility projects, direct top management involvement is unlikely. Nevertheless, top management can still have a major impact on how the project is carried out, because it sets the tone for the whole organization. For example, if top management establishes an atmosphere of free and open communication in the organization, project managers and their staff are more likely to be honest in reporting successes and failures. If top management creates an atmosphere in which failure is not tolerated, it is likely that project managers and their staff will be less than honest in reporting progress (or lack of it).

## Boss

Today, the concept of "boss" is being reassessed. As modern organizations move away from traditional chain-of-command structures and drift toward team-focused structures, the issue of who reports to whom becomes quite clouded. Although we have clearly moved away from autocratic models of supervisors who possess absolute authority over their workers, bosses have not become extinct. They still exist and still must be dealt with. The importance of the boss to project professionals is obvious, since the boss plays a significant role in creating the daily working environment and is instrumental in determining the project manager's career prospects within the organization.

Our boss can make life in the organization reasonably comfortable or painful. Typically, the boss decides what our assignment is and who can work with us on our project. If things go wrong on our project (and they probably will), it is nice to have an understanding and supportive boss who will go to bat for us if necessary. If, on the contrary, the boss pounces on us at the first sign of trouble or disowns us, our lives can be very uncomfortable.

## Colleagues

Fellow project managers and other peers in the organization can be friends or foes, or—quite commonly—a little bit of both. They can be friends in at least two senses. First, they can be useful resources, providing a project manager with important information or human or material assistance. Second, they can serve as helpful allies in getting things done within the organization. For example, whereas individual project managers may not have enough clout to get their company to purchase what they perceive to be a necessary piece of equipment, in concert with their colleagues they may possess sufficient collective influence to release funds for the purchase.

Colleagues can also be foes. An obvious source of conflict between colleagues is resource scarcity. It is not uncommon for project managers to find themselves competing against their fellows to get good staff or necessary equipment. If this competition is undertaken in a friendly spirit, it need not get out of hand. Colleagues may also be foes in the sense that they are competitors for career advancement. This last point can be particularly poignant in this era of downsized and flattened organizations.

## Staff

I have noted that the staff whom project managers have available to them are usually borrowed rather than assigned to the project on a permanent, full-time basis. Recognizing this fact, project-oriented organizations occasionally organize themselves into a matrix structure.

A pure matrix structure is pictured in Figure 1.2. Running along the horizontal axis are the functional groups that serve as resource repositories. The engineering department is filled with a wide assortment of engineers, the data processing department is peopled with programmers and analysts, the finance department is filled with accountants and financial experts, and so on. On the left side of the matrix, along the vertical axis, are the individual projects that present specific resource needs. Project A, for example, has a need for engineers and data processors. When this need ends, they return to their respective functional groups, where they are available for work on other projects.

The matrix structure formally incorporates what I have noted several times: because of the temporary, unique, and complex character of projects, it makes more sense to have a project borrow resources on

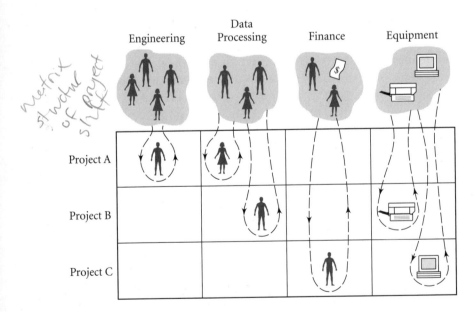

Figure 1.2. Matrix Structure.

an as-needed basis than to assign resources full time to the project throughout its duration.

Today, there are two driving forces behind matrix management. One is that when it functions properly, it leads to the efficient employment of resources. If I need editors for only two days on a three-week project, why should I hire them for three weeks? With the matrix, we use resources as we need them, and when we are done with them, we send them home to their functional areas.

A second force behind matrix management is that it allows for cross-functional solutions to problems. Today's complex problems require inputs from a broad range of players. For example, to increase the likelihood of customer satisfaction, a software development team should contain members who are aware of business concerns as well as technical issues.

Although the matrix approach may reduce resource inefficiencies and encourage cross-functional problem solving, it also is the primary source of the project managers' chief complaint: that they have little control over the resources they need, since these resources are only on loan to them and owe allegiance elsewhere—usually to their functional groups and their functional group manager.

## Managers Controlling Internal Resources

One special category of colleague that is particularly important to a project professional is other managers who control needed resources. Because project managers are typically in a position of borrowing resources, their relations with the people controlling these resources are especially important. If their relations are good, they may be able consistently to acquire the best staff and the best equipment for their projects. If relations are not so good, they may find themselves unable to get the people and material resources necessary to get the job done properly.

## Internal Customers

Projects may be undertaken to satisfy the needs of internal or external customers. Internal customers are individuals within the organization who have particular needs that will be addressed with an internally executed project. Data processing department projects, for example, are usually carried out to meet internal demands. Perhaps the data processing department wants to upgrade the corporate accounts receivable system or help an office in its automation effort.

## External Customers

External customers are individuals and organizations in the external environment. Projects can address their needs in two ways. In the first, a project may focus on developing a product or process that will eventually be marketed to outside consumers. In this case, there is no guarantee that the consumer will want to buy the product or process, so the project faces the serious risk that it might fail in the marketplace. Project managers may be ever conscious of producing something that will succeed in the market. If they are developing an important new product, it may be especially crucial that they complete their project in a timely fashion; if they do not, the product may lose its competitive edge. The business press is filled with stories of companies announcing the forthcoming introduction of a new product and then being embarrassed when the product hits the market several months behind schedule.

Projects also address external customer needs through contracts (see Chapter Seven for more details). The government, for example, commonly funds contractors to carry out desired projects. Here project managers have a clear idea of who the customers are; given this knowledge, they are obliged to maintain good communications with customers, to make sure that they are indeed meeting the customer needs.

This is easier said than done. As we shall see in Chapters Four and Five, customers often do not have a precise idea of what they want. Consequently, their needs tend to change as the project evolves and they gain a better appreciation of precisely what the project is developing. In such circumstances, project managers must balance their desire to satisfy customers with knowledge that constant changes to the project will lead to time and cost overruns.

## Government

Most project managers do not have to deal with government in their projects unless they are government contractors, in which case the government is their customer. However, those working in certain heavily regulated environments—for example, in the pharmaceutical,

pesticide, or banking industries—must be fully conversant with government regulations that bear on their projects. Not only do they face
the problems common to all other project managers, but they must
work under additional stringent regulatory constraints as well.

## Subcontractors

There are times when organizations do not have sufficient skills or capabilities to undertake all project tasks themselves. This is often true
of large, complex projects and of construction projects in general.
Under these circumstances, work is farmed out to subcontractors.
Project managers working with subcontractors must keep close tabs
on their performance, since the success of the project will depend in
part on their work.

Any number of problems can arise with subcontractors. The quality of their work may be substandard, or they may run into cost overruns, or they may face schedule slippages. Keeping tabs on them is not
easy, since they operate outside the project professional's immediate
organizational environment. It is hard enough trying to keep tabs on
individuals one encounters on a daily basis within the organization;
keeping tabs on outsiders is even more difficult.

In working with subcontractors, the project manager should have
substantial knowledge of the provisions in the contract with the subcontractor, as well as a rudimentary knowledge of contract law.

## Suppliers

Many projects are heavily dependent on goods provided by outside
suppliers. This is true, for example, of construction projects, where
lumber, nails, brick, and mortar come from outside suppliers. If the
supplied goods are delivered late or are in short supply or are of poor
quality, or if the price at delivery is higher than the quoted price, the
project may suffer seriously. Many construction projects are thrown
off schedule because required materials do not arrive on time, or because the delivered goods are of such poor quality that the delivery
has to be rejected.

Reliable suppliers are important to successful project management.
The Japanese have long recognized this in the manufacturing sector.
Major Japanese corporations dedicate a good deal of attention to their
relationships with suppliers, and the famed just-in-time system, in

which supplies arrive at the plant the day they are to be used, has been an important factor in Japan's phenomenal success at producing high-quality goods at a low price.

Project managers have so many balls to juggle that they are often tempted to downplay potential supplier problems in order to focus their attention on other crucial actors. "These suppliers are professionals, and I will assume that they will behave in a professional manner," they say to themselves. The project manager who operates on this assumption, and consequently pays little attention to possible supplier problems, may be in for a number of nasty surprises.

## THE POLITICS OF PROJECTS

Politics is the art of influence. The fundamental job of candidates running for public office is to influence a majority of the electorate to vote for them. This is what the speeches, the kissing of babies, and the paid political advertisements are all about. Once in office, the politicians are busy influencing other politicians to back them on legislative proposals, position themselves to be appointed the chair of important committees, and release funds for projects that will enrich their constituencies. The purpose of all this effort is to influence the electorate to vote for them again in the next election. This ability to influence others to do one's bidding is a politician's most important asset.

With rare exceptions, politicians are not inherently powerful people. Generally, they do not have large sums of money that they can use as an instrument of power. They do not flex large biceps to intimidate people into doing what they want. They do not possess invaluable knowledge of the secrets of nature that gives them a hold over others. The power they possess is rooted in their ability to influence others. When they lose this ability, they no longer function effectively as politicians. Even the seemingly omnipotent—such as Winston Churchill during World War II—fall quickly when they can no longer exert sufficient influence over their fellows.

Project managers are something like politicians. Typically, they are not inherently powerful, capable of imposing their will directly on coworkers, subcontractors, and suppliers. Like politicians, if they are to get their way, they have to exercise influence effectively over others. We saw previously in this chapter that one way to get others to do one's bidding is to create and nurture authority. But politicians need more than the simple possession of authority; they also need to possess a keen understanding of the overall environment in which this authority is to be exercised. They need to be realists.

Block (1983) defines a process that good project politicians follow. It is reduced here to six steps:

1. Assess the environment.
2. Identify the goals of the principal actors.
3. Assess your own capabilities.
4. Define the problem.
5. Develop solutions.
6. Test and refine the solutions.

The first four steps are designed to help the project professional acquire a realistic view of what is happening. Most project professionals, when tackling a project, skip over those steps and immediately begin offering solutions to problems. They are not good project politicians.

Because all projects involve politics and these politics often have an important bearing on whether projects proceed smoothly or roughly, it is worthwhile to examine these six steps in some detail.

## Step 1: Assess the Environment

The most important elements in the environment are the other actors involved either directly or indirectly with a project. In assessing the environment, the project professional should try to identify all the relevant actors. This is harder to do than it may seem at first blush.

Consider, for example, a project to introduce a new accounting system into an office. Good project management practice suggests beginning with an analysis of the needs of the users of the accounting system. Who are the users? An obvious set of users are accountants who maintain the company's books and the finance experts who use the accounting data to carry out financial analyses of the company's business performance. Another important set of users are all managers who engage in any sort of financial transactions. Their principal need is for an accounting system that generates reports with the information they require to do their job. For example, department heads need data on expenditures incurred by their departments, and the payments office requires information on accounts receivable. Clerical personnel who input data into the accounting system are a type of user as well. Their principal need is for a system that accepts data readily and is easy to use.

Beyond these obvious users are additional stakeholders that need to be considered. Because implementing an accounting system requires substantial cooperation from the IT department, the views of IT personnel about approaches to implementing the accounting system should be solicited. Their chief concern is that the system that is implemented makes technical sense. The executive committee of senior managers comprises important stakeholders. They want to be sure that the accounting system that is adopted serves the organization's overall needs. A stakeholder we often overlook who has a role to play on many projects is the purchasing department. If we plan to purchase goods and services in the course of the project, we better consult with the folks in the purchasing department, because they have a set of procedures that we need to follow; if we ignore them, we may not get the goods and services we need in a timely fashion.

Once the relevant actors have been identified, we try to determine where the power lies. In the vast cast of characters we confront, who counts most? Whose actions will have the greatest impact?

## Step 2: Identify Goals

After determining who the actors are, we should identify their goals. What is it that drives them? What is each after? In examining their goals, we should not shy away from speculating about psychological motivations, since these may be more powerful than purely work-related motivations.

We should, of course, pay attention to stated goals. However, we should also be aware of the hidden agenda, that is, goals that are not openly articulated. In the example of updating the computerized accounting system, one overt goal of the project sponsor might be to increase productivity and accuracy of financial data; a hidden goal might be to be recognized as the foremost guru who promotes best practices in the organization. To satisfy both the overt and hidden goals, the project professional should consider purchasing high-quality accounting software that also has a nifty look to it.

In dealing with both overt and hidden goals, we should focus special attention on the goals of the actors who hold the power. By knowing who holds the power and recognizing their overt and hidden goals, we reduce the likelihood of making gaffes that upset those people whose actions have great impact. Furthermore, we can use our knowledge in a positive way to determine how we can influence these people to help us achieve our project goals.

## Step 3: Assess Your Own Capabilities

Know thyself. Project professionals should have a good idea of their strengths and weaknesses and should be able to determine how those traits bear on the project. Self-assessment is a crucial step in developing a realistic outlook on the project and its environment. If project managers have a distorted view of their own capabilities, the project is likely to run into trouble.

Particularly important capabilities are the abilities to work well with others and to communicate well. Project professionals who are basically inarticulate should not offer to make weekly progress presentations to higher management, since these presentations will only highlight their poor ability to communicate. If weekly management reviews are necessary, inarticulate managers should rely heavily on articulate staff members.

In assessing their own capabilities, project professionals should also be sensitive to their personal values. To a large extent, our own value systems define who we are. They are the perceptual filters that determine how we view the world and offer us guidance on how to behave.

Project professionals are not automatons emerging from a common template. Their decisions are governed by their value systems. Some project professionals may see their project as one small element in their broader life, whereas others may subordinate everything to the project. Operationally, the first will be less willing to put in overtime on weekends, while the second may eat, sleep, and drink project efforts round the clock. Project professionals who are sensitive to their personal values will avoid situations that generate value conflicts, or, if these conflicts are unavoidable, they will at least understand the sources of the conflicts.

## Step 4: Define the Problem  *Takes the next time*

Only now, after project professionals are thoroughly familiar with their project environments and their own capabilities, are they ready to intelligently define the problems facing them. The problem definition effort should be systematic and analytical. The facts that constitute the problem should be isolated and closely examined. The basic assumptions underlying the approach to defining the problem should be understood.

Over and over again, the following question should be raised: "What is the *real* situation?" Project professionals who take this approach are unlikely to define the problem according to superficial realities.

## Step 5: Develop Solutions

Too often, project staff begin the whole process at this step. They start offering solutions before they fully understand the problem. With such an approach, the solutions they offer are not very useful.

If instead they can exercise self-control and refrain from offering premature solutions while they carry out the first four steps, the ultimate solutions they develop will have the important advantage of being realistic and relevant to the *real* problem that must be addressed. Consequently, they diminish the likelihood of project failure—that is, of producing deliverables that are rejected, underused, or misused by customers.

## Step 6: Test and Refine the Solutions

The solutions devised in step 6 will be rough, requiring further refinement. Solutions must be continuously tested and refined. If project staff have done the proper spadework with the first five steps, this last step should involve no major rework effort, but rather should focus on putting the finishing touches on intelligently developed, realistic solutions.

## Using the Steps to Develop Superior Solutions

There is nothing novel about these six steps. They incorporate a good commonsense outlook. The most remarkable thing about them is that they are rarely followed, even after project management staff have acknowledged their importance.

I have conducted about fifty nonscientific experiments on my project management students to see how they tackle problem solving. I give a group of students a case study that describes a typical situation and requires them to offer management advice on how the organization should proceed. I have *never* had a group that systematically attempted to identify the full roster of actors affected by the project, or a group that consciously took account of the actors' motivations, or a group that spent any time trying to uncover the hidden agenda implicit in the project situation. Rather, what they typically do is to immediately begin offering solutions to the problem as stated in its most superficial form. It is usually apparent that these early solutions are woefully inadequate, so the groups spend most of their time refining and reworking their original efforts. Generally, the problem they are working on remains superficially articulated, a one-dimensional solution in a three-dimensional world.

After the students have finished with their exercise, I point out that they have ignored the fundamental precepts of developing deep, rich, and realistic solutions to problems. I give them a new case study and explicitly ask them to employ the six-step methodology discussed here. The resulting solutions are vastly superior to the earlier ones. The solutions now take into account a broader array of actors, hidden agendas, and personal values; consequently, they are more viable than their one-dimensional counterparts.

## CONCLUSION

Projects are carried out in organizations, and a thorough understanding of their organizational context is necessary for project success. This obvious point is easy to lose sight of as project managers wrestle with the intricacies of PERT/CPM charts, resource loading charts, and budgets. Too often, we confuse the management of projects with mastery of the well-known budgeting and scheduling techniques that have been developed as project management tools. The tools are easy to learn. An understanding of organizational intricacies is not. The most effective project managers are those who are as skilled at understanding the organization in which they work as they are proficient in using the basic scheduling and budgeting tools.

# CHAPTER TWO

# Finding and Working with Capable People

In this chapter, we look at the role of people in projects. First, we focus on a number of broad "people" issues that are pertinent to projects. Who makes decisions? What do we look for in our project staff? What can we do to cope with chronic shortages of personnel to help us get our projects completed?

We then examine a valuable tool that can help us improve our insights into what makes us, our staff, our boss, our vendors, and our clients tick: the Myers-Briggs Type Indicator, based on the work of psychoanalyst Carl Jung. It helps us avoid putting square pegs in round holes and enables us to understand that conflict is rooted, to a large extent, in differences in the ways that people perceive and judge the world around them.

In the third section of the chapter, we turn our attention to the project manager. We know that project managers are concerned with getting the job done—on time, within budget, and according to specifications. But what other responsibilities do they have? What management styles do they practice, and under what circumstances?

## GENERAL ISSUES

Project managers, like people who fish or play the ponies, enjoy telling others the secrets of their effectiveness. One of the most successful project managers I know, formerly vice president of operations of a Fortune 500 firm, is particularly proud of his ability to pick good people for his projects. "You know, good people are the scarcest resource on a project," he says. "The way I find the best people is to look for the busiest people. During my twenty-five years as a project manager, I always selected for my projects the busiest people I could find. I stayed away from those people who were readily available."

The point this man makes is that the best project staff are heavily in demand. They are kept busy because everyone wants to use them. What is especially interesting is that although impossible demands are placed on their time, these people figure out ways to get the job done. Sometimes it seems as if the more work you pile on them, the better they do. Available people, in contrast, make this vice president nervous. "Why are they so available?" he asks. "Is there a reason why no one is using them?"

People are a project's most important asset. Whether a project succeeds or fails will likely be determined by the caliber of the people working on it. Unfortunately, this is often forgotten by many of us who write project management textbooks and offer project management seminars. Rather than focus on people, we focus on techniques. We spend most of our time teaching approaches to selecting projects, networking project tasks, and estimating costs.

There is a good reason for this preoccupation with technique: it is readily teachable. As an educator, I like teaching techniques, because in a matter of a few hours, I can show students how to master PERT/CPM scheduling; what's more, I can determine through tests whether they have learned their lessons well. Students conspire with instructors in this little game, because they want tangible benefits from their studies—palpable evidence that their time was well spent.

The focus on technique distorts our view of what happens on projects. For the most part, projects do not fail because people do not know how to employ advanced project scheduling and budgeting techniques. I have never heard of a project failing because a PERT/CPM network crashed. However, I have heard of many projects becoming unglued because top management issued unrealistic directives to project staff, or the skills level of project staff was inappropriate to project needs, or lack of leadership led to aimlessness in project implementation.

It is widely recognized today that people are the key to an organization's success. This is reflected in the large-scale abandonment of the impersonal hierarchies that so dominated the management scene from the onset of the industrial revolution. Today, the talk is of empowered employees, flattened organizations, and team management. Whereas not long ago, the conventional wisdom held that management's job was to direct and control, today's conventional wisdom is that management's key function is to support—to create an environment that enables the workforce to do the best job possible. Two forces have led to this situation: the obsession with customer satisfaction and the growing complexity of the world.

The focus on customer satisfaction is one of the most significant developments in the history of management. Although lip-service has long been paid to customer satisfaction (witness the age-old marketing adage, "The customer is always right"), it was only in the 1980s that businesses and governments began to recognize that customer happiness is the key to survival. The quality assurance craze of the 1980s, accompanied by the near deification of quality gurus such as W. Edwards Deming, Joseph M. Juran, Philip B. Crosby, and Kaouru Ishigawa, was early evidence of the new power of customers.

As organizations frantically strove to gain customer approval, customers' expectations of what they deserved began to rise. Organizations that could not meet these expectations fell to the side. Those that could thrived.

It quickly became apparent that traditional top-down hierarchical structures were not able to meet customer expectations. For example, decision making in hierarchical structures tends to be slow, yet customers were demanding rapid responses to their requests. It was obvious that rapid response meant that the lower-level people who worked with customers had to be empowered to make decisions on the spot. In this case, the move toward worker empowerment was not driven by humane concerns but rather by a desire to generate quick responses to customer requests.

The high level of complexity associated with today's world also contributed to the requirement that managers *support* their workers rather than *direct* them. In this complex world, no one person possesses the wisdom to address adequately the issues that need to be resolved. Even Solomon would have to ponder carefully before pronouncing judgment on the most basic issues facing today's workforce. This complexity requires that decisions be achieved through cross-functional teams that possess the collective knowledge needed to make decisions on nontrivial issues. In this situation, the manager's job is to create an environment where cross-functional team members can achieve an efficient consensus on what course of action should be pursued.

Traditional project management has been top-down, particularly in the construction industry. On routine construction projects, where building plans have been worked out to the last detail, a fairly substantial degree of top-down management can be tolerated. If building codes say that studs must be set eighteen inches apart, we do not want our carpenter, in an outburst of creative expression, setting them thirty inches apart. However, for information age projects that are less predictable, decision making must be distributed throughout the project team. There is too much specialization, complexity, and uncertainty for management to serve as an all-knowing decision maker. With information-based projects, knowledge workers are hired because of their special skills and knowledge; in order to apply their expertise effectively, they must be able to make independent decisions.

## WHO'S IN CHARGE HERE?

One of the hard-to-answer questions that arise frequently in projects is, "Who's in charge here, anyway?" Decision making in projects is often very diffuse, as is illustrated in the following case.

### VIDEOGRAPHICS, INC.

Videographics is a small company that produces industrial training videotapes and films. Its marketing department has identified a strong demand for fire prevention training videotapes. The head of marketing prepares a two-page document in which she broadly describes the nature of the perceived demand and the potential size of the market. She brings her document before Videographics' executive committee, comprising the company president, the head of operations, the chief financial officer, and herself. Together, they estimate the cost of undertaking the new videotaping venture, compute financial returns, and weigh the contribution of a fire prevention training tape to the company's position in the video training market.

The committee decides to proceed with the venture and authorizes a $90,000 project budget. It charges the head of marketing with putting together a project plan. Before the project can go full steam ahead, the plan must be approved by the executive committee. Within two weeks, the marketing department puts together a project plan, in conjunction with the production department and the executive committee. It is approved with minor modifications.

Emily Ando, who has an excellent track record in producing successful training tapes, is selected as project manager and given six months in which to complete the project. She is asked to present detailed progress reports to the executive committee at the end of the second, fourth, and sixth months. Ando puts together a core project team comprising two script writers and a videotape production specialist. In due course, the writers produce a script, and the production specialist works out the technical details of filming the production. Five actors are hired to play the principal roles written into the script. Meanwhile, the marketing department is putting together promotional material and targeting likely customers.

At the first and second progress report meetings, the executive committee suggests some major changes in the production, and these are adopted. Ando completes the project according to plan, and one month later, Videographics launches an intensive effort to sell the new videotape.

The Videographics case illustrates something that is common to many projects: important decisions are made by many different individuals throughout the project. The decision to explore the possibility of launching a project is made by the marketing department in this case. The decision to launch the project is made collectively by the executive committee. Planning decisions are made jointly by the marketing and production departments. Decisions on coordinating project efforts during the implementation stage are made by the project manager. Detailed decisions on how the script should be formulated and how production should be carried out are made by the script writers and production specialist, respectively. Course correction decisions are made by the executive committee members during the scheduled project review sessions. In answer to the question "Who's in charge?" I am not being frivolous by answering, "To a certain extent, *everyone's* in charge."

The dispersion of decision making throughout the project structure can, of course, lead to confusion and conflict. This was graphically illustrated in the tragic explosion of the space shuttle *Challenger* in early 1986. Investigations of the accident made it clear that many people inside and outside the National Aeronautics and Space Administration (NASA) made decisions that ultimately contributed to the disaster. There was no single culprit. Had the space shuttle project been organized in such a way that decision making was more unified, perhaps the *Challenger* disaster could have been averted. Nevertheless, it is not at all clear that a more unified decision-making approach is viable with a project of such complexity. A more unified approach would no doubt have given rise to other problems (for example, micromanagement) and probably would have increased overall project costs dramatically. Decision making is distributed throughout projects because projects are too complex to be dealt with in a rigid hierarchical fashion with a clear-cut chain of command.

Once again, we see, as we did in the previous chapter, that project managers are not bosses in the conventional sense. In part, this condition is a reflection of the organizational realities covered in Chapter One. Project managers typically do not have staff over whom they have direct control, for example.

In the Videographics example, we see that project managers are not bosses in another sense as well: they are not top-down decision makers, the final arbiters in all important project decisions. Typically, they are excluded from some of the crucial decisions made at the outset of a project that set the tone for how things will be carried out. For example, they may not be involved in project selection or planning decisions. Once the project is under way, they often have to defer to judgments made by others—sometimes because the realities of project politics take decisions out of their hands, often because the novelty and complexity of the project require them to depend heavily on the expertise of their colleagues.

This last point is illustrated in Figure 2.1, which shows that project managers are often practitioners of management by exception. With this approach, staff are given wide latitude in making decisions, so long as the individual decisions do not have a major impact on budget, schedule, and resource use, and do not lead to major political problems. Only when it is obvious that the project is substantially off target does the project manager become directly involved in decision making.

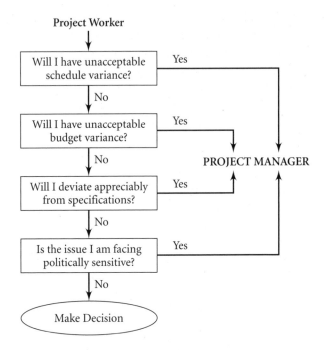

Figure 2.1.  Management by Exception.

## The Perfect Project Staff Member

Let us use our imagination for a moment and conjure up an image of Charles, the perfect project staff member. What is it about Charles that puts him in such heavy demand in his organization?

First, and perhaps most important, Charles is thoroughly committed to the projects he works on. He will do whatever is necessary to get the job done. This means that you can call him during his son's birthday party, and he will willingly drop everything to help you out. It also means that he will gladly work eighty-hour weeks, even though he is on salary and is being paid a flat rate for a forty-hour week. What's more, if there is a project emergency and the secretary is out sick, he will type and photocopy his material himself and will personally deliver it to the client.

Second, Charles is intelligent and possesses a strong share of common sense. He readily comprehends his assignments and follows instructions carefully. When unanticipated events arise, he is not afraid to deal with them. By the same token, he knows his limitations and does not rush in where angels fear to tread.

Finally, Charles is competent technically. He knows his subject matter well, and when the project manager gives him a task to carry out, she is assured that it will be done efficiently and competently.

In sum, Charles makes his manager's life easier. Because she can count on him to help her out and do a good job, he is freeing her to focus on potential problems that may jeopardize the success of the project.

For many of us, Charles is pure fiction. I know a number of project managers who believe that they are more likely to encounter the tooth fairy than a staff member like Charles. The trait that makes Charles particularly rare is the first one: strong commitment to the project.

The scarcity of project commitment has two roots, one organizational and the other psychosocial. We deal first with the organizational issue.

ORGANIZATIONAL PERSPECTIVE. The matrix structure found in many organizations discourages strong staff commitment to individual projects. With a matrix system, project staff are drawn out of functional departments and assigned to projects on an as-needed basis. They are temporary visitors who stay with a project long enough to carry out their technical tasks; when the tasks are completed, they leave. In addition, they may be applying their expertise to several projects simultaneously, further attenuating their commitment to any single project.

The reward system in a matrix structure does not encourage project staff to put in long hours on projects. Why should they work extra hours for an undertaking in which they have no personal stake? What will their extra effort earn them other than a pat on the head and a nice letter of thanks written by the project manager and sent to their functional boss?

Under these organizationally rooted circumstances, it is hardly surprising to encounter a reluctance on the part of project staff to commit extra time to projects.

PSYCHOSOCIAL PERSPECTIVE. I am going to offer a simple observation here, which for all of its obviousness is surprisingly difficult to drive home: *there is life outside the office.* Many hard-driving managers resist this idea mightily.

Typical project workers are not one-dimensional characters whose lives are completely governed by their jobs. Work is generally only one feature of their life environment. They have families and friends and a personal set of values that colors their outlook. When they arrive at work, they do not check these nonwork elements at the front door.

Our values strongly affect how we carry out our work. If in our hearts we believe that hard work will invariably pay off, we may be willing to put in eighty-hour weeks for our project. If, in contrast, we hold the view that we live only once and that the world is meant to be experienced and enjoyed, we may cherish our time away from the office, especially weekends, holidays, and vacations. If we feel that people should be dealt with forthrightly, we may not have the stomach for the political machinations that projects often involve us in.

The point here is a very simple one that is often overlooked: people working on projects are multidimensional. If project managers do not take this into account and instead treat people as if their jobs were the only thing that mattered, they face two consequences: first, they will be continually disappointed in their staff, because they will not live up to these unrealistic expectations; second, they may find that the only people who truly fit into their setting are one-dimensional people. Good people are hard to find. Why narrow the choice only to those prospects who are one-dimensional?

## Rules for Working Smart

For better or for worse, projects managers are not going to encounter many perfect staff members like Charles. We live in an imperfect world; rather than rue its imperfections, let us recognize that our time is better spent trying to determine how to use the imperfect resources we have as effectively as possible.

Most project managers focus their efforts on identifying ways to get their staff to work harder. They rack their brains devising carrots to motivate people and sticks to prod them on. If they could, they would measure the number of calories people expend on the job—the more calories burned, the better, because calories burned mean hard work.

Such efforts are largely misdirected. For one thing, if project staff do not have a strong commitment to a project, carrots and sticks will not be very effective in getting them to work harder. For another, staff typically are not fully productive on projects, so the issue is not how to get workers to work harder—that is, to prolong the time during which they are ineffectively applying themselves to tasks—but, rather, how to get them to work smarter.

Our efforts should be directed at increasing the productivity of the resources we have. There are several rules that should be followed to help us work smarter.

DO THINGS RIGHT THE FIRST TIME. Project managers should strive to make sure that staff members do things right the first time, a sentiment captured in the adage, "Measure twice, cut once." Studies of manufacturing operations show that reworking defective parts is far more expensive than producing them correctly in the first place. This also holds true for project work. If it takes people two or three tries before they carry out their tasks properly, enormous amounts of project energy are being wasted. The solution is not to extend the workers' work week by forty hours but to identify ways to get people to do things correctly the first time.

For example, you may find that your staff are not following your directions properly, and rework is common. The problem here is likely rooted in miscommunication. For whatever reason, your staff do not fully understand what is expected of them, so they produce results that have only marginal bearing on the true project requirements.

As project manager, you can take steps to reduce such miscommunication. You can explain project requirements carefully to the staff, give them time to reflect on these requirements (two or three days), and then, when they think they understand them, have them repeat their understanding of the requirements to you. You will probably be surprised at the discrepancy between what *you* thought you communicated to them and what *they* thought you communicated.

The problem of miscommunication is so prevalent in projects that throughout this book, I offer several different strategies for dealing with it. (See especially Chapters Four and Five.)

SET REALISTIC GOALS. If your project is based on a set of unrealistic expectations, you are guaranteed to have insufficient resources to get the job done according to plan. This means that you will be pressured to convince staff to put in extra hours on the job. Yet, as we have just seen, if—for organizational or psychosocial reasons—people have a low commitment to the project, they will be reluctant to work late at night and into the weekend for you. Furthermore, to the degree that they realize that the need for overtime work is a consequence of bad planning, they will resent your requests for help.

The solution to this problem is simple—at least in theory: plan realistically. Set realistic goals for project staff. Don't put yourself into the position of depending on people you don't have: perfect project staff members who will do whatever is necessary to get the job done. With realistic planning and goal setting, there is less need to have people work overtime, so there is less need to have superdedicated workers on your project.

The chief drawback to this solution is that project managers often have little input into the planning process. Plans are often drawn up before a project manager is assigned to the project. When the project manager finds that the plan is woefully optimistic, he or she might try to renegotiate the plan to make it more realistic. Should this approach fail, the project manager can expect to face pressures to get staff to put in overtime hours on the project.

GET TECHNICALLY COMPETENT PEOPLE.  There are dramatic variations in people's abilities to carry out different kinds of tasks. We have all encountered writers who can write two or three times more polished text than the norm. In software projects, a superprogrammer may be able to generate ten times as much good code in an hour as the average programmer can. The obvious lesson here is to employ highly competent people on projects.

I recall clearly the most trouble-free year I had as a manager of a portfolio of several projects. In that year, I was blessed with several staff members who were exceptionally competent technically. My project plans were based on the assumption that I would have average workers helping me. What a delight to find that many of the scheduled tasks were being completed in half the planned time. Because the staff had time to spare, they were able to help out less fortunate project workers in other parts of the organization. There wasn't much need for overtime work that year, and the quality of our output was the best ever.

Often productivity on tasks is low not because we lack supermen and superwomen but because the workers carrying out the tasks are not technically competent. I regularly come across office automation projects on which project staff have not received training on information systems. Typically, one or two staff members rush around grabbing any literature they encounter that discusses office technology. They are amateurs and, in spite of their efforts, obviously do not know what they are doing. In the end, they spend great amounts of time miseducating themselves on office automation issues and then blindly make important decisions based on highly imperfect knowledge. What they do poorly over a long period of time could have been done far better by an expert in a fraction of the time.

"We're doing the best we can with what we've got. We don't have any technically competent experts on our staff," is a common comment. In such a case, it is usually worth the price to hire an outside consultant. The cost of a competent consultant is generally far less than the price paid for poor work produced by highly paid amateurs.

## PSYCHOLOGICAL TYPES

Over the years, psychologists and management specialists have developed an array of tests designed to help us better understand why people behave the way they do. The popularity of these tests is based on the insights they give managers on the roots of conflict, human motivation, and human productivity. They are used for many different purposes—for example, hiring new workers, assigning people to job slots compatible with their personalities, determining special competencies, weeding out workers with obsolete skills, and helping people gain greater self-awareness.

One such test, the Thomas-Kilmann Conflict Mode Instrument, measures how much people display competing, collaborating, compromising, avoiding, and accommodating behavior in conflict situations. The T-P (Task-People) Leadership Questionnaire examines the extent to which individuals focus on tasks versus people in work situations. The FIRO-B Awareness Scale examines people along three dimensions: inclusion ("Do you desire strongly to be included in group activities? Do you like to include others?"), control ("Do you prefer being in situations that are well under control? Do you feel a strong need to take control of situations?"), and affection ("Is it important to you to be liked? Do you express affection toward others?").

These tests are not a panacea for resolving organizational difficulties. In fact, there is always a danger that they will be misused. However, when the tests are employed properly, the useful insights they offer managers can be substantial.

Possibly the most useful test for project managers is the Myers-Briggs Type Indicator, and that is the test we will examine here in detail. What is appealing about the Myers-Briggs approach is that it is grounded in solid Jungian theory, has been subjected to extensive empirical testing, is easy to understand, and lends itself nicely to project situations.

## The Myers-Briggs Approach

People do not behave in uniform ways. They do not possess uniform aspirations. They react differently to different stimuli. In short, people are behaviorally unique. Nevertheless, despite their uniqueness, we can make rough generalizations about them, and from these generalizations we can better understand what motivates them and makes them tick. Some people are aggressive, some passive. Some work well with others, some don't. Some are curious, some aren't.

Carl Jung, the famous Swiss psychoanalyst, was interested in categorizing people into what he called *psychological types.* In 1923, he published a work describing those types. His work dovetails nicely with research later performed by Katharine C. Briggs, who took Jung's theory and melded it with her ideas. Ultimately, Briggs's effort was refined by her daughter, Isabel Briggs Myers. The final result is the Myers-Briggs Type Indicator, which is operationalized in a number of psychological tests designed to determine one's psychological type.

The Myers-Briggs approach categorizes people according to where they lie on four scales, each scale reflecting a different dimension of human behavior: extravert-introvert, sensing-intuitive, thinking-feeling, and judging-perceiving. These four scales give rise to sixteen possible psychological pigeonholes that people can be placed into. For example, you might be an extraverted, intuitive, thinking, perceiving type (characteristic of innovators) or an introverted, sensing, thinking, judging type (characteristic of administrators).

Each psychological type has a number of well-documented behavioral traits associated with it. If we know someone's type, we can quickly develop a good idea of how that person will behave in different circumstances. Such information can be useful for project managers, who typically deal with many different people in different kinds of circumstances and can use guidelines on understanding what makes these people tick.

I will briefly outline the rudiments of the Myers-Briggs approach but skip over the theory behind it. Though it won't be covered here, the theory—incorporating the views of Jung, Briggs, and Myers—is rich, interesting, and worth investigating. (For a highly readable and informative explanation of psychological types, see Keirsey, 1998.)

**THE EXTRAVERT-INTROVERT DIMENSION.** An extravert, in the Myers-Briggs schema, is someone who is oriented toward the outer world of people and things, whereas an introvert is oriented more toward the inner world of concepts and ideas. Because they are attuned to what is going on around them, extraverts tend to be practical. They also like to deal with several things at once—to walk and chew gum at the same time, as it were. Introverts, being inner directed, mull over ideas and live mostly inside their skulls. They tend to be deeper thinkers than extraverts.

Things get interesting from a managerial point of view when you put an extravert and an introvert together in close quarters. Here is what might happen. The extravert has problems coping with the introvert, whom he perceives to be slow, impractical, and positively Teutonic in his dealings with the world. He is particularly irked by the introvert's insistence on tackling only one problem at a time and then pursuing a solution to the problem over a seeming eternity. The introvert, he concludes, is a Johnny-one-note. He doesn't seem to be very bright either.

Meanwhile, the introvert has problems coping with the extravert, whom he perceives to be rather superficial—a jack of all trades and master of none, an individual with no depth. The extravert's instant analyses of problems and his insistence on jumping from topic to topic are especially irritating. Overall, he doesn't seem to be very bright to the introvert.

This scenario shows that two competent individuals of equal intelligence can develop unflattering opinions of each other's abilities *simply because of differences in their orientations to the world.* This circumstance has practical implications for project managers.

Consider, for example, the extraverted project manager in charge of running a state-of-the-art software development project. Her technical staff are likely to be introverts who, because of their introversion, are not fully sympathetic with or responsive to external realities such as task deadline dates. She should recognize that their cavalier attitude toward deadlines is a consequence of their introversion rather than a conscious effort on their part to make her life difficult or an indication that they are disorganized. She should also recognize that from the staff's viewpoint, her extraversion may make her appear overly concerned with what they see as the superficial aspects of the project, such as deadline dates, and insufficiently interested in the content of the project.

Armed with these insights, she can deal with her staff more intelligently than if she based her actions on her gut response to their seeming intransigence. She should recognize that her introverted staff are not stubborn and irresponsible. To the extent that they may see her intrusions as reflecting superficial thinking, she might explain to them how missing deadline dates might trigger contract penalties, and certainly will result in customer unhappiness. Also, she should avoid hovering over the staff members, thereby constantly invading their space.

THE SENSING-INTUITIVE DIMENSION. Jung pointed out that there are two basic ways in which people perceive the world around them. Sensing individuals make full use of their five senses. They base their perceptions of the world directly on information garnered from sight, sound, touch, taste, and smell. Operationally, they have a high regard for facts—that is, data gathered directly through the senses. Like Sergeant Friday in *Dragnet,* a popular police drama of the 1950s and 1960s, they are principally interested in "the facts, ma'am, just the facts." They also derive great pleasure from using their senses. Intuitive individuals take information they gather through their senses and "massage" it. They are not concerned with facts for the sake of facts, but rather with the possibilities that the facts suggest. Using their imagination, they are more interested in how things might be than with how they actually are. Imaginative people are often strongly intuitive.

As with extraverts and introverts, conflicts can arise between sensing and intuitive types. Sensing individuals tend to see intuitive individuals as playing fast and loose with the facts, while intuitive individuals see sensing types as prosaic and unimaginative.

THE THINKING-FEELING DIMENSION. After people perceive reality (by sensing or intuition), according to Jung, they make judgments about its meaning. Some people do this through a cool, detached, logical process. They are thinking types. Operationally, they are more comfortable dealing with things and concepts than with people. Pointy-eared Mr. Spock in the television series *Star Trek* was a pure thinking type. Others base their judgments on more subjective considerations, that is, responses from the heart and gut. Operationally, they are more comfortable dealing with people than with things. They are feeling types.

To illustrate the different judging styles associated with these two approaches, a colleague of mine who is a Myers-Briggs aficionado relates the following tale. When they were first married, he and his wife spent a great deal of time house hunting. He recalls visiting one house in particular. Upon entering the house, he did his usual rounds: checking out the plumbing and wiring, inspecting the gutters and shingles, looking for signs of termites, and so on. After ten minutes, he decided that the house would require a large amount of fix-up work and for this reason would not be worth buying. Having reached this conclusion, he looked for his wife to give her his opinion. He searched several rooms and finally located her in the living room, where she was seated cross-legged in the middle of the floor. She hadn't made it beyond the living room! "This is it, honey," she said. "This is the house. I can feel it in my bones."

This story illustrates an additional interesting feature of the thinking-feeling dimension: there are sex-related differences in our preference for one approach over the other. Some 60 percent of males are thinking types, and some 60 percent of females are feeling types. It is interesting to speculate on how deeply the battle of the sexes is rooted in the fundamentally different processes men and women employ in drawing conclusions about the world around them.

**THE JUDGING-PERCEIVING DIMENSION.** The fourth dimension in the Myers-Briggs schema examines the degree to which people feel compelled to draw conclusions about the world around them. Some people are quick to make judgments; they hold opinions on any and all matters. The idea of loose ends makes them nervous. They would rather make a decision instantly than defer it. Operationally, they are comfortable with order and planning. On the negative side, they may be rigid and closed-minded, and they run the risk of making premature judgments. These are judging people.

Others would rather defer making judgments until there is more information available. They are flexible and open-minded. Unfortunately, they run the risk of being disorganized and falling into the pitfall of procrastination as they await more and more information before making a decision. These are perceiving people.

The conflicts that can arise between judging and perceiving types are obvious. In fact, Neil Simon's play *The Odd Couple* focused on just this difference in outlook between two roommates, one fastidious and organized, the other free-wheeling and disorganized. This play is a veritable case study of the problems that can arise when an extreme judging type and an extreme perceiving type have to deal closely with each other.

## Applying Psychological Type Theory to Projects

People who take a Myers-Briggs test are often amazed by its accuracy in describing their psychological characteristics. After receiving the results of his test, one man told me, "It's uncanny how it describes me. It knows me better than my own mother does. I wonder how it does it?"

There is no magic here. In taking the test, you are asked a number of questions that identify your preferences. For example, one question asks whether as a teacher, you would prefer to teach factual information or theory. If you answer "factual information," this suggests a preference for sensing over intuition. By answering a whole series of questions, you reveal your overall preferences on each of the four dimensions. Taken together, this information puts you into one of sixteen categories. People who fall into a given category tend to share a large number of common psychological traits. Thus, if I know your Myers-Briggs type, I can accurately describe some crucial aspects of your personality even without knowing you personally.

Knowledge of the Myers-Briggs approach can help project managers deal more effectively with people in several important areas: selecting staff, diagnosing the roots of conflict, improving relations with staff, and helping managers know themselves better.

SELECTING STAFF. The most obvious—and perhaps least useful— application of Myers-Briggs theory is in staff selection. Here, management may require all prospective staff members to take a Myers-Briggs test. Routine engineering projects are then staffed with ESTJs (extraverted, sensing, thinking, judging types); design teams are composed of ENTJs or INTJs (extraverted or introverted, intuitive, thinking, judging types); project marketers are made up of ESFJs (extraverted, sensing, feeling, judging types); and so forth.

Among the problems with using the Myers-Briggs approach in this way, two stand out. First, the Myers-Briggs test does not measure intelligence, drive, or technical competence. It may give a manager insight into whether an individual will fit psychologically in a particular environment, but it will not tell whether this individual is sufficiently knowledgeable or motivated to carry out the required assignment. Second, it is usually not practical to rely heavily on the Myers-Briggs Type Indicator for staffing in a project environment, where many factors, including personnel availability and politics, go into staffing decisions.

**DIAGNOSING THE ROOTS OF CONFLICT.** Knowledge of the Myers-Briggs approach can be very useful to project managers in diagnosing the roots of conflict in projects. Conflict can arise in many different ways and among many different combinations of actors in the project environment—for example, between project managers and their staff, between project managers and their bosses, and between staff and clients. To the extent that this conflict is based on psychological factors, the Myers-Briggs approach can suggest tactics for managing the conflict effectively, as the following case illustrates.

### SOFTWARE HANDLERS INC.

Software Handlers Inc. (a fictitious name for a real company) employs about seventy-five programmers and systems analysts and designs and develops software to meet client needs. A few years ago, Software Handlers struggled with a nagging problem that is not uncommon in this field: ineffective staff interaction with clients. Staff felt that clients were often naive about computer capabilities, didn't know what they wanted, and changed their minds frequently. By the same token, Software Handlers' management was receiving an alarming number of complaints from clients about the technical tunnel vision of its staff, their abruptness in dealing with clients, and their inability to do anything that lay beyond their limited ken.

Management instituted a number of policies to deal with this situation, one of which was requiring staff to undergo training on the Myers-Briggs approach. All staff members took the Myers-Briggs test and had the results explained to them by a Myers-Briggs specialist. They were instructed that in dealing with a client, they should make a mental assessment of the client's psychological type. Armed with this information, they would, in conjunction with an in-house Myers-Briggs specialist, map out an approach for dealing with the client. For example, if the client were a highly technical type of person (for example, an INTP scientist), his or her principal contact in the company would be a staff member of a similar type (for example, an INTP or INTJ). If the client were a nontechnical ESFJ (for example, a manager in a social services agency), it would be advisable to avoid assigning an

INTP or INTJ staff person to the project and instead have the client work with someone of a similar type. The management of Software Handlers claims that this approach has substantially decreased staff-client conflict.

**IMPROVING RELATIONS WITH STAFF.**  The responsibilities of project managers are different from those of project staff. Typically, project managers oversee, coordinate, control, and troubleshoot. Project staff, in general, have far more focused responsibilities; their perspective is narrower. This means that the basic traits that make a good project manager may be substantially different from the traits that make good project staff. In Myers-Briggs terms, we say that a project manager's psychological type is likely to be different from that of the staff.

In general, we want project managers to be people who are practical and aware of their environment. We want them to have a high regard for factual detail and to be logical and rational. Finally, we want them to be orderly and capable of making decisions. What we have described here, in general terms, are ESTJ individuals.

What of managers who are in charge of basic research projects, where it is probable that a large fraction of their staff will be ENTP, INTP, and INTJ? It is likely that conflicts will arise between them and their staff on the basis of differences in psychological types. ESTJ project managers who are unaware of the differences in psychological type are likely to be exasperated by their workers, whom they may perceive to be dreamy, impractical, disorganized, and always speculating about what might be rather than what is. If these project managers try to fit their staff into an ESTJ mold, chances are that the staff will champ at the bit and resist. From the staff point of view, management is trying to impose its superficial and arbitrary sense of order.

If ESTJ project managers are sensitive to differences in psychological type, they will use their knowledge to enhance the output of their staff rather than try to turn their workers into something they are not. For example, they may encourage staff to publish their research findings and attend professional conferences, where they can meet other scientifically creative people with similar interests. If project work is humdrum and not challenging, managers may allow staff to spend a certain amount of their time pursuing highly speculative and creative efforts. With such policies, staff are likely to see their project managers as being sensitive to their needs, and they will be more willing to tolerate what they perceive to be superficial and arbitrary project requirements.

SELF-KNOWLEDGE. As we saw in Chapter One, for project managers to be good politicians, it is vital that they know their capabilities—their strengths and weaknesses. The Myers-Briggs approach can help them in this effort. It forces them to realize that they cannot be all things to all people. If managers are very practical extravert types, they will probably be a bit weak in doing the things introverts do well—for example, working on a single problem over a long period of time. If they are superlative in dealing with facts (that is, if they are sensing types), perhaps they will be uncomfortable in the realm of speculation, where intuitive types are at home.

Knowing that they cannot be all things to all people, successful managers have the wisdom to surround themselves with staff who can cover their weak points. For example, the project manager who is a bit disorganized and has trouble coming to decisions (a perceiving type) would do well to have a highly organized assistant and advisers who are judging types.

# THE PROJECT MANAGER

In this section, we direct attention to project managers. We examine responsibilities they may be assigned, situations in which they work with a co-manager, management styles they may adopt, and games they may be forced to play.

## Project Manager Responsibilities

If project managers are asked what their responsibilities are, they are likely to respond, "To get the job done—on time, within budget, and according to specifications." Of course, project managers' responsibilities go beyond this. They are also responsible for developing staff, serving as intermediary between upper management and the project staff, and conveying lessons learned to the organization.

DEVELOPING STAFF. Project management is, as we know, the accidental profession. People stumble into projects. Rarely do they receive formal training on basic management principles. Project management know-how is conveyed informally; managers learn to carry out projects by working on them and learning the ropes from experienced project managers.

In order to get things done on projects, project managers teach their people the tricks of the trade—sometimes out of a sense of altruism but more commonly out of necessity. If you want people to do things right so that you can carry out your project on time, within budget, and according to specifications, you have to show them how best to undertake their tasks. In doing so, you are making them more valuable members of the organization. Whether you realize it or not, you are developing staff. One day, these staff members may assume major project responsibilities and, in their turn, convey project wisdom to their own project staff.

**SERVING AS MANAGEMENT-STAFF INTERMEDIARY.**  Project managers are situated between higher levels of management above them and the troops below. They occupy a delicate position. On the one hand, they are a part of management and are expected to behave accordingly. They are a conduit for upper-management information directed at the workers. Through them, project staff have a glimpse of organizational goals and upper management's desires. Unfortunately, project managers run the risk of being identified by project staff as flunkies or errand runners for upper management.

On the other hand, project managers are part of the troops and provide upper management with a glimpse of the needs, capabilities, and desires of the organization's workers. In this capacity, they must be careful not to be seen by upper management as "going native."

**CONVEYING LESSONS LEARNED.**  Project managers are great storehouses of practical project knowledge, which they gain through firsthand experiences with projects, initially as project staff and then as managers. Project successes and failures are burned indelibly into their memories. They can serve their organizations well by effectively conveying lessons learned to their upper management, fellow project managers, and project staff.

Project managers convey their lessons in many different ways, most of them informal. We have already seen that they pass their knowledge on to new staff. They also convey lessons to upper levels of management by various means. During the selection phase, for example, they may provide advice on whether a given project should be supported, and they may serve as useful members of project evaluation teams. Project managers also convey lessons to their fellow project managers when they are asked advice or during informal sessions in which they exchange war stories.

## Co-Management of Projects

In the 1990s, a number of companies began experimenting with the co-management of project teams. Instead of assigning one person to have responsibility over the entire project, they divide the management effort into two components, each with its own lead manager. One co-manager serves the role of technical lead on the project. This individual is called the development manager. The other takes charge over general management matters. This individual is called the business manager. Neither one is a project manager in the traditional sense. Working together, the two managers carry out the project management function. That is, they make sure the project is properly scheduled and budgeted, they recruit resources to carry out the tasks, they strive to make sure the project is implemented effectively, and they monitor progress and take whatever action is necessary to keep the project on track.

Some organizations have carried the co-management process further, using more than two managers to run projects jointly. For example, projects in a manufacturing organization might be run with three managers—a development manager, a business manager, and a manager who monitors what's happening in the manufacturing division—to keep project work closely aligned with developments in the factory.

In the 1990s, NCR Corporation carried the co-management approach to its logical extreme by creating customer-focused teams (CFTs) to run projects. A typical CFT would comprise five people: representatives from the sales, operations, IT, and finance departments, plus someone called the project manager, who would serve as chief shepherd of the project. At different stages of a project, different players play lead roles. For example, in the business development stage, the salesperson is the key contact with potential customers. Once the project is sold and a contract is signed, the salesperson steps back and lets a colleague (perhaps the technical person from IT) take the lead. Meanwhile, the CFT members meet regularly to examine project developments and keep the project moving ahead.

The CFT's project manager is not a traditional project manager. His or her role is primarily that of a committee chair. This person coordinates the work of the CFT and serves as the voice of the project when dealing with upper managers, colleagues, and the customers.

The move to co-management reflects recognition of the fact that many projects are too complex for one person to manage effectively. Anyone who has managed projects recognizes that their efforts usually divide along two lines: one technical, the other business. People with a strong business background may find themselves foundering when dealing with technical issues. They have no problem dealing with budgets and schedules but do not fully grasp the technical details of the project. By the same token, technical people often lack sufficient business knowledge to handle the business dimensions of their projects. They may be experts in designing state-of-art software systems, but they have difficulty dealing with financial and human resource matters. If present-day Leonardo da Vincis who can master all aspects of projects are scarce, then it makes sense to share project management responsibilities among two or more people.

The potential problem with this approach is captured in an old adage, "When everyone is in charge, no one is in charge." Experience shows that when co-managers are introduced to their responsibilities on a co-managed project, the first question they ask is, "Okay, so who's the *real* project manager? Me or the other guy?" They are concerned that without a clear sense of where the buck stops, they will come into conflict with each other. Each co-manager might aggressively demand ultimate authority in certain areas, resulting in a destructive power struggle between them. Or the co-managers may be so deferential to each other that each is afraid of pressing his or her point of view on issues, with the result that there is no strong leadership on the project.

The record suggests that co-management can work, but it requires a high tolerance for ambiguity. Co-managers must work out between themselves how they want to partition responsibility. The allocation of responsibility should reflect their capabilities and preferences. It may even happen that one manager assumes a dominant role with the acquiescence of the other. For example, the business manager might be technically adept, and the development manager may choose to work in the background.

The rise of co-managed projects shows that in today's fast-paced, messy world, the traditional imprecation for order and clarity that is taught in business schools becomes increasingly difficult to follow. Many of the old shibboleths (for example, always link responsibility and authority; only one person can be in charge of something) are becoming irrelevant in today's business environment.

## Management Style

Management style is concerned with the way managers interact with their staff. I focus here on the three basic styles that are frequently discussed in the management literature: autocratic, laissez-faire, and democratic.

Typically, autocratic management is associated with the traditional image of Boss (with a capital B). In this management style, Bosses make all the decisions. They exercise tight control over their staff and march around the office with grim expressions. You don't cross Bosses. If Genghis Khan were alive today and working in a modern enterprise, he would be an autocratic manager.

Laissez-faire management lies at the other extreme. With laissez-faire management, anything goes. Staff can do whatever they want. It might even be argued that laissez-faire management is nonmanagement: nobody's in charge.

Democratic management is participative. Managers and staff make decisions jointly. I call it red-white-and-blue management, because it heavily incorporates some of the most cherished American cultural beliefs: everyone is equal, we should all have a voice in decisions that affect us, and so forth.

To understand the dynamics of these three styles and to appreciate their differences, it is helpful to analyze each of them with regard to information flows (see Figure 2.2 for a graphic presentation).

AUTOCRATIC MANAGERS. Autocratic managers are not interested in processing information from anyone else. They are not interested in feedback from staff, for example.

Autocratic
Style

Laissez-faire
Style

Democratic
Style

**Figure 2.2. Information Flows Associated
with Different Management Styles.**

Note that autocracy has little to do with congeniality. The traditional view is that autocrats are gruff and nasty in their dealings with their staff. This is not necessarily so. Skilled autocrats can be people with a ready laugh and a great sense of humor. They can project an image of openness that leads their staff and colleagues to see them as democratic. They can have an open-door policy, encouraging staff to come in and air their views. However, to the extent that they call the shots and do nothing with the information they receive from their staff, they are autocrats.

An autocratic management style has its pluses and minuses in a project management context. On the plus side, the autocratic approach may be appropriate for routine, low-risk projects, where the staff merely carries out the plan exactly as specified. In such a situation, feedback from staff is not as crucial as in a high-risk, high-flux project. The autocratic approach is also effective when quick decisions need to be made. Because autocrats are not concerned with achieving consensus and gathering large amounts of data on which to base their decisions, they are able to make decisions speedily.

On the minus side, the autocratic approach may lead to demoralization of the staff, since they contribute nothing meaningful to the decision-making process. Creative and intelligent knowledge workers want their views to count; if they determine that their bosses don't want to hear their views, they will be unhappy. Another drawback of the autocratic approach is that it may lead to bad decision making, since the boss often bases decisions on insufficient outside information.

LAISSEZ-FAIRE MANAGERS. In contrast to the highly centralized decision making of autocratic management, decision making in a laissez-faire environment is very diffuse. (The term *laissez-faire* itself is a French term meaning "let do.") We generally find little or no flow of information, or else we may find many flows that are scattered every which way and are not effectively channeled.

In a laissez-faire system, project staff may be able to direct feedback to their managers, but, unfortunately, the managers do not act meaningfully on this feedback. As a consequence, we find that at their heart, the diametrically opposed autocratic and laissez-faire approaches hold one very important feature in common: in both cases, little or no meaningful information flows from project staff to project managers.

The laissez-faire approach may be effective in state-of-the-art projects on which project managers want to encourage creativity and are reluctant to impose their views on staff. Such freedom of action is likely to bolster morale among highly creative workers who do not like to work under close supervision.

On the minus side, the laissez-faire approach may lead to a ship-without-rudder syndrome. At first, project staff may be delighted to be able to do what they want, but before long, the sense of freedom metamorphoses into a feeling of aimlessness. Another important minus associated with laissez-faire management is that it may be disastrous in situations where quick decisions are necessary.

DEMOCRATIC MANAGERS. Managers with the democratic approach actively seek input from staff before making decisions. Overall, this is probably the most effective management style to employ with American knowledge workers, since it dovetails nicely with the American democratic culture. This approach cannot be employed very effectively in certain other cultural environments, however. Russian workers, for example, are not likely to know how to respond to a democratic approach, since it is alien to their culture. This can be seen in the complaint of many Russian émigrés now living in the United States: one of the biggest problems the United States faces, they say, is lack of authority and structure!

There are various pluses associated with the democratic approach. First, it meshes well with American cultural notions. Second, it can lead to better decision making because it reflects a broad spectrum of viewpoints. Third, it increases the commitment of staff to carry out decisions, because they themselves played a role in making the decisions.

The democratic approach also has drawbacks. One is something that political scientists call the *tyranny of the majority.* This results when a given majority in a democratic system always gets its way, much to the chagrin of what becomes a perpetual minority. An analogue in a project management scenario occurs when one clique always calls the shots. It will not take long for individuals outside the clique to become discouraged and disillusioned with how decisions are made.

A second drawback of the democratic approach becomes evident when the wrong "voters" are polled on their views and decisions are consequently based on incorrect information. For example, a democratic manager may make a great show of getting feedback from his staff before making some important decisions, but if the staff he consults are not technically competent to offer meaningful advice (that is, if he has polled the wrong voters), his decisions will not be based on valid information. A third drawback of the democratic approach is that it may be ineffective when quick decisions are needed.

CHOOSING A MANAGEMENT STYLE.  In actual project situations, it is neither possible nor advisable for project managers to pursue one style 100 percent of the time. The best project managers adapt their style to reflect the circumstances they face. A project manager may adopt a laissez-faire manner with her closest staff during the creative design phase of a project and then use a democratic approach during the more routine implementation phase. She may determine that the only way she can get good results out of a troublesome supplier is by behaving in an autocratic fashion with him, yet she may take a laissez-faire approach with another supplier who has proved to be very reliable over the years.

The style that project managers employ can have a dramatic impact on the outcome of their projects. Let me give you an example. The worst-run construction project I have ever come across was headed by a new construction superintendent who came out of his company's sales department; he had been given project responsibilities as a reward for good sales performance. Because this individual was unfamiliar with the nuts and bolts of construction, he deferred all project decisions to his subcontractors—that is, he adopted a 100 percent laissez-faire approach. Anyone familiar with the building industry recognizes that one major role played by the construction superintendent is that of autocrat. The superintendent often has to crack the whip with subcontractors, whose own agenda may not correspond to the project needs. On the project in question, progress ground to a halt as subcontractors did whatever they felt like doing.

The trick is to know which style to apply in different circumstances. This decision depends largely on the good sense of the project manager and his or her capacity to size up situations accurately. It also depends on personality factors. What style or styles is the project manager most comfortable with? Some may be constitutionally incapable of adopting a style radically different from their basic temperament.

## Playing Games

I once spent several days visiting an engineering firm that produces telecommunications hardware and software. On the first day, I had lunch with the president and two other executives, and we discussed the president's approach to project management in his organization. His approach was a standard one—perhaps more enlightened than the average, since he was actively concerned with project management issues. However, something he said disturbed me: "One thing I've learned after working with engineers for thirty years is that when you ask them to estimate how long it will take to do something, they always hem and haw and give you a figure that's 20 percent larger than it should be. So whenever one of my engineers tells me it will take so much time to complete something, I lop 20 percent off the figure and tell him to do it more quickly."

Over the next two days, I had an opportunity to talk to many of the company's project managers about their work. Most expressed general satisfaction with the work environment, but one critical comment surfaced a number of times: "We're always under tremendous schedule pressure. We're asked to make good estimates about how long it will take to do the work, but when we submit our estimates, we're always told we have to do it faster. So we spend an awful lot of time working after hours and on weekends so that our schedules don't slip." One project manager confessed to me that he deliberately exaggerated his estimates so that when upper management cut it back, the resulting figure would be reasonable.

A month later, I visited a U.S. government research laboratory, where I presented a project management seminar to middle managers. In the morning of the second day, we were reviewing three charts showing three projects in various states of disarray in their schedules and budgets. Toward the end of the discussion, I pulled out a fourth chart, which showed a project perfectly on budget and ahead of schedule. It was labeled "Fantasy World," and I told the group that it pictured something that rarely happened in projects. Several of the project managers burst out laughing. They told me that virtually all their projects looked like the one pictured in the Fantasy World chart.

These project managers had learned to manipulate to their advantage the arbitrary fiscal year requirements of their agency's budget system. Furthermore, each project was structured so that it would consume only 80 percent or so of its budget. A large margin of error was thus built into budget and schedule estimates. When money was left over on a project (and it often was), staff would undertake unofficial projects that were technically challenging and entertaining. (A number of these unofficial projects produced results that were viewed as important and useful to the laboratory.)

We have here two examples of a phenomenon that is common in project management: game playing. It comes in many shapes and sizes. What most project games have in common is players who are trying to outfox each other or the system. What is troublesome is that the process of outfoxing others entails the manipulation and distortion of information, yet accurate information is important for carrying out projects effectively.

It is equally troublesome that game playing tacitly encourages wholesale dishonesty in projects. In selectively manipulating budget data and distorting schedule data, we are being dishonest. It is easy for this dishonesty to get out of hand. Our initial manipulation may lead to false reports that milestones have been accomplished and deceptive accounts of how project funds have been expended. A project that ultimately rests on distortions and lies is a recipe for disaster.

Is game playing to be avoided at all costs? Absolutely not. Frequently, it is unavoidable. Sometimes project managers are forced to play system-induced games. Anyone who has worked in an organization with fiscal year budgets recognizes that you have to be good at budget games if you want to thrive. Sometimes project managers must play games foisted on them by their bosses (like the boss mentioned earlier who automatically cuts time estimates by 20 percent). Sometimes game playing is part of the macho corporate culture, as described in captivating detail in Kidder's *The Soul of a New Machine* (1981). In this case, if you don't play games—and play them roughly— you are perceived to be some kind of sissy.

Although project managers may have no choice but to play games initiated by others and by the system, they do have a choice as to whether they will initiate games. For the most part, it is advisable to avoid doing so. As we will see later, in the discussion of project planning and control in Part Three, project managers should do everything in their power to build their projects on a foundation of accurate and timely information. Playing games undermines this effort.

## CONCLUSION

People lie at the heart of projects. With white-collar projects in particular, success hinges on people issues. Are staff members committed to the project? Are they intelligent? Do they display initiative when it is needed? Are bosses supportive? Do they make clear what they expect of staff? Do we have good rapport with customers? Are we dealing with the right set of customers? Answers to these and related questions give us a good idea of how we will do on our projects.

Many of the issues addressed in this chapter are obvious. We all know that people are multidimensional, that excessive autocracy will lead to the demoralization of creative staff, and that people come in a rich variety of types. Yet as managers, we too often treat our workers as unidimensional, as if the only important things for them should be their jobs. We too often practice an autocratic management style, feeling threatened by legitimate feedback, which we perceive as unwarranted criticism of our judgments. And we too often pigeonhole people into simplistic types: smart and stupid, cooperative and uncooperative, good and bad.

Thus, for all the obviousness of human relations issues, we find that we inexorably drift away from them in our management practice. It is useful, now and again, to review them carefully.

# CHAPTER THREE

# Structuring Project Teams and Building Cohesiveness

very autumn, a certain sports madness overcomes many Americans on Sunday afternoons. Week after week, millions sit in front of their television sets for three or four hours, cheering their favorite football teams, booing the opposing teams, vilifying referees for what they perceive as unfair calls, flicking off their sets when it is obvious that the home team is spiraling down into defeat. For half an hour before the contest, sports commentators examine the players, coaches, and possible game plans in excruciating detail. For half an hour following the contest, they perform postmortems, trying to determine the whys and wherefores of success and defeat. Frequently someone comments that the winning team made a good team effort, while the losing team could not seem to bring things together.

Just as teams are the basic work unit of sports competition, they are the basic work unit of projects. Because of the central role that teams play in projects, it is worthwhile spending some time examining them to gain a better understanding of what they are and to determine how they contribute to project success and failure. With this knowledge, we can then structure project teams to maximize the likelihood that our projects will be carried out effectively.

*team-worthy*
*together to achieve a goal*

# CHARACTERISTICS OF PROJECT TEAMS

A team is a collection of individuals who work together to attain a goal. For them to work together, their individual efforts must be co-ordinated. In sports, coordination is directed by an all-powerful coach and coaching staff. It is achieved through hours of drills and practice sessions. In projects, we have a fundamentally different perspective on teams, since, as we saw in earlier chapters, project managers are rarely all-powerful and the unique and transitory nature of projects does not make them amenable to repetitive drills.

Project teams, like projects themselves, come in a great variety of shapes and sizes. Some are large, some small. Some must grapple with highly complex problems, others with routine affairs. Some are highly dynamic, with team members constantly changing, while others are stable.

These last points have interesting implications. In sports teams, a large amount of effort is directed at developing team spirit, which re-quires team members to have a clear image of what the team is and to identify strongly with it. The presence of team spirit may give a team the competitive edge that allows it to win over equally competent teams lacking team spirit. With project teams, however, team mem-bers are often borrowed and may have only the briefest exposure to the project effort. They work on a piece of the project, and when they are done they move on to other projects. Because of this, they may not recognize that they are part of a team. Without such recognition, they are incapable of developing team spirit, or what I have referred to as project commitment.

*\* importance of spirit of team*

Of course, from the perspective of the project manager, there *is* a team, whether or not the team members recognize this. The project manager is aware of project goals and knows how the pieces fit to-gether. To the extent that project workers do not realize they are part of a team, however, the project manager's work is more difficult. Clearly, one important task of project managers is the development of some sense of team identification among their staff.

Project teams have structure: there are established rules governing the relationships of team members with each other, with the project manager, with the client, and with the product being developed. How the team is structured will have a strong bearing on a project's prospects for success. A well-structured team can enhance the prob-ability of project success, while a poorly structured team will surely

*good team structure*

lead to trouble. Good team structure is a necessary, though not suffi-cient, condition for success; poor team structure is a formula for failure.

One question naturally arises: How can we structure the project team in such a way that it will facilitate the effective management of projects? One answer is to structure the team to enhance team efficiency.

## TEAM EFFICIENCY

In engineering, the concept of efficiency is straightforward. It is de-fined as the ratio of output to input. If a device consumes 100 energy units of coal (input) and produces 60 equivalent energy units of elec-tricity (output), we say the device is operating at a level of 60 percent efficiency.

With projects, we are unable to measure team input and output precisely, so any treatment of team efficiency is necessarily rough. For purposes of discussion, let us loosely define team efficiency as the frac-tion of potential team performance that is actually achieved. Thus, if a team is accomplishing only a small portion of what it could accom-plish under ideal circumstances, its team efficiency is low. If it is achieving as much as is physically possible, its team efficiency is high.

Our concern here is not with how to measure team efficiency pre-cisely but with how to achieve it. How can we structure project teams to enhance team efficiency?

To answer this question, it is useful to understand better why sys-tems are inefficient. Mechanical engineers know that two common and interrelated sources of inefficiency in machinery are machine de-sign and friction. If a machine is poorly designed, it will be inefficient. Poor design often means that the machine is not configured in such a way as to minimize the effects of friction. But even a well-designed machine can operate at less than peak efficiency if, through poor maintenance (for example, improper lubrication), it is subject to the effects of friction.

Team efficiency can be viewed analogously. We can say that a proj-ect team can be inefficient because its basic design ensures inefficiency, or because organizational friction keeps it from operating as smoothly as it could—or both. Major structural sources of team inefficiency in projects are matrix-based frictions, poor communication, and poor integration of the efforts of team members. The inefficiencies in all three cases are interrelated and are rooted in both design inadequa-cies and organizational friction.

## Matrix-Based Frictions

Projects that are heavily dependent on temporarily borrowed staff—that is, projects employing the matrix approach—often have built-in inefficiencies. One important cause of inefficiency in a matrix-structured project is lack of staff continuity.

Let's say that Arthur is assigned as a computer programmer/analyst to a project to revamp a hospital's accounts receivable system. He works actively on the project during the early design phase. When the preliminary design is done, he returns to the data processing department, where he is promptly assigned to an office automation project. Two weeks later, top management signs off on the accounts receivable preliminary design and releases funds for a detailed design phase.

Because Arthur is now working on another project, Linda is assigned to the accounts receivable project as the computer programmer/analyst. This is new material for her, so she spends her first week reviewing overall project requirements as well as Arthur's specific contributions. Only after this review period is she ready to work actively on the detailed design phase. When this phase is completed, she returns to the data processing department, where she is immediately assigned to a new project. During the implementation phase of the accounts receivable project, still another programmer/analyst is employed. And so on.

In this kind of situation, which arises commonly in projects, organizational friction is high, with people spending substantial time simply reviewing what others before them have done. Couple this with the lack of project commitment characteristic of high-turnover jobs, and it is evident that team efficiency will be low.

Another important matrix-based source of friction is the project manager's lack of direct control over project staff and material resources. Without direct control, it takes more effort and time to acquire needed human and material resources. Project politics also may enter the picture, so that acquisition of even a simple piece of equipment may trigger a contorted Rube Goldberg chain of events.

## Poor Communication

Information is the lifeblood of projects, and communicating this information effectively to the relevant parties is vital to project success. When communication breaks down, the project is in serious trouble.

Of the various kinds of communication-based friction that contribute to team inefficiency, three will be examined here: communication that becomes an end rather than a means, communication channels that suffer from information atherosclerosis, and garbled messages that lead to work being done improperly.

Although this discussion focuses on communication within the project team, communication between the project team and the customers of the product emerging from the project is also very important. If customers' needs are improperly conveyed to the team, the team may produce a deliverable that is rejected and requires rework. This issue is so important that a large amount of space is devoted to it in Chapters Four and Five.

**COMMUNICATION AS AN END RATHER THAN A MEANS.**  As projects become increasingly bureaucratized, proportionately more and more effort is expended on transmitting information and coordinating tasks. On large projects, as much effort may be directed toward communication and coordination as toward carrying out the required tasks.

As is illustrated in Figure 3.1, the number of communication channels can grow quadratically as projects become larger. When a project

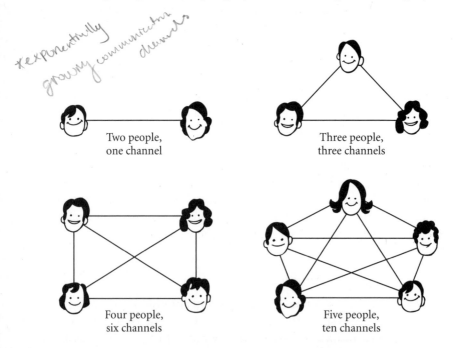

Figure 3.1.  Communication Channels.

team consists of two members, there is only one communication channel to maintain. When it consists of three members, there are three channels; four members, six channels; five members, ten channels. In mathematical terms, if the team comprises $n$ members, there are potentially $n(n-1)/2$ channels to be maintained. Thus, even a modest team of 20 members has a possible 190 communication channels!

On most projects, not everyone has a need to communicate with everyone else. Nonetheless, the potential exists to overwhelm projects with communication requirements. When an inordinate amount of time is spent sending and receiving messages, team efficiency is bound to decline.

**INFORMATION ATHEROSCLEROSIS.** Atherosclerosis is a condition in which arteries become so clogged that blood can barely trickle through them. Information atherosclerosis occurs when communication channels are so clogged that important information has difficulty making its way through them.

The clogging is largely a consequence of requirements that information be processed in a bureaucratically sanctioned fashion. Thus, an important piece of information sent from team member A to team member B may have to pass through five hands before B receives it. Clogging may also be caused by large amounts of useless information floating through channels and blocking the flow of important messages. Here, great effort must be expended to separate useful information from chaff.

The principal consequence of information atherosclerosis is that information flows are retarded, contributing to inefficiencies in the team effort.

**GARBLED MESSAGES.** We are all familiar with the parlor game "Telephone," in which ten or fifteen people sit in a line or a circle while someone whispers a message in the ear of the first person, who whispers it in the ear of the next person, who passes the message to the next individual, and so on. Typically, by the time the message is passed on to the last person, it has undergone some modification.

I clearly recall a personal experience with message modification. Many years ago, when I was a freshman in college, the college president invited me and two dozen other freshmen to his house for a get-acquainted tea. Upon entering his house, I encountered a reception line of three school officials (the admissions director, the assistant dean, and the dean), and at the end of the line stood President Lowry.

I introduced myself to the first person, saying, "Hello, I'm David Frame from Donelson House [my dormitory]." After greeting me, he turned to the woman standing beside him and said, "Professor Jones [or whatever her name was], I want to introduce you to Mr. David Frame from Donelson House." "So nice to meet you," she said. "Are you related to Jim Frame from Schenectady?" I told her I was not, and after a few more seconds of pleasantries, she passed me on to the next official in line, introducing me as Jim Frame from Donelson House. This official chatted with me for a moment and then introduced me to President Lowry as Jim Donelson. Over the next four years, whenever I encountered Dr. Lowry on campus he would smile and say, "How do you do, Mr. Donelson?"

This experience illustrates something that frequently occurs in organizations: messages get garbled. The consequences of garbled messages range from neutral to disastrous. In projects, garbled instructions may lead staff to carry out their tasks incorrectly. If their work has to be redone (assuming the mistake is caught), or if their efforts cause spinoff problems with other tasks, team efficiency drops.

## Poor Integration

As we have seen, one of the basic traits of projects is that they are systems, composed of many interrelated pieces. For the system to work, those pieces have to be brought together and fitted into their proper places. This process of bringing things together is called *systems integration.*

Systems integration is an important function of project professionals. They must integrate the pieces of their projects, bringing everything together so that both the project and its product work properly. If integration is not carried out properly, tremendous inefficiencies will be introduced into the project.

Consider, for example, an editor who is compiling a handbook on gardening. The handbook will contain twenty-five chapters, each written by a recognized expert. If the editor does not carefully spell out what she expects of each of the chapter authors—if she does not take steps to integrate the pieces into a whole—she will have a hodgepodge of chapters turned in to her. Some will be long, some short. Some will be narrated in a folksy manner; others will be rigidly academic in tone. Some will be filled with footnotes; others will lack any references to related material. Many will repeat material covered in other chapters.

Ultimately, if the editor wants a work that hangs together nicely, she will either have to return the chapter manuscripts to the authors, with instructions on how to revise them so that they dovetail with each other, or she and her staff will have to spend enormous amounts of time editing and rewriting the submitted material. In any event, a poor initial effort at integrating the separate chapters into a cohesive book will cause burdensome rework and yield low levels of team efficiency on the project.

This matter of integration is especially crucial in software development projects. In developing complex software, programmers typically work separately on different pieces of the system. Different pieces of equipment that will employ the software may be produced by different vendors, leading to problems of marginal interoperability. Major problems often arise when attempts are later made to integrate the pieces into a whole. What happens, using the jargon of systems analysis, is that "bugs arise at the interfaces." Although the pieces may be internally consistent and bug free, they don't quite fit together, leading the system to malfunction. A great deal of time and effort must be dedicated to trying to get the pieces to fit together. More time is usually spent testing and debugging the system to ensure integration than writing lines of computer code.

To the extent that project managers are effective systems integrators, they dramatically increase the efficiency of their project teams.

## STRUCTURING TEAMS

The issue of structuring organizational effort became popular in the 1990s with the promotion of the concept of organizational architecture, which was most fully explicated in a book with that title written by David Nadler and coauthors (Nadler and others, 1992).

Because we want to structure project teams in such a way that the structure leads to team efficiency, we clearly want to avoid structures that result in the organizational and design frictions just discussed. Thus, a desirable project team structure is one that copes with staff turnover and lack of direct project manager control over resources, enhances effective communication among project team members, and facilitates the integration of the many pieces of the project.

No one structure fits the bill for all projects. A structure that is ideal for one project may fail dismally with another. Various things must be taken into account in configuring a team structure. What is the size of the project? Can staff be permanently assigned to it, or will there be high levels of staff turnover? What is the technical nature of the project? What is the corporate culture like? What are the psychological characteristics of the team members and other relevant project actors?

To illustrate team structure considerations concretely, we will examine the consequences of structuring a hypothetical project in four different ways. The project is a common one faced by professional consultants: to write a technical report on some topic of interest to a client.

## Isomorphic Team Structure

The adjective *isomorphic* comes from the Greek *iso,* which means equal or same, and *morph,* which means form or shape. Two things are isomorphic when they share the same structural appearance.

If we configure a project team so that it closely reflects the physical structure of the deliverable—the thing that is being produced—the team and the deliverable are isomorphic with respect to each other. Figure 3.2 shows an isomorphic team configuration for the project to write a technical report for a client. Figure 3.2a shows what the report will look like: a simple document with five chapters. Figure 3.2b shows how the team can be configured to match the structure of the deliverable. The project manager corresponds to the fully integrated report, and each of five team members corresponds to one of the report's five chapters.

With a project structured this way, there is always a real risk that the pieces (the chapters in the example) will not fit together nicely, since each is being developed independently. Clearly, then, a major

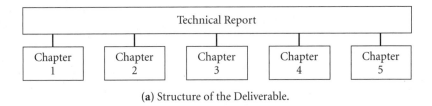

(a) Structure of the Deliverable.

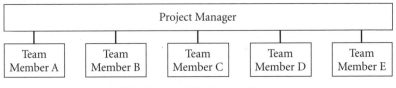

(b) Structure of the Project Team.

**Figure 3.2. Isomorphic Team Structure.**

function of project managers is to serve as integrators. They must interact closely and continually with their staff to make sure that staff members produce pieces that will fit in the final product.

In our example, the project manager should focus on maintaining a consistent writing style among the team members, avoiding duplication among the different chapters, and linking together the material through cross-references between the chapters. One way to accomplish this integration is to hold weekly staff meetings at which team members briefly describe their efforts and compare notes.

There are several advantages to the isomorphic approach. One is that it is organizationally simple. In our example only five communications channels exist out of a potential of fifteen (six players can be connected together in a total of fifteen pairs). Accountability is crystal clear, since each team member is responsible for developing one piece of deliverable. If progress on one chapter of the report begins to lag seriously, the project manager immediately knows whom to talk to in order to find out what the problem is.

Second, if the different modules of the system are independent, the isomorphic approach allows parallel implementation of tasks, which may considerably shorten the amount of time it takes to carry out the project. Thus, in the example, if the chapters are independent of each other, all five chapters can be written simultaneously.

Third, this approach is well suited to projects where new staff members are getting their first exposure to a project management environment. Its simplicity eases novices into their new jobs rather than overwhelming them with complexity. Furthermore, the project manager can take on the role of mentor to the new staff, watching over them closely and providing them with important guidance on how projects are carried out in the organization.

In general, the isomorphic approach can be highly effective in dealing with projects on which the different pieces that make up the deliverable are relatively independent of each other. In such cases, problems of systems integration are much smaller than in projects on which the pieces are inextricably tied together.

## Specialty Team Structure

The specialty approach to structuring teams is illustrated in Figure 3.3. A little thought will show that the specialty team structure is simply a variant of matrix management. With this approach, team members are

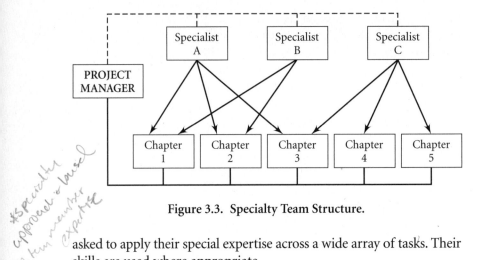

Figure 3.3. Specialty Team Structure.

asked to apply their special expertise across a wide array of tasks. Their skills are used where appropriate.

With this approach, project managers face the classic dilemma of matrix management: they have high levels of responsibility (to produce a deliverable), but lack corresponding levels of authority (they do not directly control the borrowed resources who are working on the project).

A quick review of Figure 3.3 shows some possible deficiencies of the specialty team structure. For one thing, accountability is rather diffuse. If there is a problem with Chapter 1 in the report, we may find specialist A pointing a finger at specialist B and B pointing back at A. Another problem is rooted in the unequal distribution of work. Specialist C clearly has her hands full: she is working on half the document's chapters. She presents another problem as well: she is working alone on two of the chapters, so there is a risk that these chapters will not be well integrated into the document.

The specialty team structure nevertheless offers some advantages. For one thing, it requires a fairly high degree of self-management, something that most knowledge workers value. That is, it is primarily up to the team members to determine how they will coordinate their activities. Decision making shifts substantially from the project manager to the team members. Another advantage is that expertise is applied where appropriate. If team member A's skills span Chapters 1 and 2, then it makes sense that A works on both chapters.

## Egoless Team Structure

In the early 1970s, Gerald Weinberg noted in *The Psychology of Computer Programming* (1971) that a major cause of problems in com-

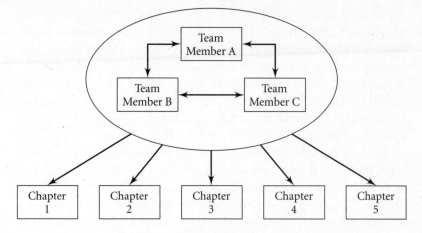

**Figure 3.4. Egoless Team Structure.**

puter programming projects is the ego of computer programmers. They are often more interested in developing tour-de-force programs than in doing what is necessary to come up with a well-integrated product. Too often, they are not good team players. To deal with this common problem, Weinberg suggested that project teams should be structured to minimize the ill effects of egos. When we look at the product of an egoless team, the results of a truly collaborative effort, it should be difficult to determine who produced what portion of the product.

The structure of a three-person egoless team is shown in Figure 3.4. Note that there is no obvious leader on the egoless team. Decisions are achieved through consensus, and project tasks often reflect the input of all the team members. For example, in the technical report example, team member A may write a draft of the first chapter and then turn it over to team member B, who edits and reworks it. After all the chapters are done, team member C may do a final editing of the report, to make sure that it is well integrated. To the extent that team members collaborate jointly like this, problems of ego will be minimized.

The egoless team structure encourages high levels of interactivity and communication among project members. They are continually in touch with each other and make decisions through consensus. If communication is good and team members are working together toward a common goal, problems of systems integration should be low.

I have heard many scathing criticisms of the egoless team approach by those who have tried to implement it in their organizations. One of the most common is that "the egoless team doesn't work, because people have egos." Project workers, especially those with great talent, possess pride of authorship. They want to make their unique contributions, to stand out from the crowd, and they strongly resist attempts to downplay their egos. Another criticism focuses on the lack of leadership. "Without strong leadership, there is a tendency for egoless teams to drift," comments one project manager who worked in a company that espoused the egoless approach to team structure.

To those who declare that egoless teams go against human nature (and I often hear this comment), I point out that in Asian cultures, with their stress on harmony and consensus, egoless teams are more the rule than the exception. The Western concept of leadership, based on individualism, is alien to the East. Consider the Japanese dictum that states, "The nail that stands up is hammered down."

I believe that egoless teams can work effectively in Western cultures in certain situations. First, team size must be relatively small, since with larger teams, communication channels proliferate, leading to bureaucracy and its attendant inefficiencies. Furthermore, with large teams, it becomes difficult to achieve a meaningful consensus.

Second, egoless teams require continuity in team membership. They are very much like a sports team in this respect. In the 1980s, there was a college basketball team that had four starting players who were brothers. "I spend most of my time trying to get team members used to playing with each other," said the coach. "These brothers have been playing together a whole lifetime. They're remarkable." As with sports teams, team efficiency on egoless teams is highly dependent on the team members' knowing one another's operating styles, technical capabilities, weaknesses, and so on. This knowledge can develop only if staff work together continually. You cannot have egoless teams functioning effectively as a matrix.

Third, egoless teams may function well on ill-defined state-of-the-art projects for which the final deliverable is at first only vaguely conceived. Basic research projects typically have these characteristics. A synergistic team (one on which the effectiveness of the combined team is greater than the effectiveness of the individual team members) may be able to pool the talents of the team members and come up with creative solutions that they could not achieve if working alone.

Finally, egoless teams may be effective on projects where highly creative team members resist the imposition of strong leadership, which goes against their grain and which, they feel, restricts creativity.

The egoless team concept is particularly interesting today, because many of its basic tenets have been resurrected in the concept of self-managed teams. While self-managed teams possess enormous capacity to tap into the hidden strengths of team members, proponents of this approach should recall some of the lessons learned from our experiences with egoless teams.

*Self - managed teams*

## Surgical Team Structure

Frederick P. Brooks, in his classic work on managing software projects, *The Mythical Man-Month* (1995), promotes use of an approach he calls the surgical team. (In software project management, this approach, developed originally by Harlan Mills of IBM, is called the chief programmer team concept.) Brooks asks us to consider how a surgical team functions. At the heart of the team is the surgeon, who performs the surgery on the patient. The surgeon is surrounded by assistants—an anesthesiologist, nurses, and interns—who provide her with all manner of assistance. In the final analysis, however, it is the surgeon who carries out the surgical procedure. She calls the shots. The primary function of the assistants is to help the surgeon carry out her task most effectively, with *the* surgeon defining effectiveness.

One fundamental objective of the surgical approach in medicine is to allow the surgeon to pursue her work freely, unencumbered by administrative and technical obligations. The surgeon's task is to perform surgery. Billing of the patient can be handled by administrative staff, anesthesia can be administered by an anesthesiologist, surgical tools can be maintained by the nursing staff, examination of removed tissue can be carried out by a pathologist, and so on. Similarly, in project management, one individual is given total responsibility for carrying out the main body of project work while being shielded from administrative paper pushing.

The surgical approach to team structure stands diametrically opposed to the egoless approach. With the surgical approach, all attention focuses on a single individual and his or her abilities. With the egoless approach, it is the overall group effort that counts.

Figure 3.5 shows how the surgical approach can be applied to our project to write a technical report. A chief writer stands at the heart of the undertaking. This individual will write the entire technical report. She has been chosen for this position because she writes quickly and clearly and understands the technical content of the study. She is

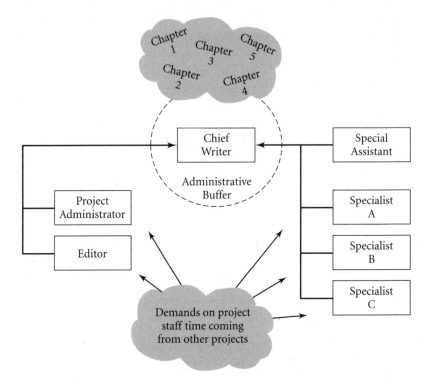

Figure 3.5.  Surgical Team Approach.

buffered from administrative concerns by a project administrator, who keeps track of hours devoted to the project, progress reports, and the like. She is relieved of editorial burdens by an editorial staff member, who at the end of each day reads her writing, corrects misspellings and grammatical errors, spots and removes minor factual inconsistencies, and so on. In addition, she is provided with technical backup: individuals who are specialists on the material covered in the technical report. If at any point she needs detailed information on a particular topic, she will confer with the appropriate specialist to obtain this information.

At her side is her special assistant, an alter ego who is also a good writer, though perhaps with less experience. The special assistant plays numerous roles. For example, he may serve as an intermediary between the chief writer and the specialists. His most significant role, however, is to keep fully abreast of what the chief writer has done and to take over the project if necessary. The special assistant is an insurance policy against what in project management is called the Mack truck syndrome, which gets its name from the question, "What happens to the project if, on the way to work, the project manager gets hit by a Mack truck?"

A major advantage of the surgical team approach is that it tackles the issue of systems integration head on. Since project output flows from the mind of a single individual, the pieces being produced are likely to fit together nicely. Stylistic and factual inconsistencies and duplication of effort will be minimized. The final product will be well integrated.

One disadvantage of the surgical approach is that it requires a superlatively capable individual to play the role of surgeon. If such an individual is not available, the resulting product may be mediocre.

Another disadvantage is that the surgical team may end up with three bosses. The surgeon is clearly a boss, but principally in regard to technical matters. The project administrator is a boss in the sense that he or she is in charge of maintaining and controlling budgets, schedules, and material resource allocations. Finally, the special assistant may assume responsibility for coordinating and controlling the technical personnel who serve as project specialists. If these three individuals do not communicate with each other clearly and frequently, or if they hold differing perceptions of project goals, team efficiency will be low.

The surgical team approach is most effective on design projects, computer coding projects, and projects that entail large amounts of writing, such as our technical report. Brooks (1995) claims that it can also be used effectively on large projects if each project module is given a surgical team structure. When used in this way, according to Brooks, this approach combines small-project efficiency and consistency with large-project scope.

## The Impact of Team Structure

This discussion of four approaches to structuring a project team is not meant to be exhaustive; many other approaches can be undertaken. Rather, it is illustrative. It shows that—for a single project to write a technical report—team structure has a dramatic impact on the way in which a project is carried out. It also shows that there is no one perfect structure for management projects. An approach that addresses the issue of systems integration (the surgical team) may lead to confusion as to who is in charge. An approach that fosters intense and open communication among team members (the egoless team) may suffer from lack of leadership. An approach that is conceptually simple and straightforward (the isomorphic team) may yield systems integration problems. And an approach that dovetails nicely in a matrix environment (the specialist team) may have associated with it all the problems that can come with matrix management.

By examining an organization's architecture, project staff develop the ability to predict many of the things that happen on projects, since so much of what happens is structurally induced. Thus, organizational architecture reviews enable project staff to operate proactively. They can anticipate problems and opportunities and work to deal with them early on.

## AN EMERGING STRUCTURE FOR KNOWLEDGE-BASED PROJECTS

Knowledge-based organizations have gradually adopted a project superstructure that is designed to bridge the business-technology gap that many projects encounter. This structure is commonly encountered in the financial sector but can be employed in other sectors as well.

The basic business of financial organizations is engaging in financial transactions. Banks, for example, take deposits from citizens, issue loans to borrowers, offer investments in an array of investment vehicles, make payouts in CDs, and so on. Brokerage firms deal with large volumes of trades of different types of securities. Real estate companies have consortia investing in large development projects. And insurance companies gather premiums from clients and reinvest the money in many ways.

The level of financial transactions in these companies is gargantuan. What makes their businesses viable is heavy use of information technology, specifically computer and telecommunication technologies. Those who carry out projects in the financial sector face an interesting situation of dealing with business in its purest form (the conduct of financial transactions) interacting heavily with technology.

This situation leads to interesting management challenges for people running these projects because the business culture and technology culture are radically different from each other. In business, the principal concern of practitioners is making money. The niceties of process and technique are subservient to the bottom line. Furthermore, the educational background of businesspeople tends to be in the liberal arts and management areas. Most have a limited grasp of technology.

In the technology arena, knowledge and method reign. What you know and your mastery of tools is the key issue. Many technical people have educational backgrounds in computer science, engineering, or the natural sciences. Most of them are committed to designing and implementing optimal technical solutions to problems. Business concerns are secondary.

To deal with the business-technology schism, IT organizations in a wide array of businesses have begun adopting a common approach to managing their software development and maintenance projects. In this approach, key decision making is distributed to a number of significant players in both the business and technology domains rather than put into the hands of a single individual. Like co-managed teams, this structure acknowledges that most projects have a technical and business component to them, so it is designed to serve and integrate these two components.

The new way of structuring project efforts is pictured in Figure 3.6. Although the specific labels attached to the players may vary from organization to organization, their underlying roles remain constant. The roles of each player will be discussed briefly.

*roles in knowledge-based projects*

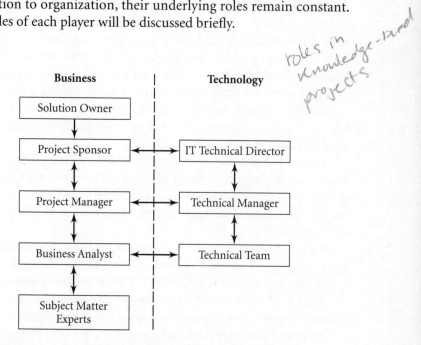

**Figure 3.6. Team Structure for Knowledge-Based Projects.**

## Solution Owner

Although all deliverables have multiple customers, solution own-ers are in effect the ultimate customer of the deliverable. They are the people who are given primary responsibility for serving customers' interests. On internal projects, they are the senior executives who fund the project. On external projects, they are the most senior executives who have responsibility for making sure that the customer organiza-tion receives what it wants.

## Project Sponsor

The senior executives who serve as guardian angels of the project within the organization are the project sponsors. By virtue of their senior posi-tion, they have power that they can use to support the project effort. For example, if a project team is having difficulty obtaining resources from the design shop, the project sponsor can talk to its head to see if the needed resources can be released quickly. They also serve as the cham-pion of the project in meetings of the organization's most senior execu-tives, to make sure that the project remains visible in the organization.

Project sponsors also play a mentoring role to the project team. Be-cause they are experienced in the ways of the organization, they can offer guidance on what is possible (and not) within the organization. They can also deal with problems arising outside the organization. For example, when the project team has a conflict with a significant cus-tomer, they can deal directly with the customer to reduce the level of friction. In this sense, they serve as political godfathers, helping the team to navigate tricky political waters.

Project sponsors also serve the needs of senior management. They keep watch on project developments and make sure that it is achieving goals that meet the organization's requirements. If the project is mis-managed or drifts from its objectives, sponsors can intervene to help set things right.

The importance of project sponsors for enabling project success has been recognized only since the mid-1990s. Prior to that time, projects might have had senior managers helping them out, but this was done on an ad hoc basis for the most part. After that time, sponsors were formally assigned to projects and were given defined roles in the project effort.

In view of the importance of project sponsors to project teams, sponsors must be effective. Often they are not, for the following rea-son. In many cases, project managers are the ones who recruit sponsors, and they frequently make a common mistake: they try to recruit sponsors from the most senior levels of management on the grounds that these men and women are very powerful. The problem with this approach is that while the executive vice president may agree to serve the sponsor role, it is unlikely that he or she has the time to do a good job. This person may not show up for important meetings, or review significant reports, or champion the team's cause on the executive committee.

*[handwritten: x rules for selecting project & sponsors]*

After encountering this problem in many organizations, I have established what I call *Frame's Rule for Selecting Sponsors*. The rule goes like this: *Identify the highest-level sponsor that you would like to have to protect the project's interests. Then choose someone one or two layers beneath this individual in the organization's hierarchy.* The rationale for this rule is simple. Having a powerful sponsor on paper is not helpful if the sponsor cannot commit to giving the project's affairs the attention they need. So recruit as a sponsor someone who is both willing and able to help out. If they are close to the high-level executive, they have his ear and can influence support from him when appropriate, so you still can get support from the highest ranks of the organization.

## IT Technical Director

The project sponsor is principally a sponsor from the business side of the organization. It is also important to get support from the highest levels of the technical organization to make sure that the project receives the technical resources it needs. If the project team finds that its technical counterparts are not being cooperative, then their project sponsor can approach the IT technical director to see if she can correct the problem. Interestingly, if the technical team members realize that their boss is committed to enabling a project to achieve its goals, they usually function in a cooperative way without prodding.

The project sponsor should work to gain the IT technical director's support for the project, thereby reminding her that the project has strong support from the highest levels of the organization.

## Project Manager

With the project team superstructure we are looking at here, project managers play the same role as business managers described in the discussion on the co-management of project teams. Their principal concern is to make sure that business requirements are achieved on time and within budget. A substantial portion of their energy must be devoted to collaborating with their technical counterpart in the IT organization: the technical manager.

## Technical Manager

Technical managers play the same role of development managers on co-managed teams: they strive to make sure the project achieves its technical requirements on time and within budget. They muster the technical troops to do their jobs as effectively as possible. They devote substantial energy to collaborating with their project manager counterpart.

## Business Analysts

The central role of the business analyst is another new development in managing knowledge-based projects. Traditionally, systems analysts had the job of making sense of what customers needed and wanted and wedding these needs and wants to the technology that would be used to satisfy them. They would study the existing system, identify features of the desired system, and take stock of possible technical solutions. Then they would use this information to identify technical requirements, which would be converted into specifications. Though this process, customer needs and wants would be transformed into technical solutions.

Unfortunately, this process led to solutions that were only partially on target: project teams were building deliverables that did not fully address customer needs and wants. Not surprisingly, customers would be unhappy with the outcomes. A big source of problems was that the systems analysts did not understand the business they were dealing with. For example, there might be nonaccountant systems analysts gathering requirements for an accounting system. Although they might be masters of software design and programming, they didn't know the difference between cash-based and accrual-based accounting.

To deal with this problem, large portions of the systems analyst position slowly evolved over the 1990s into the business analyst role. Unlike systems analysts, who see themselves fundamentally serving a technical function, business analysts have an explicit charge to make sure the customers' business requirements are captured correctly in the technical requirements. Thus, they must know both the business and the technology. In many organizations, business analysts are people who once worked in the technology arena and then migrated to the business side of the enterprise. To make sure they do not forget that their job is to serve the customers, they usually are part of the business team on projects, as indicated in Figure 3.6. Often, they are the key point of liaison between business team members and technology team members.

## Subject Matter Experts

The content experts who provide business analysts with the detailed information they need to understand how business processes work are referred to as subject matter experts, or SMEs (pronounced *smeeze*). For example, in developing a comprehensive accounting system, business analysts might draw on the expertise of tax specialists, financial managers, database experts, and general accountants. If the accounting system is going to function over the Web, they would also add Web experts and network specialists to the list of SMEs they need to work with.

Working with SMEs can be challenging. If they are busy doing their regular jobs, they may have trouble freeing up time to help business analysts. Typically, they are experts on the periphery and not major stakeholders in the project, so they may not feel strong commitment to providing insightful responses to the queries of the business analysts. Furthermore, they often have limited knowledge of the technology that is being employed, so they do not know how to phrase their guidance in ways that are meaningful in a technical context. Because of this, business analysts must be trained to communicate effectively with SMEs to help them understand what is needed of them, and then to take the SMEs' lay insights and convert them into technical solutions.

## Technical Team

The technical team members are the people who will implement the requirements presented to them by the business analysts. They often have little in-depth knowledge of the business content of the solutions they are working on. Their primary interests are in solving technical challenges with the tools available to them. If these men and women are to develop meaningful technical solutions, their technical director must convince them of their need to commit themselves to meeting project goals and the business analysts must make sure that they understand exactly what needs to be done.

### Working Collaboratively

The track record of this project team superstructure has been good. By employing it, we have some assurance that both business and technical issues will be handled effectively. In addition, this superstructure requires businesspeople and technical staff to operate in a collaborative way. Collaboration starts at the top, with the project sponsor and IT technical director agreeing at the outset that they will do what they can to support the project so that it is delivered on time, within budget, and according to specifications and that it ultimately leads to customer delight.

## CREATING TEAM IDENTITY

The focus of the discussion thus far has been the mechanical aspects of putting a team together. Beyond mechanics, there is the question of creating a sense of cohesion among the team members. The stumbling block is the familiar problem: people working on projects are typically on loan and have little opportunity or motivation to develop a commitment toward the projects. It is clearly in the interest of project professionals to stimulate a sense of project identity among workers attached to their projects.

There are many ways in which they can do this. What sometimes pulls a team together is the personality and special management style or expertise of the project manager. Charismatic managers or those with a legendary reputation for technical prowess easily catch the attention of their staff, who recognize that they are privileged to work with these managers.

Those who lack exceptional charismatic or technical prowess must work hard at developing a sense of project identity among project staff. Some research I have carried out suggests that team-building efforts on projects should focus on three things: making the team as tangible as possible, building a reward system, and building team spirit by effective use of a personal touch.

### Making the Team Tangible

People are not easily motivated by intangibles, so it stands to reason that project professionals should aspire to make their teams as tangible as possible. This is difficult on projects that depend on borrowed resources. Designers are brought in to do their design work. When they are done, they return to their homes in the design shop. The same process is repeated with implementers, testers, sales personnel, purchasing agents, and all the other people who constitute the project team. To these people, the project is largely an abstraction.

A survey I conducted of project professionals suggests that they commonly carry out a number of actions to make their teams more tangible. In particular, they use meetings to good advantage, devise a common working space, and give the team a name.

EFFECTIVE USE OF MEETINGS. The obvious purpose of team meetings is to communicate information. A less obvious function is to establish a concrete team identity. During the meeting, team members get to see that they are not working alone. They are part of a larger group, and the success of the group undertaking depends on the efforts of team members doing their individual parts.

One important event that makes the team tangible is the kickoff meeting, when all the project team members assemble at the outset of the project. A number of actions should be carried out at this meeting:

- Players should be identified and a team roster should be distributed.
- A first shot at identifying roles and responsibilities should be made.
- The project charter, which identifies the rationale for the project, should be distributed, with key milestones highlighted.
- If possible, a high-level manager should be present to demonstrate top management's commitment to the project effort. If the project has a project sponsor, his or her presence is absolutely vital.

*— meetings to communicate info*

Another important meeting is the status review. Status reviews are periodic meetings (say, biweekly) to examine project performance. These reviews offer team members a chance to get together and reaffirm their commitment to serving the interests of the larger group.

Meetings need not be formal. Beer and pretzel parties, team softball games, and other social activities are meetings of sorts. Just as with more formal meetings, they enable team members to develop a palpable sense of team identity.

**COLOCATION OF TEAM MEMBERS, WAR ROOMS, AND WEB SITES.** The most obvious way to make the team tangible is to have team members work together in a common space. The problems with this approach are practical: Who has the space to colocate team members? Does it make sense to locate people physically in the team space if they are going to be on the job for only a couple of days?

An effective substitute for colocation is the creation of a war room. The war room can be as elaborate as the high-tech electronics-filled rooms serving the defense community or as humble as a converted closet. War rooms contain the most significant project documentation. Frequently, their walls are covered with PERT/CPM charts, cost charts, and the other appurtenances of project planning and control. Their primary significance from the perspective of this discussion is that they serve as a tangible sign of the project effort. Even when they are far removed from the core team activities, project personnel can associate their rather abstract team with its physical embodiment, the war room.

Today, war rooms are increasingly being replaced by project Web sites. It is a rare project today that lacks a Web site, which is really a virtual war room. Team members can access the site twenty-four hours a day, seven days a week, to determine whatever information they need about the project. A good Web site provides information on schedule status and job assignments and contains the minutes of status meetings. Through the Web site, team members can access important documentation, such as the project charter and the statement of work.

**CREATION OF A TEAM NAME.** The creation of a team name is a common device for making the project team more tangible. Frequently, an associated team logo is also created. The name and logo might be affixed to such things as stationery, T-shirts, coffee mugs, and caps. If done with good humor, this collection of "trinkets and trash" (as project staff have dubbed them) can serve a significant role in developing team identity.

## Building a Reward System

So long as project professionals lack the carrots and sticks needed to catch people's attention, it is difficult for them to motivate project team members. Lacking the standard corporate rewards and punishments, they must invent their own reward systems. Here are some suggestions from the creative project professional's bag of rewards:

*Letters of commendation.* Although project professionals may [→benefits of a ping a team] not have responsibility for their team members' performance appraisals, they can write letters commending their project performance. These letters can be sent to the workers' supervisors, to be placed in their personnel files.

*Public recognition for good work.* Superlative workers should be publicly recognized for their efforts, and not just at the end of the project but on various occasions. For example, it might be a good practice to begin each status review meeting with a brief mention of project workers who have exceeded their project goals.

*Job assignments.* Project professionals should recognize that although they may not have much budgetary authority, they have substantial control over how the team members spend their time. They should recognize that job assignments can be used to reward and punish team members. Good work should be rewarded with challenging job assignments.

*Flexible work time.* Good project workers who need adjustments in their working hours might be rewarded with some measure of flexibility. Workers who have put in many hours of overtime might be given an occasional day off as a reward.

*Job-related perquisites.* Most work environments have special features that can serve as motivational perquisites. Common examples of perks include a convenient parking space, access to a company car, nice office space, and use of a cellular phone. Such perks should be offered to the best workers.

*New equipment.* Whenever new equipment is to be allocated among project workers, the first pieces should be distributed to the best workers as a clear sign of appreciation for their efforts. This is a particularly useful motivational approach when dealing with technical people, who take great interest in their tools.

[incentives]

*Recommendation for cash awards or bonuses.* Many organizations have established cash awards for their best performers. Project professionals can use these awards as an incentive to do good project work.

## Using a Personal Touch

The third general means by which project professionals can build a sense of team identity is the effective use of the personal touch, the one-on-one relationship between project professionals and their borrowed staff. When managers establish a personal rapport with their team members, they create an environment where the team members are willing to walk the extra mile to achieve project goals. The list of things managers can do to strengthen their personal touch can go on for pages. Following is a short list of actions that have been particularly effective in building team spirit on projects:

*Be supportive.* Team members appreciate a supportive manager. There are various ways in which managers can support their teams. Physical support may be achieved by doing everything possible to make the work environment pleasant. Psychological support may be reflected in such actions as defending project workers against attack by outsiders and expressing appreciation for the efforts of the project team.

*Be clear.* One of the most common complaints that employees express about their managers is unclear expectations, muddled instructions, and lack of meaningful feedback. Team members appreciate working in an environment where clarity dominates and confusion is minimized.

*Learn something about the team members.* Many effective project professionals go to great lengths to learn as much as possible about their team members, including their personal interests, information about their family, and their accomplishments.

*Celebrate special occasions.* Project professionals can further demonstrate their interest in their team members by celebrating the occurrence of special occasions of importance to the workers—for example, birthdays, anniversaries with the organization, and special achievements.

*Be accessible.* Project managers will not build much team spirit if they are perceived as cool and distant. They should be accessible, enlisting an open-door policy. They should encourage team members to offer their views on project-related issues.

## CONCLUSION

Projects are carried out through teams, but these teams are typically fragmented and poorly defined owing to the exigencies of matrix management. An important function of project managers is to consciously create a team structure where no discernible structure exists. This is not a trivial matter, since there are countless ways teams can be organized. One prime consideration in structuring a team should be to select a structure that contributes to team efficiency.

It is not enough simply to select an appropriate team structure, however. Team members must be encouraged to identify with the team, develop team spirit, and do whatever is necessary to make the project succeed. The problem is that team members are usually on temporary loan to the project and have little stake in whether it succeeds or fails. Project managers must create a sense of identity in an environment that does little to encourage a cohesiveness and make stakeholders out of their staff. They can do this through a number of ways, particularly by making the team as tangible as possible, creating a reward system to reward good behavior, and displaying a caring personal touch in their dealings with team members.

# PART TWO

# Project Customers and Project Requirements

# CHAPTER FOUR

# Making Certain
# the Project Is Based
# on a Clear Need

T his book looks at project management from the perspective of the pitfalls that project professionals are likely to encounter. The purpose of focusing on pitfalls is not to accentuate the negative and thereby discourage people from assuming project management responsibilities, but to introduce a strong dose of reality. Although the road traveled by project professionals is littered with potholes and debris, this does not mean that the road is impassable. Many of the problems that project professionals encounter are created by the very nature of the project management process and human organization. They are predictable and therefore can be anticipated. With foreknowledge of pitfalls, project professionals can avoid them or mitigate their harmful effects. At the very least, unpleasant surprises can be minimized.

The previous three chapters concentrated on identifying and dealing with organizationally rooted problems. Now we turn our attention toward identifying and resolving problems associated with the formulation of customer needs (this chapter) and the specification of project requirements (next chapter).

# EVOLUTION OF NEEDS

Projects arise in order to meet human needs. A need emerges and is recognized, and then management determines whether the need is worth fulfilling. If it is, a project is organized to satisfy the need. Thus, needs are the fundamental driving force behind projects. This seminal aspect of needs makes them important for project management. Their emergence sets off the whole project process. If at the outset we do not fully understand a need and its implications, articulate it incorrectly, or mistakenly address the wrong need, we have gotten off to a bad start and can be certain that our project will be trouble filled.

Needs evolve from something very amorphous to something well structured and clearly understood. The following case study illustrates how needs evolve:

### RALPH'S DRUGSTORE

Ralph's Drugstore is located in a small midwestern town. While visiting Minneapolis on vacation, Ralph Amdahl, the owner, was impressed by the volume of business carried out by the city's discount drugstores. When he returned home, he converted his drugstore into a discount operation, a complicated process that took six months.

Business volume soon increased dramatically. People came from miles away to take advantage of Ralph's discount prices. The store aisles were constantly jammed, and a long line regularly snaked from the store's single cash register. Ralph witnessed the crowds with mixed emotions: it was good to see that his new discount policy was bringing in the crowds, but he realized that customer dissatisfaction was growing. Complaints were primarily directed at three things: the crowded conditions in the store, stockouts of special sale items, and long waits in the checkout line. Ralph was concerned that his success would backfire and that customer dissatisfaction with service would stymie growth.

Ralph expressed his concerns to Marie, his wife and business partner. One evening, the two of them sat down after dinner to discuss the future of the business. They determined that although their discount business was dramatically different from their previous operation, the basic way they conducted their business had not changed. For example, the physical layout of the store was no different than it had been before, and it was now apparent that this layout was inadequate to deal with the growth in customer traffic. Ralph and Marie decided that they needed more floor space, more shelf space, more cash registers, and more sales staff. They would have to remodel their current facilities, build new facilities, or rent different facilities. With paper and pencil, they roughly calculated their requirements: to meet anticipated customer traffic, they would need to double floor space and shelf space and add at least two cash registers. They concluded that to satisfy these requirements they would have to move to new facilities.

At this point, they met twice with a local architect to identify how best to configure a store to make it better suited to the new kind of business they were doing. Using the information garnered from these meetings, the architect designed three different store configurations. Ralph and Marie were excited by the second design, which required them to build rather than rent a new structure, and after suggesting some minor modifications to the plan, they authorized the architect to proceed with detailed drawings of the new facility. He completed the architectural plans within six weeks, and three months later, groundbreaking for the new store was initiated.

## THE NEEDS-REQUIREMENTS LIFE CYCLE

The case of Ralph's Drugstore illustrates the evolution of needs from something vague and nascent to something quite tangible that serves as the basis of a project plan. First comes the *needs emergence phase:* customer traffic at Ralph's Drugstore increased dramatically after Ralph converted his store into a discount operation, and this growth in traffic led to a number of problems. Then there is a *needs recognition phase:* Ralph became aware that his facilities could not adequately handle the increase in customer traffic. This is followed by a *needs articulation phase:* Ralph and Marie consciously addressed the perceived need and attempted to describe its boundaries and implications.

After the needs have been articulated, they can serve as the basis for establishing *functional requirements*—a narrative description of what a project would have to do if it were to meet the articulated needs. In the case of Ralph's Drugstore, functional requirements emerged from Ralph's and Marie's paper-and-pencil exercise in their after-dinner conversation and continued in their early meetings with the architect. From these functional requirements, the architect was able to articulate *technical requirements* (for example, blueprints), around which a project plan to build a new facility would be structured.

Because needs are the driving force behind projects, it is useful to examine these different phases of the needs-requirements life cycle in more detail.

## Needs Emergence

Change is the generator of needs. With the status quo, needs remain constant; with change, new needs emerge and old ones fall away. Because we live in an age characterized by change, we face the continuous emergence of new needs.

Needs can arise from within or outside an organization. Internal needs are typically related to improving organizational performance. An agency overwhelmed with paperwork may have a strong need to simplify procedures. A company periodically facing the prospect of worker strikes may have a need to improve management-employee relations. A law office establishing branches in different cities will have a need to communicate effectively with these branches. The popular term describing attempts to improve organizational performance by re-forming business process is *business process reengineering.* Its best-known articulation is found in *Reengineering the Corporation* (Hammer and Champy, 1993).

Organizations are also vitally interested in needs that arise in the environment outside the organization. These environmentally generated needs are the lifeblood of for-profit companies. Emerging needs for more powerful computing capabilities, better-tasting TV dinners, harder drill bits, more durable handbags, and so on are what keep companies in business and drive them to innovate. Environmentally generated needs are also important to nonprofit and governmental organizations. The growing need of individuals to avoid having obsolete skills is what enables universities to thrive. The whole rationale of organizations such as the Red Cross is to respond to needs created by natural disasters, such as floods and fires. Similarly, government, the servant of the people, is predicated on addressing societal needs.

## Needs Recognition

It is not enough simply to have needs emerge. These needs must be recognized for what they are. If they are not seen to exist, no action will be undertaken to satisfy them. This is an obvious point, yet the recognition of needs is not a trivial matter. It is not easy to spot emerging needs. Often we are so accustomed to doing things in a certain way that we do not see that as things change, new needs emerge; we fail to notice that the old ways may no longer be effective.

The transistor, developed as a substitute for the vacuum tube, is a case in point. The U.S. military underwrote the considerable expense of developing transistors because they had a need for components more reliable than vacuum tubes in military hardware. Thus, the commercial development of transistors was largely a response to military needs.

American manufacturers only vaguely perceived new applications of transistors to meet consumer needs. The Japanese, however, saw how transistors could lead to miniaturization of electronic devices, and they further saw how miniaturization could satisfy consumer needs to, say, take a radio on a picnic or to the beach. This recognition of consumer needs for portable electronic devices launched Japan on its enormously successful journey into the realm of consumer electronics. Akio Morita, former head of SONY Corporation, describes SONY's insights into the commercial value of transistors in his readable *Made in Japan* (1986).

Recognition of needs requires conscious effort. People in organizations must constantly ask, What are our needs? What are the needs of our clients (consumers, taxpayers, victims of disaster, students, and so on)? Procedures must be established for systematically identifying needs. The information resource management department in an organization may hold monthly meetings to identify newly emerging information needs within the organization. The marketing department may require its sales force to submit a brief statement of their perceptions of client needs each time they meet with a client. A municipal government may establish a liaison office to obtain feedback from citizens on their needs.

Attention must focus not only on existing needs but on anticipated needs as well. Thus, effective needs recognition requires forecasting. This forecasting can be very simple. For example, a department manager can meet with three or four staff members once a month and, through a one- or two-hour brainstorming session, develop ideas of possible future needs. This type of forecasting is called scenario building. Forecasting also can be elaborate, quantitative models designed to predict future conditions. The important thing is not the degree of sophistication of the forecasting effort but the fact that a conscious effort is being undertaken to anticipate the future emergence of needs.

## Needs Articulation

After a need is recognized, it must be clearly articulated. Needs articulation entails an in-depth scrutiny of the recognized need. With such
a scrutiny, our understanding of the need will change.

Too often we accept needs at face value and lose sight of the reality that lies beneath the surface. We are overwhelmed with paper in
our office, and we immediately jump to the conclusion that we should
computerize to create a paperless office. The quality of our products
is declining, so we conclude that we need more inspectors to examine
the products for defects. In both instances, we have zeroed in on superficial needs. In most office environments that are drowning in
paper, the need is not for computers but for better information management procedures. In production environments where quality is a
problem, the need is not for more inspectors, who catch defects only
*after* they occur, but for new processes that will reduce the number of
defects.

In other words, if we thoroughly examine a particular need, we are
less likely to grab onto the superficial. Often the very act of trying to
describe something precisely gives us a better understanding of what
we are looking at.

Needs articulation has a practical side to it: it serves as the basis for
the development of functional requirements. What this means is that
after a need has been clearly articulated—that is, after it has been fully
and unambiguously stated—we can go about the business of stipu-
lating in concrete terms what we have to do to achieve it. Obviously,
if we have done a poor job of articulating the need, our functional requirements will be misdirected and the resulting project will be non-
responsive to the true need.

In practice, needs can be articulated in a number of different ways.
One approach to articulating needs effectively is to carry out the following five steps:

*Step 1: Ask those who have the need to define it as clearly as possible.*
It is important to see the need through the customers' eyes, even
though at this point they usually have only the vaguest notion of what
that need is. Individuals with a need usually have a sense of the need
rather than a solid grasp of what it is. Frequently, they cannot precisely
articulate their need because they are too close to it and lack the technical competence to do so. Thus, although it is important to deter-

mine how customers view their needs, you should not accept these views at face value.

*Step 2: Ask a full set of questions about the need.* It is wise to maintain a set of stock questions to ask when you are trying to articulate needs precisely—for example:

- How do those who have the need define it?
- Is the need real? Is this need the true need, or is it masking a more basic need?
- Can we resolve the need? Can someone else resolve it? Is it resolvable at all?
- Is the need important? Is it worth trying to satisfy?
- What are the implications of the need? If fulfilled, will it give rise to other needs? By satisfying it, will we also be satisfying other needs? Does the emerging need replace an existing need?
- Who are the actors most directly touched by the need? Do they agree that it is a worthwhile need? How will satisfaction of the need affect them? How will they react to efforts to satisfy it?
- How does the need affect my organization? How does it affect me?

These questions should force you to address the needs from different perspectives. When answered, they will provide a multidimensional view of the needs.

*Step 3: Carry out whatever research is necessary to enable you to understand the need better.* Before you can properly articulate a need, you must understand it in all of its aspects, including those that are technical. How can we adequately formulate needs to enhance the productivity of the office, for example, if we are ignorant of existing and potential office technologies? You may carry out research on the technical aspects of the need within your organization; if your organization lacks sufficient expertise, you can tap the expertise of outside consultants.

*Step 4: Formulate the need as best you can in view of insights gained in the first three steps.* At this point, you have a far better grasp of the need and its implications than you did at the outset. When you formulate the need now, it will probably look much different from the original.

*Step 5: Ask the customers to respond to your formulation of the need, and revise your formulation accordingly.* One widely recognized pitfall in needs formulation is that the needs eventually articulated are not those of the customers whose needs are supposedly being addressed but, rather, those of the professionals who are trying to articulate the needs on behalf of the customers. During the needs-requirements life cycle, it is common for experts to modify needs so that they satisfy the experts but not the customers.

The problem here is obvious: the ultimate product that is created on the basis of the modified needs will probably be underused, misused, or not used at all by the customers. To reduce the likelihood of this happening, the needs formulator should make a great effort to be sure that what he or she has articulated does indeed reflect customers' needs. This can be done by working closely with customers, getting their reactions to the newly articulated needs, and revising the needs statement to reflect customer desires.

## Functional and Technical Requirements

After needs have been carefully defined, we can use them as the basis for developing a project plan. We do this by formulating the needs as *functional requirements*. Functional requirements describe the characteristics of the deliverable—what emerges from the project—in ordinary language so that nontechnical people can understand them. A functional requirement flowing from a school's need to improve the mathematics abilities of its sixth graders might be stated as follows: "We want to have 95 percent of our sixth graders scoring in the top six deciles of the Smith-Jones Mathematics Achievement Test by the end of the next academic year." Functional requirements might be strengthened by the use of graphic images. For example, one component of functional requirements in the building of a shopping mall might be an artist's conceptual drawing of what the mall will look like.

*Technical requirements* emerge from the functional requirements. Although functional requirements should be clearly stated, they typically do not offer enough precise guidance for project staff to use them as targets for guiding their efforts. While functional requirements are designed to ensure that customers know what they are getting out of a project, technical requirements are written for the technical staff. Consequently, technical requirements are often incomprehensible to the customers, who lack the training to know what they mean.

In a software project, for example, the functional requirements may stipulate that a database system will be developed to allow access to financial data through a remote terminal; the corresponding technical requirements would spell out the architecture of the data structure, the language in which the database management system will be written, the hardware on which the system will run, telecommunication protocols that should be used, and so forth.

The effective specification of requirements is one of the most challenging undertakings project planners and managers face. Inadequately specified requirements will guarantee poor project results. (Requirements are addressed in detail in the next chapter.)

## Business Requirements

The term *business requirements,* increasingly common in project-centric organizations, is loosely employed to describe requirements from the perspective of business users. As Chapter Three made clear, there is a clear trend to organize project efforts along two lines: a business line and a technical line. This demarcation has arisen because we are dealing with two distinct cultures, a business culture and a technical culture, each with its own philosophy, vocabulary, and skill sets.

So when we talk about business requirements, we are describing the business users' perceptions of what a deliverable needs to address. These requirements are consciously developed in isolation from the knowledge of possible technical solutions so that customers do not begin confusing their requirements with solutions that might be open to them. Once they have been stated, they are given to the technical team, which then tries to see how they can be formulated as *technical functional requirements.*

A little reflection shows that the elicitation of business requirements is built into the needs-requirements life cycle described above. When articulating needs and then converting them into functional requirements, we should avoid jumping the gun to describe technical solutions. Our attention should focus principally on business issues. As the functional requirements are refined, they may begin taking on a technical cast, but only after the business concerns have been fully addressed and articulated.

Is it necessary to identify business requirements as a distinct step in the needs-requirements definition process? The answer to this question is a matter of personal choice. If an organization has a clear demarcation between business team members and technical team members on its project teams, then using the term *business requirements* might reduce confusion when people are talking about what requirements a project should address. Otherwise, it is not necessary to introduce this concept into managing a project, because when articulating needs and converting them into requirements, we are, in effect, defining requirements from the perspective of business users.

## PITFALLS IN DEFINING NEEDS

There are many ways in which the process of defining needs can go awry. Some of the problems are subtle, and we may not even realize we have a problem until the project starts to unravel.

It is worthwhile exploring common pitfalls that arise in defining needs, so that we are alerted to their existence and are prepared to deal with them. Three broad categories of problems are examined here: problems with inherently fuzzy needs; problems with identifying solutions prematurely, before needs have been fully defined; and problems with addressing the needs of the wrong customers.

### Dealing with Inherently Fuzzy Needs

The most fundamental cause of difficulties in defining needs is their inherent fuzziness. When needs first emerge, they are rough and ill defined—just a glimmer of an idea. They represent something new, something different. The more unique they are, the greater is their imprecision. Their articulation is undertaken iteratively. At first, they are only vaguely perceived; after we address them systematically and refine them, they gradually take on shape and substance.

Two related characteristics of needs contribute to their natural fuzziness: needs are dynamic and rarely understood by customers.

DYNAMIC NEEDS.  Needs are dynamic and ever changing. One project manager told me that articulating needs is like shooting at a moving target. Another, choosing a more imaginative metaphor, described it as trying to nail jelly to the wall.

The reason for this dynamic nature of needs is that they are defined in relation to the environment in which they emerge. In our Ralph's Drugstore case study, for example, increases in customer traffic resulted in a need for Ralph to initiate some fundamental changes in the way he did business. Unfortunately, as needs emerge and we wrestle to articulate them precisely, the environment does not stand still but continues to change. No doubt by the time Ralph's new drugstore opens, the needs it was designed to serve will have changed somewhat, and new needs will have emerged.

Specific sources of changing needs include:

• *Changing players.* One of the dramatic realities we must cope with today is the continuing turnover of personnel in our organization, in the customer organization, and among vendors. Each time new players come on the scene, they bring their own perspective to the project. They may want to change the rules outright, or they may hold a different interpretation on the meaning of needs and requirements than their predecessors did.

• *Changing budgets.* Most project professionals routinely see money being budgeted for a particular work effort and then withdrawn. A Government Accounting Office study of problems on government projects identified this "budgetary instability" as a leading contributor to cost and schedule overruns. In government, a major contributor to budgetary instability is the turnover of politicians after elections. In the private sector, this instability is rooted in the perpetual reorganizations being carried out in companies.

• *Changing technology.* Technology is constantly changing. Each new technology introduced to the marketplace stimulates people's wants and may lead to a reconsideration of their needs. And just as adjustments are made to reflect the impact of a technological change on a need, the technology changes again, leading to further adjustments.

• *Changing business environment.* The business environment outside an organization is undergoing continuous change. A rise in the exchange rate of the yen suddenly makes importing critical components from Japan unattractive, and we must find some affordable substitute. Our competitors produce a new product that detracts from our existing product line, so we must rethink what we should produce. A new government regulation requires that we phase out use of a particular chemical in our manufacture of plastic goods.

In order to cope with this ever-changing character of needs, project planners and managers first must recognize that it exists. They should avoid inscribing needs statements in stone as if they were immutable. Beyond this, they should be aware that the changing nature of needs may require changes in the project plan once implementation has begun. Given the dynamic nature of needs, it is a good idea to create flexible project plans.

Something else project planners and managers can do is to anticipate changes in needs through forecasting. In articulating a need, they should define it not only in terms of the existing environment but an anticipated future environment as well. This is difficult to do. It is hard enough to get a handle on existing needs; it is much harder to articulate needs that don't exist now and may never exist.

MISUNDERSTOOD NEEDS.  Customers generally operate according to the dictum, "I'm not sure what I want, but I'll know it when I see it." Although they have a sense of their needs, they may not fully understand them and their implications. Their ill-defined perceptions of their needs are likely to shift with the slightest change in circumstances.

This is not to say that their needs are not real. They *are* real. However, they are only vaguely perceived, and they cannot be satisfied effectively as long as they are conceived in their current form. The implications for project planners are clear: if managers base their plans solely on customer statements of needs, they are not likely to produce deliverables that will satisfy the customers' true needs.

Newcomers to project management are often frustrated in their dealings with customers, because they see them as wishy-washy and a bit dense—individuals who don't know what they want and are never satisfied with what they get. This attitude will invariably lead to an us-versus-them mentality that will undermine project effectiveness.

Project staff must recognize that one significant role they play is guide to customers. Working closely with customers, they must help them to identify clearly what it is they need. Project staff will derive benefits from such an approach in at least three ways. First, by working closely with customers, they will have a better understanding of the customers' point of view so that they are better able to plan a project whose deliverables address customer needs. Second, by encouraging active customer participation in the needs development process, project staff are gaining customer acceptance of the emerging solution: when people participate meaningfully in a decision-making process, they ultimately achieve a strong commitment to supporting its outcomes. Finally, when customers see that project team members care for them and their concerns by focusing so much attention on their needs and wants, they are far happier with the experience than when working with a distant and uncaring group.

## Identifying Solutions Prematurely

The inherent fuzziness of needs is clearly a major pitfall facing project planners. Another common pitfall is shortcutting the needs articulation process, causing us to come up with answers before we have formulated the right questions.

Performing an analysis of needs requires a good deal of patience and self-control. From the moment we perceive the existence of a need, ideas enter our heads on how to satisfy it. Frequently we are ready to offer a solution before we fully understand the need. This is illustrated in the following case.

### AN EDIFICE COMPLEX

The dean of an urban engineering school determines that the school's physical plant—its administrative offices, faculty offices, classrooms, and laboratories—is decaying and no longer meets the needs of the faculty and student body. He decides that what the engineering school needs is a brand-new physical plant—a six-story building that will cost $50 million. He and his staff begin a major three-year drive to raise the money necessary to build the new facility.

When news of the dean's plans leaks out to the engineering faculty, some professors express concern about the building project. One wag jokes about the dean's "edifice complex." They recognize that their facilities are in bad shape, and they all would like to have more posh accommodations. However, they see the investment in a new plant as increasing the school's operating costs, which translates into higher tuition for students at a time when tuition rates are already astronomical. If the new plant is built, it seems inevitable that the engineering school will price itself out of the market.

A consensus emerges among these faculty members that the school should be pursuing avenues that will enhance the teaching and research environment and at the same time contribute to a decrease in tuition—for example, with distance learning. When the dean hears about this view, he says, "That doesn't sound like much of a suggestion to me. How can we simultaneously build a first-rate facility and reduce tuition? The problem is that these teachers want to have their cake and eat it too."

The divergence in outlook held by the dean and the dissenting faculty is explained by the ways in which they identify the engineering school's needs. The dean walks through the existing facilities and sees plaster falling off the walls, peeling paint, shabby whiteboards, linoleum flooring that has completely worn through in spots, and dingy and underheated professors' offices. His conclusion: "What we need at the engineering school are new facilities." He may be right; he may be wrong. What is important to note is that his *expression* of the school's need has embedded in it the *solution* to the need. His solution is to build new facilities. Other possible solutions have been shut out.

The dissenting engineering faculty members have a different perspective. They are concerned that the building program will ultimately lead to a loss of students, which may lead to the loss of teaching jobs. Their perception of the school's need is this: "We must strengthen teaching and research, and also ensure that the school is affordable for engineering students." No obvious solutions are inherent in this statement of needs. The construction of new facilities may satisfy the need, as might refurbishing the old facilities, developing distance-learning capabilities, and so on. Having stated their needs in the way they do, the dissenting faculty raise a broad array of options (including the dean's sole option) to consider in deciding what should be done.

This case illustrates a common pitfall encountered in the definition of needs: the premature offering of a solution to the needs problem. Recognizing and articulating needs is an evolutionary process. It is important that at the outset, we leave as many options open as possible. As we go through the effort of articulating needs, we obtain more and more pertinent information that allows us to narrow down the options. Only after we have gone through this process do we have enough information to consider seriously the specific solutions to satisfying needs.

## Addressing the Needs of the Wrong Customers

In the earliest stages of the needs-requirements life cycle, that is, grappling with trying to identify and formulate needs, we should find ourselves struggling to clarify *whose* needs should be addressed. If we do not raise that question, there is a good chance that we will address the needs of the wrong customers.

Two possible pitfalls stand out here: there are multiple customers, and we address the needs of the wrong set of customers; and our personal values so color our interpretation of customer needs that we wind up addressing our own needs rather than theirs.

**SORTING OUT THE NEEDS OF MULTIPLE CUSTOMERS.** Thus far, I have been talking about satisfying customer needs as if it were clear who "the customer" is. In practice, there are often multiple customers to contend with, and their needs typically do not dovetail. In fact, their needs may actually conflict. Given these circumstances, a project planner must sort through the contending needs, determine which needs are most important, and articulate a composite need that captures their most significant features. The following case study offers an example of some of the struggles people had in defining needs on early office automation projects in the 1980s. It shows that even in a relatively simple situation, it is not easy to determine whose needs should be addressed.

### LEGAL OFFICE OF THE DEPARTMENT OF NATIONAL WELL-BEING

The legal office of the U.S. Department of National Well-Being has fifty attorneys. All office records regarding internal administrative matters are maintained manually by an administrative assistant. Office automation is limited to the use of four stand-alone word processors (although the great bulk of paperwork is still produced on standard electric typewriters).

John Roberts, the new chief counsel who has just joined the department from a major law firm, is surprised to find such low usage of new information technology. Not only are administrative matters handled manually, but staff attorneys have no access to computerized legal research databases such as LEXIS, which are employed routinely in law firms and law schools.

Unfortunately, Roberts shares with most other attorneys anxiety and befuddlement regarding technical things and is not certain how to go about remedying the office's information processing deficiencies. Indeed, he is not even absolutely certain that a true deficiency exists.

Allen Kaye is the only attorney in the office with a technical background. He has recently become fascinated with personal computers and their day-to-day applications. He purchased a Micro-G computer for use at home and now wants to turn his attention to the Stellar Max personal computer, which is fast becoming the standard for the workplace. He meets with Roberts and argues forcefully that their office is living in an information Stone Age. He shows Roberts a recent *New York Times* article describing the power of the Stellar Max in the workplace and points out that this machine, if equipped with a modem, could be used to access legal research databases. After half an hour of persuasive argument, he convinces Roberts to order a Stellar Max for the office.

Several months pass before the computer arrives. Meanwhile, another attorney, Robin Smith, has become intrigued with the possible uses of the computer in her work. She talks to Kaye about her desire to learn something about the Stellar Max, and Kaye, delighted to find someone who shares his interest in computer applications, eagerly enumerates the computer's possibilities. At the end of the discussion, however, he turns serious for a moment and warns Smith that she should try to contain her enthusiasm so that not too many attorneys become interested in using the computer. Should this happen, he anticipates that both he and Smith will have to fight toot and nail for time at the machine.

Unfortunately for Smith, enthusiasm is no substitute for substantive knowledge of how computers operate. She recognizes this and decides that the most efficient way to learn about software and computer operations is through formal training. She receives permission from Roberts to approach the department's training office about providing training assistance on use of the Stellar Max. The training manager responds that although the department has capabilities to train agency personnel to use microcomputer software and hardware, it has already overcommitted its meager resources and will be unable to assist the legal office. Furthermore, he refuses to approve the use of outside contractors because his office cannot adequately monitor the quality of such training—and because such outside training undercuts the raison d'être of his office.

Five months later, a visitor to the legal office sees Allen Kaye bent over a Stellar Max, lost to all things save his machine and his software. An attorney laughingly tells the visitor that Kaye is the office's computer nut, spending eight hours a day, five days a week on the machine. He adds that no one else in the office knows the first thing about computers, so no one has the slightest idea what Kaye is doing.

**MULTIPLE CUSTOMERS, MULTIPLE NEEDS.** The preceding case illustrates how most organizations typically deal with the needs-requirements life cycle. Needs are identified and articulated in the most haphazard way. A systematic needs assessment would have shown that the overall need to automate the legal office could be broken into a number of specific needs that differ according to different customers. If John Roberts, the chief counsel, had asked Allen Kaye to articulate the office's information needs more precisely and if he had required Kaye to raise the questions listed earlier in this chapter during the discussion of needs articulation, he would have learned that the different constituencies in his office have their own specific information needs. Consider the following actors in the legal office and their needs:

- *John Roberts.* As chief counsel, Roberts would like to have his office run as smoothly and efficiently as possible. To the extent that office automation increases office productivity, he sees it as good. In addition, with an automated office, he may be able to improve his access to timely information on legal and administrative activities within the office. Finally, by replacing machines that clunk with machines that hum, he may impress upper management with his grasp of modern technologies, which could help satisfy his need for career advancement.
- *Staff attorneys.* Perhaps the strongest information need facing the attorneys (including Allen Kaye and Robin Smith) is rapid and full access to legal information. This information is crucial for them to formulate effective legal opinions. The most important aspect of office automation for them is access to the computerized legal databases.
- *Allen Kaye.* Kaye has expressed a need to upgrade his computer skills. Perhaps this need is rooted in a desire to do the best job he can, or in satisfaction of curiosity about computer technology, or in a desire to upgrade his skills to make him more attractive in the job market.
- *Administrative assistant.* Since the administrative assistant is charged with maintaining all office records (for example, time sheets, budgets, and personnel files), her information needs focus on data creation, manipulation, and retrieval. On a more personal level, she may see automation as filling a need for greater authority and prestige, since as chief administrative staff member, she would clearly play an important role in maintaining a computerized system.
- *Secretaries.* Secretarial information needs revolve around their principal clerical task: typing reports and legal opinions. These needs are addressed primarily by word processing equipment, which allows a handful of secretaries to do the work of many secretaries working only with typewriters. It should be noted, however, that satisfaction of their professional need may create problems for secretaries, since it may lead to their unemployment.
- *All actors in the legal office.* One need that all the actors in the legal office share is to receive training on the new technology. Allen Kaye is the only one in the office who uses the Stellar Max because he is the

only one who knows how to use it. He learned to use the computer through self-instruction, and he was successful in this because he was highly motivated. Because they lack microcomputer training, the other staff members never warmed up to the Stellar Max and were never able to see how it could help them improve their productivity.

In the final analysis, the only need that was fully addressed and satisfied was Allen Kaye's need to upgrade his computer skills. The project to automate the legal office was an outstanding success from Kaye's viewpoint and a failure from the perspective of the other actors. The project could have been handled more effectively if a systematic needs analysis had been carried out. A good needs analyst would have unearthed the full array of needs that had a bearing on office automation: professional, personal, and psychological needs.

**ESTABLISHING PRIORITIES: THE NEEDS HIERARCHY.** When there are multiple customers—and there often are—the needs recognition and articulation effort can become complex and politically charged. In part, this is a function of the fact that there are more needs to deal with when there are multiple customers than when there is only one. It is hard enough to get a handle on a single need and far harder still to come to grips with several, particularly when they reflect the different orientations and requirements of different customers. Multiple needs are not likely to dovetail perfectly. They may even conflict with each other. It is clear that priorities must be established among them. Not all needs are equal in importance, and they do not have equal costs and technical risks.

How do we reconcile the different, often conflicting, needs of the different customers? How can we generate a set of reasonably consistent and focused needs that will serve as the basis of our project plan? The answer is to create a *needs hierarchy* during the needs articulation phase of the needs-requirements life cycle.

The needs hierarchy is a diagram that shows the full range of needs that exist for a given problem and the relationship of these needs to each other. A view of a partial needs hierarchy for the legal office case is offered in Figure 4.1. We will assume that this needs hierarchy was put together by a small cross-functional team of staff workers in the legal office of the Department of National Well-Being (DNWB) working closely with the chief counsel, administrative assistant, staff attorneys, and secretaries; thus, we have reasonable assurance that the hierarchy

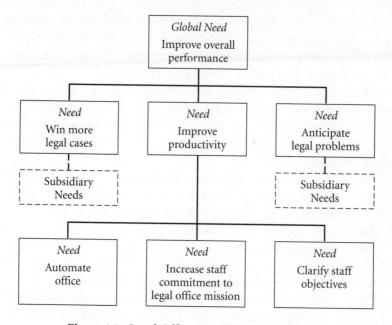

**Figure 4.1. Legal Office Overall Needs Hierarchy.**

has incorporated the input of most or all of the relevant actors. Each item was included only after the team achieved a consensus that the item belonged in the hierarchy.

As Figure 4.1 shows, eliciting needs occurs in a top-down fashion, starting with a rather abstract statement of a need and then gradually drilling down to gain a more precise understanding of it in its various dimensions. This approach to eliciting needs is called *peeling the onion*.

Let's say a business analyst assembles the needs definition team in a conference room. She may start the elicitation process by making the following comment: "In defining needs, we must avoid identifying solutions before we really understand the basic nature of the needs. So let's start the process by getting a high-level sense of what DNWB needs in the broadest sense. Then we can gradually become more specific and focus on office automation issues. So at the highest level of abstraction, let's identify DNWB's premier need associated with running its operations."

In practice, the needs identification team can quickly reach agreement on this high-level need, since it is a noncontroversial mother-and-apple-pie statement. Figure 4.1 shows that the team agrees that the highest-level operational need at DNWB is "To improve overall performance." They debate other possibilities, such as, "To optimize the use of corporate assets" and "To serve the public," but in the context of the problems the agency is facing in functioning effectively, they zero in on "To improve overall performance."

The business analyst moves on: "See how easy it is to achieve agreement on what our needs are? Okay, now we all know this stated need is too abstract to have real content, so let's try to be more specific. In order to improve our performance at DNWB, what subsidiary needs ought to be addressed?"

After fifteen minutes of discussion, where a dozen possibilities have been articulated, the group agrees that the three key subsidiary needs are to (1) win more legal cases, (2) improve productivity, and (3) anticipate legal problems rather than react to them.

The business analyst continues: "Very good. Now we have a sense of the context in which we are functioning at DNWB. It seems clear to me that 'To improve productivity' is the need that has the greatest bearing on our general counsel's charge to us to improve operations at DNWB. So let's pursue this line of exploration further. What are some subsidiary needs that must be achieved if our legal office is to improve its productivity?"

Once again, a list is generated of possibilities. The team prioritizes them and identifies three sub-sub-needs that go to the top of the list: (1) automate the office, (2) increase staff commitment to the office's legal mission, and (3) clarify staff objectives.

The business analyst continues: "Now we're getting somewhere. We can explore each of these possible sub-sub-needs in detail. However, I want to stick to 'automate the office' since it is clear that our senior management believes we need work in this area. As we examine 'automate the office' in more detail, keep in mind that we have identified two other sub-sub-needs that should be addressed if we are going to improve our productivity.

"By now, you know the drill. What subsidiary needs should be satisfied in order to achieve the sub-sub-need, 'To automate the office'?"

Figure 4.2 shows the results of applying the needs hierarchy technique to "Automate the office." Three items are ranked most highly: (1) improve access to legal data, (2) improve efficiency of report production, and (3) improve maintenance of office records.

Note two things about where the team is in the peeling the onion process. First, it has moved from a statement of a highly abstract need at the outset to the statement of something that is beginning to sound

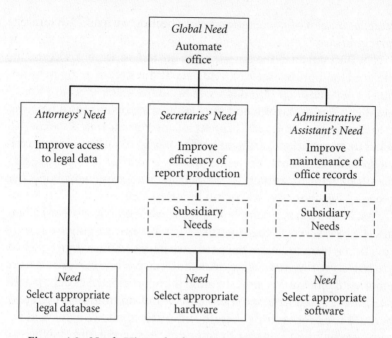

**Figure 4.2. Needs Hierarchy for Legal Office Automation Project.**

like a solution. Normally, when defining needs, we adhere religiously to the admonishing, "Don't confuse solutions with needs." But in this case, the solutions that the team is approaching are directly traceable to the office's abstract needs. We aren't jumping the gun in identifying solutions.

Second, it is only at this point that the stakeholders' specific interests have been raised. Attorneys are primarily concerned with better access to data, the secretaries are concerned with better report production, and the office administrator is concerned with the maintenance of records. There is little overlap among the different stakeholders' principal interests. This could be a source of conflict, but it turns out that with the needs hierarchy process, it seldom is.

Normally, when needs assessments are carried out, the stakeholders are asked at the outset to define what they think their particular needs are. Regrettably, this approach can set up a conflict situation among the stakeholders as they jockey to have their specific needs addressed. With the needs hierarchy approach, we start the process by identifying high-level needs that everyone has and then gradually work our way to specifics. Thus, the needs definition team has a chance to establish a habit of cooperation before dealing with difficult territorial matters.

The business analyst continues: "We are almost there! Let's examine the need to improve access to legal data. If this need is going to be fulfilled, what subsidiary needs should be addressed?"

After some discussion and the highlighting of a handful of items, the team focuses on three: (1) select an appropriate legal database, (2) select an appropriate hardware platform, and (3) select an appropriate software platform. The same process is applied to "Improve efficiency of report production" and "Improve maintenance of office records," but those results are not reported here.

What do we gain by employing the needs hierarchy process? There are several answers to this question. First, because we employ a cross-functional team to define the needs, we have some assurance that we are reflecting the views of key stakeholders. No one can accuse us of ignoring them. Furthermore, because they participated in defining the needs, we should have some measure of buy-in from them. Second, because the process is deliberate and disciplined, we can avoid the common pitfall of jumping to solutions. As noted earlier, by the end of the process, the solutions we hint at are clearly derived from more abstract needs that we have identified. Third, by using this process, we minimize territorial struggles. The technique is geared to getting people to define their needs in a collaborative way.

Once the needs elicitation session is ended, the business analyst writes up her findings. Ultimately, these findings will be forwarded to senior management, and if approved, they will be delivered to a technical group that will use them to develop functional and detailed requirements. In her report, she describes the overall discovery process so that senior management and the technical folks have a deep understanding of the context in which the defined needs emerged.

DISTORTING THE CUSTOMERS' NEEDS.  There is always a danger that the individuals analyzing the needs of the customers will alter the statement of those needs so that they more closely reflect their own biases than the customers' true needs. Sometimes this alteration is undertaken consciously, but I suspect that usually it is not. If you were to point out to needs analysts that their articulation of the customers' needs was strongly distorted by their own values and perceptions, they would probably be surprised.

There are a number of ways that customer needs are distorted in this fashion. Three common ways are gold-plating of needs, selective filtering of customer needs, and practicing the father-knows-best approach:

- *Gold-plating of needs.* We live in an era where new technology is glorified and obsolescence is abhorred. Purchasing agents in organizations are extremely sensitive to the issue of obsolescence. One of their big questions is, "Will the hardware I buy today be obsolete one or two years from now?" Since this is often difficult to answer, the safest course of action may be to buy the most advanced hardware available.

This orientation carries over to defining needs. A customer may have a need to get from A to B in a certain period of time. This need may be perfectly well served by providing the customer with an entry-level Honda Civic. However, the needs analyst, who is aware of state-of-the-art automobile systems, may upgrade the customer's needs to include a need for climate control within the vehicle, quadraphonic sound, cruise control, and so on. While the customer may need only a Honda Civic, she may get a Mercedes Benz—to satisfy the needs analyst's enhancements of her needs.

The problem here is largely one of waste, of underused capacity. But at least the customer can use the Mercedes Benz to get from A to B. Things could be worse. Consider the case of a needs analyst who is an extreme technology enthusiast. He may articulate the customer's simple need in such a manner that the only way to satisfy this need is to order a state-of-the-art Stealth fighter, which will get the customer from A to B very quickly indeed!

In this case, of course, the problem is that the system as defined by the needs analyst does not satisfy the customer's needs at all; consequently, the system emerging from the gold-plated needs will not be used.

The problem of gold-plating needs is fairly common in organizations that do not face serious resource constraints. The military services have been a prime example, although in this era of funding constraints, this is becoming less so. New projects are often conceived as simple and relatively cost-effective, but needs may be redefined so that they take into account every conceivable contingency a weapons system might encounter. By the end of one or two years, the original, simple conception metamorphoses into something extremely complex—and expensive. Lean and hungry organizations do not engage in much gold-plating of needs, not because they are inherently less inclined to obtain the most advanced technology but because the discipline of the small bank account forces them to take a more parsimonious view of their needs.

• *Selective filtering of customer needs.* There is an old saying that has important implications for the analysis of customer needs: "To a four-year-old boy with a hammer, all the world is a nail." We can just as well say that to an accountant, all the world is a spreadsheet; or to a scientist, all the world is a set of mathematically describable physical relationships; or to a politician, all the world is potential voters. Each of us sees the world through a filter that has been developed over a lifetime and reflects our experiences, values, and training.

Our filters clearly color our perceptions. A difficulty arises when our perceptions deviate dramatically from reality. In such a situation, our response to problems may bear little relationship to what is needed to solve them. In the context of articulating needs, we may find a customer telling a needs analyst, "I need a better way to keep track of the services my clinic offers to clients." What a computer-oriented needs analyst may hear is, "I need a computerized, client-directed management information system." Consequently, what is ultimately delivered to the customers may be an elaborate and expensive computer system, when their needs could have been adequately satisfied with a stack of three-by-five-inch index cards. Once again the consequence of distorting customer needs may be the underuse, misuse, or nonuse of a project's deliverables.

The best way to bypass this problem is to have the needs recognition and articulation tasks carried out by a cross-functional *group* of people, each with a different background and each capable of viewing customer needs from a different perspective. Close contact with customers is also important, and the cross-functional group may have customers as members.

• *Practicing the father-knows-best approach to needs recognition and articulation.* I know a man who in the mid-1960s served in the Peace Corps in an Andean village. One of his goals was to carry out a small demonstration project to show the local Indians how to raise healthy, plump hogs by using modern animal husbandry. At the end of several months, the two objects of his attention, Napoleon and Josephine, were the finest-looking hogs in the region, a tribute to modern agricultural science and the Peace Corps worker's diligence. The Indians admired the outcome of this demonstration project, yet none of them adopted the methods employed by my acquaintance. He asked several of them, "Don't you want to raise nice hogs like Napoleon and Josephine?"

"Certainly we do," they responded.

"Well, why don't you employ the hog-raising techniques I showed you in my demonstration project?" he persisted.

"Because we figure that in your approach, it costs more to raise the hogs than we can recover by selling them. Right now, it costs us nothing to raise hogs because we give them scraps and let them eat whatever they can find in the streets and fields. Whatever price we get for them in the market is almost all profit to us. So our hogs are small, but at least they're profitable."

This story illustrates something that often happens during the needs articulation phase—what I call the *father-knows-best syndrome.* Usually the people working on the needs articulation task have been selected to carry out this task because they have the experience and technical competence to translate customers' often vague perception of a need into something concrete and workable. In these circumstances, it is easy for the needs articulators to assume a paternalistic posture and to feel that they know what is best for their customers, even when these customers show resistance to their suggestions.

Because they are experts, they often *do* know what is best for the customers. However, if they encounter customer resistance to their approach and choose to ignore the customers' deeply felt concerns (believing these concerns are silly and uneducated), the project emerging from the needs they articulate is likely to produce a deliverable that will be underused, misused, or not used at all.

Sometimes, of course, the experts do *not* know what is best for the customers, as was the case in the hog-raising example. In any event, individuals involved in articulating needs should avoid taking a paternalistic approach to their work, since there is nothing to be gained from it and much to be lost.

## CONCLUSION

I have devoted a whole chapter to the issue of recognizing and articulating customer needs because projects arise in order to address needs. Needs are the driving force behind projects. If we do a bad job of articulating needs, our project will be built on a foundation of sand, and major problems *will* arise.

Articulating needs is serious business but has received little attention in either the theory or the practice of project management. In regard to the practice of project management, my personal experience suggests an overall disregard for the issues covered in this chapter. Not surprisingly, there does not seem to be much goodwill between customers and project staff. When the two sides continue to miscommunicate and frustration levels get high, customers often harbor the view that project staff are unresponsive and suffer technical tunnel vision, while project staff see customers as fickle, aimless, unknowledgeable, and naive.

The pity is that so many project problems are rooted in poor needs recognition and articulation. When these matters receive sufficient attention at the outset of the project, many of these problems never arise.

# CHAPTER FIVE

# Specifying What the Project Should Accomplish

F or most of us, being misunderstood is a common occurrence, something that happens on a daily basis. At the restaurant, the waiter brings our dinner and we note that the baked potato is filled with sour cream, even though we expressly requested *no* sour cream. For Mother's Day, we order a dozen roses to be sent to our mother and are aghast to receive a call from her thanking us so much for the lovely carnations. Our mail-order drapes arrive—eight inches shorter than we ordered.

Projects are filled with similar misunderstandings between customers and project staff. What customers order—or, more accurately, what they *think* they order—is often not what they get. Consider the following conversation between an office worker and a painter contracted to paint his office:

OFFICE WORKER: Not only did you paint my office walls blue, but you painted the ceiling blue as well.

PAINTER: You asked me to paint the room blue, and now you've got a blue room.

OFFICE WORKER: But the blue ceiling is oppressive. Ceilings should never be the same color as the walls. They should always be a lighter color.

PAINTER: You asked for a blue room. You're lucky I didn't paint the floor blue as well.

This conversation captures in a nutshell the essence of a major source of misunderstandings on projects: the inadequate statement of customer requirements. The office worker's description of how he wanted the room painted meant one thing to him and another to the painter. As a consequence, the room was not painted to the office worker's satisfaction. Had his requirements been more carefully stipulated, he probably would have gotten what he wanted.

The blame for the poor specification of requirements does not rest entirely on his shoulders. The painter must share some culpability. It was clearly in her interest to make sure she understood exactly what the office worker wanted. As a professional painter, she should devise an approach to dealing with clients that allows her to determine precisely what their requirements are. For example, before beginning each paint job, she might give the client a checklist asking what colors the walls should be, the ceilings, and the trim. Otherwise, clients will continue to be unhappy when she does not do what they want, and they will see to it that she is unhappy as well.

One major objective of those who are effective in designing and implementing projects is to reduce such misunderstandings to a minimum. This can be done with the careful specification of customer requirements.

## THE NATURE OF REQUIREMENTS

As we saw in Chapter Four, requirements specify what the project deliverable should look like and what it should do. They can be divided into two basic categories. *Functional requirements* describe the characteristics of the deliverable in ordinary, nontechnical language. They should be understandable to the customers, and the customers should play a major, direct role in their development. *Technical requirements* describe the features of the deliverable (for example, its physical dimensions and performance specifications) in detailed technical terms. These technical specifications offer project staff crucial guidance on what they should be doing on the project. Because of their technical nature, technical requirements are unlikely to be understood by the customers. In this chapter, most of our attention will focus on functional requirements.

Project requirements are important for at least two reasons. First, they are a tangible embodiment of the customers' needs. Needs emerge, are recognized and carefully articulated, and then are translated into requirements, which serve as the basis of the project plan. In the final analysis, project planning reduces to the effort of determining how best to meet requirements. If they are specified wrongly or even poorly, the plan will be inadequate.

Second, requirements are important because they define the project team's obligations to the customers. Carefully specified project requirements detail the team's responsibilities. On projects run under contract, the specified requirements are written as a statement of work, and compliance or noncompliance with the contract is determined by resolving whether the contractor has fulfilled the statement of work.

## PROBLEMS WITH REQUIREMENTS

Requirements-related problems are one of the principal sources of cost and schedule overruns. They may lead to rejection of the deliverable or to major reworking of project tasks. Furthermore, they contribute substantially to what I perceive to be the most serious category of project failure: the production of a deliverable that is never used or is misused. Requirements-related problems result in several ways: the requirements that are specified are incorrect, they are imprecise and ambiguous, or they shift as the project is carried out.

Regardless of the specific nature of the requirements-related problem, its consequences unfold with consistent regularity. Here is what happens. During the course of the project, the customers become aware that what the project staff are developing is not what they want. This may reflect the fact that the project staff are working on something completely at variance with what the customers want (incorrect requirements), or they have misinterpreted the customers' stated desires (imprecise, ambiguous requirements), or the customers have changed their minds about what the project staff should develop (shifting requirements). Whichever problem it is, the customers and the project staff are out of sync, and the flow of the project is interrupted.

If the project staff respond to the customers' concerns and do what the customers want—and they should if they have grossly misconstrued the desires of the customers—the project will have to be replanned, delays will occur, and cost overruns are likely. If they do not act in accordance with the customers' desires, the project's deliverable is not likely to be very meaningful to the customers, suggesting that the project was a waste of time and resources.

Project professionals are faced with a no-win situation here. When requirements-related problems arise, those working on the project encounter either the likely prospect of cost and schedule overruns or strong customer dissatisfaction. Their best bet is to avoid this problem before it surfaces; once it arises, there will be serious trouble. The problem can largely be avoided if they take care to articulate customer needs carefully and then work closely with customers to develop unambiguous functional requirements. They should also recognize that customers are often fickle and should take precautions to avoid being taken by surprise by sudden customer shifts in requirements.

## Incorrect Requirements

We saw in Chapter Four that there are many ways in which customer needs can be misconstrued and misrepresented. The needs addressed may be those of the wrong customer, the articulated needs may reflect the biases of the needs articulator, and inherently fuzzy needs may be misinterpreted. In any such cases, functional requirements built on poorly articulated needs will be off the mark. This is a certainty. The final deliverable (assuming the project gets that far) will bear little or no relationship to what the customers need and want.

A large share of Chapter Four was dedicated to suggesting ways to carry out the needs recognition and particular tasks effectively, so it is not necessary to rehash the earlier material here, except to offer a summary of steps that should be taken.

First, project planners should recognize the inherent difficulty of articulating needs. Needs tend to be fuzzy; even those holding them generally aren't quite sure what the needs are. Recognition of the difficulty is important, because it encourages the individuals charged with articulation to give this matter the attention it deserves. Too often these individuals rush in with packaged solutions to problems they don't really understand.

Second, project planners should identify the most relevant customers. In most situations, project planners will be dealing with multiple customers, only some of whose needs should be addressed in the project. They should avoid organizing their projects around the needs of peripheral or nonrelevant customers.

Third, project planners should work closely with customers in articulating their needs. Needs articulation entails a certain amount of hand holding; the needs articulator and the customers should work closely together to hammer out a well-formulated and accurate statement of what it is the customers need.

Fourth, project planners should be aware of the most common pitfalls associated with needs articulation. They should avoid gold-plating needs (that is, offering customers more than they need), imposing their own needs on customers, and assuming a paternalistic, father-knows-best attitude in dealing with customers.

## Imprecise and Ambiguous Requirements

A major problem arises when requirements are posited in such a way that they are imprecise and ambiguous, subject to different interpretations of their meaning. Imprecise requirements are invitations to problems. When requirements are ambiguously specified, two people can look at the same statement and disagree on what it means. The disagreement can become vehement, since it is clear to each party what the specification is saying, and the fact that the other party does not view the specification "correctly" is attributed to obstinacy, stupidity, or outright dishonesty.

There are various reasons that requirements are specified imprecisely. Some of these reasons are legitimate and understandable. Others reflect sloppy thinking, impatience, or a conscious desire to obfuscate things. Following are some the more obvious reasons for the imprecise specification of requirements.

THE NATURE OF HUMAN LANGUAGE.  Human language is naturally ambiguous. While this ambiguity makes for interesting poetry, it is not well suited to describing the requirements of project deliverables. For example, we may specify that we want to furnish our waiting room with chairs that are fire-engine red. For most people, this immediately conjures up an image of a bright red color. But there are many varieties of bright red. (Of course, we could go to our local fire department to get a better idea of what fire engine red is, but this would not be very useful in my neighborhood, where the fire trucks are yellow.) We can be more precise in specifying our color if we request a particular upholstery fabric using its color identification number, or if we attach to the requirements statement a sample of the desired color. If we want to carry this matter of precision even further, we can describe the color according to its wavelength in the visible light spectrum.

This discussion points out the difficulty of depending on human language to describe requirements. For requirements to be precise, we must often supplement our verbal descriptions with additional supporting material: drawings, samples, maps, photographs, and technical data, for example. We can reduce the imprecision in the verbal portion of the requirements statement by describing what we want in excruciating detail, leaving nothing to the imagination. In this last instance, however, we run the risk of overwhelming project staff with impenetrable verbiage that they may choose to ignore.

**DELIBERATE IMPRECISION FOR FLEXIBILITY.** Sometimes requirements are stated ambiguously on purpose, simply to maintain flexibility in the project. This approach is common in state-of-the-art projects, on which there is generally great uncertainty about how the project will proceed. The fear is that the precise statement of requirements will constrict project staff in their work, discouraging them from exploiting unanticipated opportunities as they arise.

Deliberate imprecision is also common in projects that are filled with conditional outcomes. These are projects on which when asked, "What is it that you want?" a customer responds, "It depends on how things work out." The danger with this approach is that the project may drift aimlessly. As a consequence, it runs the risk of never being concluded or of producing a deliverable that meets no one's needs. This is precisely the outcome of many basic research projects.

**HUMAN CONFLICT PREVENTING CONSENSUS.** When people cannot achieve a consensus on what it is that should emerge from a project, they may be unable to generate clear-cut requirements. They may postpone hard choices until later, hoping that the conflict among them will be resolved and things will somehow straighten themselves out. What is likely to happen is that the loosely phrased requirements will take on a life of their own and lead to a deliverable that satisfies none of the contending parties.

Given the tendency of poorly formulated requirements to cause project troubles, it is usually better to make the hard choices as early as possible in the project life cycle. These choices will have to be reckoned with some day; if they are addressed later in the project and it is determined that the project has been moving in the wrong direction, the consequences for the budget and schedule may be devastating.

INHERENTLY NEBULOUS INFORMATION AGE PROJECTS. Information age projects often deal with intangibles or "semitangibles," whereas traditional projects in construction and engineering deal with things you can touch and readily see. For example, someone who is designing a project to carry out a marketing study is dealing primarily with abstractions—consumers, consumer preferences, hypothetical product prices, potential competitors, mythical competing products, and so forth. Trying to get a firm grip on these abstractions is something like trying to grab a handful of sand.

Seasoned professionals who spend their lives working with intangibles develop the capacity to "see" what the end product will look like, just as a draftsperson can look at a blank sheet of paper and "see" the drawing that will ultimately emerge. The problem is that customers are generally not seasoned professionals accustomed, say, to designing on-line information systems or undertaking sophisticated marketing studies. In trying to visualize the deliverable, they cannot see anything but an amorphous blob. Only as the project evolves and takes shape do they begin to have an inkling of what is being developed. Now that they can see what is emerging, they may not like it and may demand that the project take a different turn to produce something that is more to their liking. This is a very common occurrence with projects dealing with intangibles and semitangibles.

What project staff must do to minimize problems created by the inherently ethereal nature of their projects is to help customers "see" the results of the project as early as possible. They should make frequent use of visual tools, such as drawings, flow diagrams, and tables, and they can do what architects and engineers regularly do in their projects: create simple prototypes of the deliverable, which they can show to the customers. Rather than build a physical model of a building or an airplane, they might put together simple back-of-the-envelope mock-ups of the thing they are developing—a scaled-down computerized accounting system or a sample market study, for example.

A methodology has been created to help project planners and managers use prototypes effectively in information projects. It is called *rapid prototyping*, and I will discuss it in more detail later in this chapter.

CUSTOMERS' LACK OF EXPERTISE. Everybody knows that an expert is someone who is very good at doing something. A tennis expert is good at playing tennis, a computer expert is good at writing code, a legal expert is good at interpreting the law, and so forth. By the same token, someone who is not an expert will find it difficult to do these things well. Customers are generally not experts with regard to the technical content of the projects carried out to meet their needs. They may have expertise in other areas, but this other expertise may be only marginally helpful to them in formulating needs and requirements for their project.

Albert Einstein was a brilliant theoretical physicist of international renown. To my generation—children during Einstein's last years—his name is virtually synonymous with the word *genius*. Yet I doubt if Einstein would have been very effective in describing the precise requirements of an accounting system to help Princeton's Institute for Advanced Studies (his employer) keep better track of how he and his colleagues spent their research funds.

One important task of the project team is to educate customers about relevant features of the potential deliverable. Certainly, customers cannot be expected to know everything, but just how well educated should they be? This is difficult to answer specifically. There are dangers with both overeducation and undereducation. If too much effort is devoted to educating customers, they may be overwhelmed with detail that they cannot—and possibly don't want to—understand. In this case, the well-meaning attempt at customer education may produce a completely opposite result. Feeling themselves lost in a miasma of incomprehensible technicalities, customers may withdraw from the process and leave the project definition in the hands of the experts. These experts unfortunately often have little understanding of what the customers will ultimately find acceptable.

But if little or no effort is devoted to educating customers, they will not know enough to be useful partners in the project definition process. Their input will be ill informed and may steer the project into fruitless side excursions. Ultimately, a deliverable will be produced that will not be very useful to them.

Project staff should be sensitive to this issue. The temptation is to ignore customer education altogether—and possibly even to intimidate the customers with expertise. Let's face it: customers can be a big pain. They don't know what they want or what is good for them, yet this doesn't stop them from telling project staff how to do their job. When customers timidly offer suggestions, experts who really don't want customer kibitzing often react by overwhelming them with terms and statistics beyond their ken, hoping to intimidate them with a technical whirlwind. Perhaps this tactic gains some momentary peace for the project staff, but in the long run, it may lead to the creation of deliverables that customers do not want.

How much should customers know? In general, they should know enough to be able to contribute meaningfully to the needs articulation and requirements specification efforts. They should also know enough so that they are not surprised with the final outcome. The specific amount of education that should be directed at them has to be determined on a case-by-case basis.

OVERSIGHTS ON THE PART OF PROJECT PLANNERS. The final reason that requirements are stated imprecisely is more pedestrian than the others. Simply put, this may happen because of sheer oversight, reflecting unstated assumptions or an incomplete understanding of what the project should entail and what the deliverable should be. In asking the painter in the example to paint our office pale blue, we may exclude the requirement to keep the ceiling white because it does not occur to us that this is an issue.

These kinds of oversights occur on all but the most routine projects. There is a certain inevitability to them. They occur because we operate according to unstated assumptions and because we are not omniscient, lacking sufficient imagination to identify every possible meaningful contingency that our project should address.

One way to minimize such oversights is to go to those who will actually carry out the assigned tasks and ask them what kinds of contingencies might arise that should be dealt with in the project specifications. A good long-run approach for dealing with such oversights is to compile a project-by-project checklist of requirements that should be addressed on all projects. As more and more project experience is gained, the list will grow in depth and breadth. Workers in the construction industry are familiar with this kind of list.

## Shifting Requirements

The third and final broad area of requirements-related problems focuses on problems associated with shifting requirements. Projects are dynamic things, so it should not come as a surprise that there are strong pressures to modify the original requirements as a project evolves. However, modification may play havoc with the project plan, which is built on specified requirements and may lead to cost and schedule overruns.

Four common situations resulting in changes in requirements are illustrated in the following cases:

### BUYER'S REMORSE

Maureen Shea is the chief administrator of Marvin Gelb Memorial Hospital. This hospital is overcrowded, with three patients typically occupying a single room. Shea and her staff have long entertained a dream of building a new wing on the hospital, which would dramatically ameliorate the condition. When a three-point plunge in mortgage rates occurs, Dr. Shea seizes the opportunity and enters into a contract with a construction firm to build the new wing. It will accommodate 120 beds, a major addition to the patient-handling capability of the hospital.

No sooner is the contract with the builder signed than Shea reads in the local paper a series of articles on the growing popularity of inexpensive outpatient care facilities in the region. She begins to worry that perhaps she has bitten off more than she can chew with her expansion of the hospital. Five months into the project, after the foundation has been poured and the skeleton of the new wing has risen from the ground, Shea begins discussions with the builder to revise the construction plans so that the facility will accommodate only 60 new beds instead of the original 120. She is shocked to learn that this 50 percent reduction in the wing's capacity will save only 15 percent in construction charges.

This case illustrates a phenomenon that real estate agents and car dealers are familiar with. It is so common in these lines of business that it has been given a name: buyer's remorse. It is also common in project management, especially with controversial or high-risk projects.

After much thought and debate, a decision is made to launch a costly project, and no sooner is the decision made than those responsible for it have second thoughts. They may now try to scale down or even eliminate the project in order to reduce some of the deleterious consequences they imagine will hit them if the project does not work out as expected.

This scaling down may be very costly, especially if the project is well under way, since it entails major changes in the original project plan. When this situation arises, the project manager must make it clear to the customers that changes to the plan will be expensive.

### INSURMOUNTABLE OBSTACLES

Marsha Bronfman is a graduate student working on her doctoral dissertation, which focuses on the public health problems of a developing country. Central to her study is a questionnaire survey of public health practitioners in the country, designed to identify major obstacles to establishing an effective public health program there. She spends two months developing and testing the questionnaire. When it is ready, she sends out 350 copies to the principal public health workers in the country.

A few days later, she receives a visit from an official of the ministry of health, telling her that she had no authority to conduct the survey and that she is forbidden to do further work on it. Bronfman suddenly finds herself persona non grata in the country. What is worse from her perspective is that her doctoral dissertation is jeopardized, since it was designed to focus on the results of the survey analysis. If she is going to complete her dissertation, she will have to revise her research strategy completely.

The sudden appearance of insurmountable obstacles, such as those Bronfman encountered, is a common experience on projects. Any project that blazes new trails runs a strong risk of encountering such obstacles. With technical projects, for example, we are almost assured that technical glitches will force us to utter that age-old expostulation, "Well, I guess it's back to the drawing board!"

### FLIGHTS OF FANCY

Brian Davis and his design team are developing a new toaster for Appliance Masters Co. They spend two weeks working closely with Daniel Seligman, vice president of new product development. Seligman is a highly creative individual—the classic idea man—and he offers several novel suggestions for features that should be built into the new toaster. Davis accepts the suggestions and begins building a prototype of the new toaster.

Two months later, Seligman visits the design shop to see how the toaster is progressing. Viewing the nearly finished prototype, he becomes quite excited. "I've just had a brainstorm," he exclaims. "Let's include a voice synthesizer chip in the toaster, enabling the toaster to 'talk' to the user." The design team members, recognizing that this suggestion would require a major redesign of the product, look at Brian Davis with apprehension. "We'll do it," says Davis, and the design team members groan inwardly.

Three months later, Seligman returns to the design shop to review the nearly completed prototype of the talking toaster. The demonstration he sees causes him to jump with glee. "This is great," he says. "This is the stuff of science fiction! You know, we should carry the toaster one step further than we have. What we produce should not be a mere toaster; it should be an information center, the brains for all kitchen appliances. Look into this, will you, Brian?" Brian nods his head in agreement while performing some lightning calculations in his head. The latest request will extend the project by at least nine months and will require doubling the design team.

Seligman's vision of the toaster's possibilities evolved with the physical development of the toaster itself. As the new toaster took on tangible shape, Seligman's imagination was stimulated to come up with new possibilities. Such a phenomenon is common on projects. Although suggested changes in the project requirements may ultimately lead to a superior product, they can create serious problems for the project manager.

Changes in the requirements are not cost free. Because of them, schedules may be stretched out, costs may escalate, and other projects in the queue may have to be postponed or canceled. If changes are constantly being required, the project also runs the serious risk of never being completed.

## SEIZING OPPORTUNITIES

Nancy and David Rama buy a run-down old house with a view to refurbishing it and renting it out. They hire a contractor to carry out cosmetic improvements. Because the house is structurally sound, the contractor's efforts are largely dedicated to stripping off old paint, removing wallpaper, plastering cracks in walls and ceilings, repainting, and refinishing the hardwood floors.

While removing paint from the mantel of the living room fireplace, the contractor discovers that the wood under the paint is beautiful hand-carved chestnut. Similarly, he finds that the banister leading down the stairs is hand-carved chestnut. As more paint is removed from window frames, it becomes clear that the Ramas have bought a quality house. Consequently, they change their original plans and decide to undertake a major renovation, which will entail far more cost and effort than initially planned. They figure that the $50,000 renovation cost will enhance the value of the house by $80,000, so the added expenditure seems worthwhile.

This case is similar in many respects to the previous one; Seligman too no doubt saw himself as seizing opportunities that presented themselves to him. The line separating flights of fancy from seized opportunities can be thin.

There is an important difference between the two, however. Flights of fancy typically entail an undisciplined impulse to change requirements without regard for cost, schedule, or resources. Habitual practitioners of this "method" of project development substitute their ad hoc approach for sound project planning. In effect, they are proponents of the plan-as-you-go school of project management. The impact of this approach on project budgets and schedules can be devastating.

Seizing opportunities, in contrast, involves a measured response to unanticipated project developments. It entails capitalizing on the unexpected. For this to be successful, it must be determined that the benefits of changing requirements outweigh the costs.

Each of these four cases illustrates how easy and natural it is for requirements to change. Sometimes change is for the better and will result in improved project output. At other times, change is merely disruptive and results in delays and unwise increases in costs. Project staff can count on changes in the specification of requirements, and they must learn to identify such changes as they occur. This is not always easy. Changes in requirements can be subtle and can occur very gradually, almost imperceptibly.

Once professional staff have identified possible changes, they must learn to anticipate the consequences of these changes. If the consequences are strongly negative, they must alert their customers to this fact, particularly if the customers are the cause of the disruptive change. Without a conscious methodology for dealing with changes in the specification of requirements, project staff will be only marginally in control of their project.

# THE FUNDAMENTAL TRADE-OFF IN SPECIFYING REQUIREMENTS

There is a frustrating built-in conflict facing individuals charged with specifying requirements for a project. On the one hand, they might be wise to specify everything in detail. Their motto might be, "Leave nothing to chance." Not only might they describe the requirements in great detail, but they could give an item-by-item directive on how the requirements should be achieved. The theory here is that when project managers focus on minutiae and provide detailed instructions on all the steps that have to be carried out to meet specified requirements, there is little likelihood that project staff will interpret requirements incorrectly. In addition, the painstaking enumeration of detail will protect the project performers from potential accusations by customers that they did not do what they said they would.

On the other hand, project planners might be wise to keep things as flexible as possible, so that the project can readily respond to changes in the environment that may require changes in requirements. This more flexible approach is based on the premise that circumstances are bound to arise that will cause alterations in the specifications of requirements.

## Problems with Overspecification of Requirements

Each of the two approaches outlined above has problems associated with it. Let us begin by addressing problems with the first approach.

INSUFFICIENT INFORMATION. It is unlikely that individuals specifying requirements will have enough information to plan everything in detail because they cannot know everything that might happen. Detailed specification of requirements puts a tremendous burden on requirements analysts. Remember that they do their work before the deliverable is produced. If they really don't want to leave anything to chance, they need detailed knowledge of all the contingencies that may arise during the course of project implementation, so that they can specify different courses of action for these contingencies.

In practice, individuals writing project requirements are far from omniscient. Even the most carefully specified requirements will be based on guesswork. To the extent that these guesses are off the mark, the specified requirements may or may not be viable or relevant to the needs of the customers.

INITIATIVE DISCOURAGED. Too much detail by the planners tends to discourage initiative on the part of project staff. When all the details of the requirements are spelled out for them, staff members charged with implementing the plan are being told, in effect, not to take any initiative on the project: "We know best what it is you should be producing, so please don't deviate from the specs."

This approach carries with it at least two possible negative consequences. One is that creativity on the part of project staff will be discouraged. Even if they see a way to enhance the deliverable, or if by a change of procedures they can effect time and cost savings, they are discouraged from conveying their insights to their bosses. It is unlikely that truly creative workers would be attracted to such projects.

A second possible negative consequence is that if following the specs becomes the most significant guiding principle of a project, people will be discouraged from assuming responsibility for doing the best job they can. Responsibility is narrowed to a simple directive: meet the specs. If project staff see a fundamental flaw in the specs, they can say, "That's not our problem. We've been told to meet the specs without questioning them, and meet them we will."

REQUIREMENTS IGNORED. Excessive detail in specified requirements often results in project staff ignoring them. A leave-nothing-to-chance philosophy may ultimately backfire on the requirements analyst, creating exactly the opposite effect from what was intended. Too much detail may overwhelm those charged with implementing the project. If much of the detailed material deals with relatively obvious points, there is a temptation on the part of project staff to skim over the minutiae. If the mass of detail is too difficult to digest, project staff may prefer to work things out on their own. Anyone who has tried to put together a model airplane from a kit knows what I am talking about. At the outset, you have every intention of following the instructions carefully, but after five minutes of reading very obvious material ("Before assembling the airplane, you should make sure that the parts you have match the parts listed in Exhibit A"), you decide to skip over the simple stuff. You begin painting parts and gluing them together, using the picture on the box as a guide. Occasionally you look at the assembly diagrams, but you are bewildered by the array of code letters, lines, and curves; besides, many of the parts shown in the diagrams don't look like anything you have in your kit. In the end, you have a finished product that looks reasonably similar to the airplane pictured on the box, but there are three or four remaining parts lying on the table that you never incorporated into the model airplane.

**COSTLY REWORK EFFORTS.**  Excessive rigidity in the specification of requirements may lead to costly rework efforts. Change *will* occur on projects. Perhaps customer needs shift, or new technological developments make the deliverable obsolete in its present form, or a new labor contract escalates the salaries of project staff higher than anticipated. The details will differ from project to project, but the fact remains that *change will occur,* and this change will require rethinking the requirements. If requirements are rigid and deviations from them are prohibited, chances are that at some point, our refusal to accommodate change will catch up with us.

For example, it may become clear early in the project life cycle that meeting a particular requirement is technically unfeasible. However, owing to the rigidity of our approach to requirements, we may proceed as if there were no problem. Ultimately, we come face to face with the fact that the spec is unachievable in its present form. We have no choice but to change our requirements and redo the work we have completed. At this point, the rework effort will be quite expensive. We could have saved considerable time and money had we altered the specified requirements earlier in the project, when we first perceived the problem.

## Problems with Excessive Flexibility

Excessive flexibility in specifying requirements also has problems associated with it.

**PATCHWORK DELIVERABLES.**  The specify-as-you-go approach to defining requirements can easily yield a deliverable that lacks cohesiveness. With such an approach, the deliverable is a patchwork, reflecting many ad hoc decisions rather than a comprehensive vision. To paraphrase a well-known epigram, a camel is a horse designed as a result of the ad hoc specification of requirements.

**CHAOTIC PROJECT PLANNING.**  Excessive flexibility will result in chaotic project planning. As we shall see in the next chapter, planning is the process of identifying how to achieve the requirements, given the constraints of limited time and resources. If requirements are ill defined and evolve willy-nilly over the life of the project, our planning efforts will be chaotic. We will have no cohesive plan; rather, we will have many different plans that change in character as changes are made in the requirements.

TIME AND COST OVERRUNS. The previous two problems associated with excessive flexibility are likely to result in time and cost overruns. A patchwork deliverable that does not meet customer needs, for example, may result in rejection of the deliverable by the customers and may give rise to demands to redo the project. Clearly, a project that entails rework efforts will pose both time and budget slippages.

If excessive flexibility causes chaotic planning, this will lead to major inefficiencies in the implementation of the project. We will face false starts and about-faces. Resource utilization will be haphazard, since we will never be quite sure what resources—and how many—we should be using at any given time. With such inefficiencies, it is unlikely that we will meet our original budget and schedule targets.

## Seeking a Middle Ground Approach

We see, then, that the two extremes for specifying requirements will probably yield serious problems for project staff. In specifying requirements, therefore, we should seek some middle ground—an approach that avoids the rigidity of immoderately detailed, inflexible requirements, on the one hand, and the chaos of excessively free-form requirements, on the other. To put this in a more positive light, we want requirements that are firm and clear enough to avoid problems of ambiguity and volatility and at the same time sufficiently flexible to accommodate changes that are bound to occur during the course of a project.

## GENERAL GUIDELINES FOR SPECIFYING REQUIREMENTS

I cannot overstate the observation that along with inadequately articulated customer needs, poorly formulated requirements stand out as an enormously significant source of grief on projects. If the requirements are stipulated incorrectly, or are subject to multiple interpretations, or are too complicated, or are forever changing, the whole project suffers.

The good news is that many of the problems associated with requirements specification can be minimized if those involved with
projects—project staff and customers alike—pay attention to some
basic guidelines:

• *Rule 1: State the requirement explicitly and have project staff and
customers sign off on it.* Too often, especially on small, informal projects, requirements are implied rather than stated explicitly. For example, George says to Martha, "Write up a proposal to bid on that
Molsen job, will you?" Martha agrees, and four days later she turns in
a document that George finds to be too short, lacking in method-
ological rigor, and emphasizing the wrong issues. George calls Martha
in and chews her out. "This isn't what I asked for," he chides, pointing
out its various shortcomings to Martha in detail.

Two features of this incident stand out. First, it is ludicrous for George
to say, "This isn't what I asked for," since he never really did say what it
was that he wanted. *Of course,* what Martha delivered was not what
George asked for. This was ensured by the fact that George never conveyed anything but the vaguest sense of his requirements. A second
interesting feature is this: only after the project has failed from George's
perspective does he sit down and elucidate what he expects out of the
Molsen proposal. That is, in pointing out the problems with the proposal, he is hinting at what his requirements are ex post facto. Even
here he is *implying* his requirements rather than stating them explicitly and systematically.

In general, it is a good idea to be explicit in stating requirements.
The explicit listing of requirements can be viewed as a contract, focusing on what the customers want and what project staff have agreed
to deliver. As with any contract linking customers and producer, it is
wise to have both parties carefully review the stated requirements and,
if the requirements are acceptable, to sign off on them.

• *Rule 2: Be realistic; assume that if a requirement can be misinterpreted, it will be misinterpreted.* This rule is a variant of Murphy's Law,
which states that if something can go wrong, it will. In examining the
way a requirement is stated, do everything possible to determine how
it can be misinterpreted. Ask different staff members to offer their interpretations of the requirement. Ask customers their interpretation.
Determine the views of other people who will be affected by the project; if their opinion of what the requirement should be varies from
the customers' opinion, there may be trouble. If it is an important
project, hire independent experts to review the requirements and see

whether their viewpoints correspond with yours. If these things are done early in the project, you are likely to avoid some nasty surprises midway through or at the end.

• *Rule 3: Be realistic; recognize that there will be changes on your project and that things will not go precisely as anticipated.* We have examined this point in detail in this chapter, as well as in the previous chapter, dealing with the definition of needs. The basic lesson here is to avoid excessive rigidity in formulating requirements and to anticipate change.

• *Rule 4: To as great an extent as possible, include pictures, graphs, physical models, and other nonverbal exhibits in the formulation of requirements.* I had my first lesson on the limitations of language when I was a sixth-grade student. One day the school principal visited my class and set us a challenge: to describe a spiral verbally, without using our hands. I think we did a pretty good job of it, but it was difficult. We would have done a better job if we could have simply drawn a spiral on the blackboard.

This lesson was driven home to me a couple of years ago when I carried out a study on how patent examiners determine the technical capabilities of the inventions they review. I interviewed a number of patent examiners, and over and over they told me that the key to doing their job was to review the drawings that accompany the verbal description of the invention. Several said that a review of the drawings alone gives them almost full knowledge of what an invention can do and what the patent applicant's patent claims are.

The point here is an old one: a picture—or graph, or flowchart, or mock-up model—is worth a thousand words. Engineers and architects have long recognized this; the clarification of requirements with blueprints, drawings, and the like is commonplace in these professions. It is less commonplace—in fact, downright rare—in the more mundane, informal, white-collar projects we typically carry out in our organizations. This is a pity, since these nonverbal exhibits can dramatically sharpen the clarity of the requirements we are trying to establish.

• *Rule 5: Establish a system to monitor carefully any changes made to the requirements.* Construction companies have long recognized that they would go broke if they did not keep meticulous records of changes made to their projects, and so they have established systems to keep track of them. Systems developed for keeping track of changes should address two basic issues. First, projects are themselves systems—that is, they are made up of interrelated parts. If a change is made to one part, will it have systemwide ripple effects? Remember that the consequences of a single change may be profound and widespread.

The second basic issue is that changes have costs associated with them. The costs may be obvious, as when a change requires the disassembly of a piece of hardware and its reassembly in a new way. But the costs may also be more subtle. For example, change always has hidden administrative costs associated with it.

There is a strong relationship between these two issues. The greater is the systemwide impact of a change, the greater is the likelihood that costs associated with the change will be substantial.

The nature of the system developed for tracking changes to project requirements will vary according to the character of the project and the organization in which it is carried out. Large, complex projects require a high degree of formality in tracking changes; otherwise, countless small changes will be lost in the shuffle. The dominant approach to managing change on large projects, called *configuration management,* requires detailed documentation of all actions associated with change requests. With smaller projects, formality can be reduced. In fact, too much paperwork can measurably decrease the productivity of the smaller effort.

However, at a minimum, in large projects and small, written change orders should be required. The change order should contain the following information:

- Date of the change request
- Name of the person requesting the change
- Description of the change
- Statement of the change's impact on the project
- Listing of tasks and staff affected by the change
- Estimate of the cost of the change
- Signature of the individual making the change request, indicating that this individual is aware of the cost and performance impacts of the requested change

With such a written change order, those desiring changes—whether designers or customers—are required to take responsibility for their requests. Given this personal assumption of responsibility, they are less likely to make frivolous requests that may have serious impacts.

• *Rule 6: Educate project staff and customers to the problems of specifying requirements.* Anyone experienced in working with projects recognizes that one important cause of problems is that inexperienced staff and naive customers are ignorant of what is involved in generating and meeting project requirements. They demonstrate time and again the old maxim that fools rush in where angels fear to tread. Customers may pepper the project team with requests for changes, not realizing the enormous impact these requests may have. Staff may set up requirements in an arbitrary, slipshod way, seeing them more as guidelines for action than as blueprints that need to be followed precisely. The list of mischief that staff and customers can get into unwittingly is never ending.

To lessen requirements-related problems that are rooted in raw ignorance and naiveté, project staff and customers should be educated about the needs-requirements life cycle. They should be made aware that requirements serve as the target at which the development of project plans is aimed, so that the quality and viability of the plan are tightly connected to the quality and viability of the requirements. They should be taught that requirements are inherently slippery and that changes in them will have an impact on the project budget. Finally, they should be made to view requirements as provisions in a contract that state what the customers need and what the project team has agreed to provide.

## RAPID PROTOTYPING

*Rapid prototyping*, a project management technique that emerged in the software industry in the 1980s, recognizes that with computer software projects—or any other projects that deal largely with intangibles—it is hard to picture concretely what the project should be producing. Consequently, there is a good chance that the final deliverable, based on an amorphous understanding of customer needs, will not satisfy the customers.

To deal with this reality, rapid prototyping allows for the dynamic development of requirements rather than demanding that all requirements be cast in iron at the outset of the project. It allows the customers to play an active role in defining the requirements as the project is being carried out. It is, in effect, a method built on a partnership between customer and developer.

At the heart of the technique is the concept of iterative prototyping of an intangible deliverable. Let's say that a software development team is contracted to produce a computerized inventory control system. Working closely with the customers, the team identifies needs and from these generates requirements. Then the team begins work on the project, with the objective of quickly putting together a simple prototype of the final deliverable.

The first prototype may be nothing more than a set of computer screen images of a data entry form. When the prototype is completed, it is brought before a panel of customers to provide them an opportunity to see what is being developed early in the project life cycle. After examining the prototype, the customers may, for example, express general satisfaction with the product but note that it appears that the emerging system will not process and track incoming inventory items well.

The software team then takes account of the customers' input, refines the software, and quickly develops a new, more detailed prototype. Once again, the customer panel examines the prototype and offers comments and suggestions. This and subsequent reviews can take hours or days, depending on the nature of the project. At a certain point, they actually drive the evolving prototype using test data, thereby developing a good sense of the capabilities of the emerging system. The project proceeds in this iterative fashion until a well-defined prototype is developed.

On small systems, the final approved prototype might be handed over to the customers as a functioning system. On more complex systems, the final prototype is given to requirements experts, who review it to see what customer needs and wants are embedded in it. With this information, they specify customer-focused requirements carefully, and these well-specified requirements are used to design and build a product that leads to high levels of customer satisfaction.

For rapid prototyping to work effectively, rules for prototyping and requesting improvements to the evolving system must be carefully spelled out; otherwise, the project may never be brought to a conclusion, and costs may get out of hand. For example, how detailed should a prototype be? How many rounds of prototypes should be developed during the course of the project? What are the limitations on customer requests for improvements to the deliverable? How will the cost impacts of changes to the prototype be calculated?

The advantage of the prototyping approach is obvious. The final deliverable should make the customers happy, because they played a major role in defining what it looks like and does. This is not a trivial point, since costly rework efforts will have to be undertaken if the deliverable is unsatisfactory, and the project may even have to be redone completely. Another advantage is that rapid prototyping provides project professionals with a methodology for making the intangible a bit more tangible—for dealing proactively with some of the significant problems that arise on amorphous, white-collar, information age projects.

The disadvantages of rapid prototyping are also obvious. For one thing, there is a risk that heavy involvement of the customers in defining the product as it evolves will be taken as an invitation to make changes according to whim. Consequently, rapid prototyping efforts should employ conscious change control processes. There is also a danger that unless there is a strong commitment on the part of both the customers and project staff to bring the project to a conclusion, the project may drift from prototype to prototype without ever coming to closure.

Rapid prototyping has a substantial track record: when it is implemented properly, it leads to high levels of customer satisfaction. It appears to be a clever step in the direction of getting better control over some of the significant problems that arise in relation to the specification of needs.

## CONCLUSION *good requirements – realistic, flexible, etc.*

Writing good requirements is a formidable task. The pitfalls are bountiful: the requirements may be ambiguous or unrealistic, or they may have no bearing on the customers' true needs. They may be too detailed or not detailed enough. They may be too rigid or overly flexible. If the pitfalls are not avoided, problems will arise.

This chapter has shown that there are many ways that project staff can develop good requirements. The single most important step is the simplest: be aware of the role that requirements play in the evolution of a project. Staff should recognize that requirements form the basis of project plans, since the purpose of the plans is to describe how the requirements can be met. If the requirements are deficient, the project plan is flawed, and if the plan is flawed, its implementation is defective. An understanding of the connection between requirements and the plan also leads to an appreciation of how modifications to the requirements can yield cost and schedule overruns, since changes in the requirements necessitate changes in the plan.

With a thorough understanding of the importance of requirements, staff will be better able to identify and deal with the many big and little requirements-related problems that inevitably arise on their project.

# PART THREE

# Project Planning
# and Control

# CHAPTER SIX

# Tools and Techniques for Keeping the Project on Course

T hus far, we have focused on two major categories of pitfalls commonly encountered in project management: organizationally induced problems, arising from the very structure of projects and the organizations in which they are carried out, and problems associated with the identification of needs and the specification of requirements. In this and the following chapter, we investigate a third important source of project difficulties: poor planning and control. Project managers, staff, and customers can be sure that problems in each of these three areas will arise. With this knowledge and an understanding of the specific nature of many of these problems, they can avoid stumbling into avoidable pitfalls and can better manage the difficulties they will inevitably encounter.

In the project management literature, more attention is directed toward planning and control than any other topic. I suspect this is largely a consequence of the fact that project managers and their staff can exercise a high degree of discretion over how they carry out planning and control activities. It also reflects a philosophy that we should devote most of our study time to learning about things over which we have some influence.

On a project, many things happen that are out of our hands and beyond our control. An important subcontractor may go bankrupt, our department budget may be slashed in half, the people assigned to us may not have the skills necessary to do a good job. Project managers facing a steady flow of problems outside their realm of control often assume a reactive posture, responding to difficulties after they occur in the best way they can with a limited tool kit of project management techniques and skills. However, with planning and control, wise project managers can turn things to their advantage. They can assume a proactive posture, planning in advance for problems and finding ways to head them off. Proactive management entails initiating actions that will help project managers anticipate what needs to be done to carry out a project effectively (this is planning) and then make sure things are being undertaken as planned once the project is under way (this is control).

Good planning and control are necessary conditions for project success. It is hard to imagine how an unplanned project with no controls could possibly succeed except, perhaps, through blind luck. Sadly, good planning and control are not sufficient conditions for success. If we want to succeed, we need to be diligent in our planning and control efforts. However, diligence alone will not ensure success, since, despite our best efforts, surprises may arise that have a devastating impact on our project.

In this chapter, I focus on commonly accepted planning and control practices employed on projects. These practices have evolved over the years, arising chiefly from construction and engineering. The techniques described here are relevant to most information age projects. Their systematic application will help project managers and staff avoid creating problems that should never arise.

## THE PROJECT PLAN

A project plan is basically a road map that shows how to get from A to B. Typically, the plan is the launching point of a project—a beginning, a guide to future developments. However, it is important to recognize that a plan is the consequence of a good deal of effort. The plan emerges gradually as needs are defined, requirements are specified, predictions are made about the future, and available resources are tallied. Only after these and other matters are mulled over, pieced together, refined, scrapped, reworked, and refined again do we finally encounter a plan that can serve as our road map.

Plans are generally three-dimensional: they focus on time, money, and human and material resources. Planning tools have been developed for each of the three dimensions. The time dimension is handled through schedules. A broad array of scheduling tools—some sophisticated, some simple—is available for use on projects. These tools enable us to determine when different tasks should begin, when milestones will be achieved, and so on. In this chapter, we examine two of the most common scheduling tools: Gantt charts and scheduling networks.

The money dimension is handled by means of budgets, which lay out how project funds are to be allocated. The need for budgeting is a universal reality in organizations, and most organizations—in the private, public, academic, or nonprofit sectors—spend a substantial amount of effort putting together budgets. Although there are universal principles underlying sound budgeting practice, the specific way in which budgets are formulated varies considerably from organization to organization. Budgeting is a personal thing, reflecting organizational philosophies, attitudes, and structures.

In this chapter, we briefly consider basic budgeting principles; we then devote most attention to examining how budget variances can be used to strengthen project control. In the next chapter, we look at the budgeting issue again when we examine the earned-value technique, a cost accounting technique that is gaining great popularity in project management.

The human and material resource dimension is concerned with how best to allocate the limited resources on projects. Many resource allocation tools exist. In this chapter, we examine resource Gantt charts, resource spreadsheets, resource matrices, and resource loading charts.

## PLANNING AND UNCERTAINTY

Mastery of planning tools is extremely helpful in managing projects, but even an expert with good tools cannot create the perfect plan. Planning entails the future, and dealing with the future means dealing with uncertainty. A fundamental reality of planning, then, is that it involves uncertainty, which means that even the very best plans are estimates, mere approximations of what the future may hold. Sometimes these estimates can be highly accurate, as when, after completing work on 999 identical houses, a builder estimates how long it will take to build the last house in a 1,000-unit housing subdivision.

Uncertainty here is reduced because of ample historical experience on which to base guesses about the future. More often, though, our estimates are quite rough, because what we want to do has never before been done in precisely the way we need. This is especially true on information age projects. In carrying out these novel projects, we are to a large extent trailblazers, and the maps we devise (our plans) are much like the maps of the fifteenth-century Portuguese explorers, filled with broad, vague spaces labeled *terra incognita*.

It is important that project managers, staff, and customers recognize how uncertainty bears on the planning effort. The character of the plan is largely determined by the level of uncertainty of the proposed project. With projects involving low levels of uncertainty, we can create highly detailed plans, because we have a good idea of precisely how the project will proceed. When we are building the thousandth identical unit in a housing development, plans can specify precisely how the foundation should be poured, where studs should be placed, where nails should be driven, and so on. Because we have built this particular type of house so frequently, few surprises remain. In fact, in such a situation, we would be remiss *not* to plan in great detail, since these details will help avoid leaving things to chance.

Projects with high levels of uncertainty, in contrast, cannot support this degree of detailed planning, because there is insufficient information on how things will proceed. Consider a project aimed at finding a cure for cancer. The researchers undertaking this project have very little idea of what they will find. How they carry out their work depends, to a large extent, on their step-by-step discoveries, so their project plan must be rather vague and imprecise.

Good planning here may mean phased planning. For example, a high-risk two-year project may be broken into six planning phases, with detailed planning initially undertaken only for phase 1 (months one through four). Toward the end of phase 1, detailed planning commences for phase 2, and so on. This method is sometimes called the *rolling wave approach* to planning. To force project staff on a highly uncertain project to develop sophisticated, detailed plans for the whole project is an exercise in futility.

We should bear in mind an important distinction between complexity and uncertainty. I have had participants in my project management seminars ask, "How can you say that there are low levels of uncertainty in building houses and bridges? Even a routine bridge is highly complex and filled with uncertainty."

That is true. Even a routine bridge *is* highly complex. However, if the bridge is truly routine—that is, if bridges of this sort have been built so many times that the steps for constructing them are clearly laid out—we have a precise idea of what we will encounter in our efforts to build it. By definition, then, we are involved in a situation where uncertainty is low; that doesn't mean it isn't complex.

The difference between uncertainty and complexity is illustrated in Figure 6.1. In both parts of this figure, we are concerned with getting from A to B. In Figure 6.1a, the path from A to B is long, twisting, and complex. (This pattern is common on construction projects.) Nonetheless, the path is precisely known, and if we carefully follow our map, we will ultimately arrive at B. In Figure 6.1b, we no longer encounter the complexity of Figure 6.1a; there are few twists and turns. However, we do have a problem when we reach the fork in the road: we are not sure which path will get us to B. In fact, in projects where there are truly high levels of uncertainty (for example, in the cancer project), we are not even certain that B exists. This high level of uncertainty is common on many information age projects.

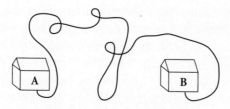

(a) High Complexity, Low Uncertainty.

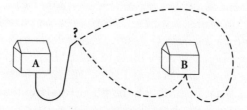

(b) Low Complexity, High Uncertainty.

**Figure 6.1. Getting from A to B.**

# PROJECT CONTROL

Project control entails looking at the plan, looking at what is actually happening on the project, and comparing the two. As in project planning, attention focuses on the three dimensions of time, money, and human and material resources.

The purpose of control is to keep the project on track by keeping track of the project. Control serves a feedback function. For example, a driver is in control of her car when, as it veers slightly to the left, she compensates by steering slightly to the right. Analogously, a project manager is in control of her project when, say, after learning from her schedule data that a certain task is falling behind, she directs more resources to the task to put it back on track.

Too often project personnel approach the control function by asking, "Are there variances between the plan and the actuals?" That is, is there a difference between the time we were scheduled to finish a task and when we actually finished it? Is there a difference between what we planned to spend on the task and what we actually spent? Is there a difference between how we thought we would use our human and material resources and how we actually used them?

Without knowing anything about the project in question, I can say yes to these questions and be quite certain that my answer is correct. One of the fundamental realities of project management is that *there will be variances between actuals and the plan.* Remember that all plans are guesses, and while our best guesses may be quite good, it is unlikely they will be perfect. And the higher the level of uncertainty is in projects, the greater is the likelihood that guesses are substantially off the mark.

The question that should be asked is, "Are the variances we encounter on our project acceptable?" By basing our approach to project control on this question, we are taking the realistic position that there will be variances. Our attention focuses on whether the variances we inevitably encounter are reasonable or wildly askew.

To answer the basic control question, we must establish criteria of acceptability for variances. On high-risk projects with high levels of uncertainty, we typically are willing to accept large variances. For example, on the cancer project, we may be willing to live with variances of 20 percent. That is, although the plan stipulates that a given task will cost $1,000, we may be willing to accept a cost overrun or underrun of up to $200. We accept such large variances because we recognize that the plan entails some rather heroic guesswork on how much it will cost to carry out specific tasks. With low-risk projects, such as routine construction efforts, our criteria of acceptability are much more restrictive, because our knowledge of how things should work out on the project is precise. For example, deviations of more than 2 percent from the plan may be viewed as unacceptable on a routine project.

Given that we have established criteria that define acceptable variances, we do not spend much time fretting over tasks that fall within the acceptable range. Instead, our management efforts are directed at reviewing tasks with variances outside this range. If we spend 8 percent more than planned in March and our criterion of acceptability is a variance of plus or minus 5 percent, we ask, "What is happening with this task that is resulting in unacceptable overruns?" In using this approach, we are practitioners of *management by exception,* which was discussed briefly in Chapter Two. With this approach, we funnel our energy toward special problems; we do not dissipate it on routine matters.

During the course of the project, some variance from the plan is acceptable; as the project comes to termination, however, variance for the entire project should approach zero if the project is to conclude close to planned schedule and budget. By the end of the project, the acceptable positive and negative variances that occurred throughout the project should more or less cancel each other out, leaving a near zero overall variance—if we have done a good job of planning and control.

Note the distinction here between *acceptable variances* and *unacceptable project overruns.* Practicality and realism suggest that we must be willing to accept some variance from the plan in the day-to-day operation of our project simply because we lack the perfect knowledge that would enable us to predict exactly what will happen. However, although we may accept 5 percent variances from the plan as the project is being carried out, we may not have the luxury of accepting a 5 percent cost or schedule overrun for the project overall. If we are willing to accept such overall overruns, we should build something called *management reserve* into our budget and schedule. This management reserve covers what we view to be an acceptable overrun for the project as a whole.

## HOW MUCH PLANNING AND CONTROL IS ENOUGH?

Anyone undertaking a planning effort or designing a project control methodology ultimately faces the question, "How much planning and control should we engage in?" There is no obvious best answer to this question. On the surface, it might seem that we should always implement a major planning and control effort in order to minimize project uncertainty and be in full control of the project. Our philosophy on this matter might be reflected in statements such as, "You can't plan too much" and "A project with weak controls is a project out of control."

Unfortunately, planning and control have costs associated with them. The relationship between project costs and the costs of planning and control is illustrated in the following simple formula:

Project costs = Production costs + administrative costs

This formula shows that increases in the costs of planning and control (that is, administrative costs) drive up total project costs. It also illustrates that increases in planning and control costs mean that we are spending smaller and smaller proportions of our project budget on directly productive activities.

What proportion of the project budget should be dedicated to planning and control costs? Ten percent? Twenty percent? Fifty percent? More? How we answer this question is related to a number of important factors.

## Project Complexity

How complex is the project? The greater the level of complexity is, the greater the need is to specify precisely what steps should be taken to carry out the project. In general, highly complex projects need greater planning and control efforts than simple projects. This is exemplified in such complex undertakings as the space shuttle project.

## Project Size

Very large projects require enormous amounts of coordination. On such projects, it is easy for details to get lost in the shuffle, easy for us to lose track of what has been done and what should be done. Consequently, planning and control must be highly formal on large projects, with detailed rules developed that describe how the project should be undertaken.

On very large projects—say, over $200 million—administrative costs associated with planning, coordinating, and controlling may constitute from one-half to two-thirds of the total project cost. Such a high overhead on a $10,000 project would be ridiculous, since the small size of the project makes it possible to keep track of things in a more relaxed, less formal way. On small projects, we should start worrying about overplanning and too elaborate controls when the administrative costs begin edging over the 15 to 25 percent range.

## Level of Uncertainty

It is often futile to develop elaborate plans and employ sophisticated control techniques on projects with high levels of uncertainty. As we know, the problem with such projects is that we have very little information about what the future holds. Given great uncertainty, it is guaranteed that the plan, however elaborate it is, will undergo continual modification, so that detailed planning and stringent controls may not work. In fact, they may actually hurt a project if they enforce rigidity on a project that needs flexibility. Projects with low levels of uncertainty can support detailed planning and tight control, because we have substantial knowledge of what is necessary to bring them to fruition.

## Organizational Requirements

Organizations vary widely in their approach to planning and control. The business press is filled with stories of companies that make it a habit to rush into projects without planning adequately for them, as well as tales of companies that go through an elaborate planning exercise before they make any important decisions. We often read of companies tottering on the brink of bankruptcy because of loose corporate control over operations, as well as companies with such tight control systems that management knows precisely how every penny is spent.

In general, organizations with a corporate culture that places emphasis on good corporatewide planning and control employ good planning and control practices on their projects. The danger here is that senior management may require project managers to go through the same planning and control procedures with a $3,000 project as with a $10 million project. Organizations in which corporate culture tolerates sloppy planning and control procedures are likely to foster projects that are poorly planned and controlled.

## User Friendliness of the Planning and Control Tools

If planning and control tools are difficult to learn or cumbersome to use, their employment on the project is likely to reduce project efficiency and drive up administrative costs. There are a large number of software solutions being sold that are designed to help organizations manage project schedules, budgets, and resource allocations. They vary substantially in learnability and usability. In selecting an appropriate software solution, buyers should consider user friendliness as well as technical features.

# PLANNING AND CONTROL TOOLS: THE SCHEDULE

A major portion of the planning effort entails determining the relationship of different tasks to each other and then scheduling these tasks in such a way that the project is carried out efficiently and logically. A number of tools have been developed over the years that make this undertaking rather routine. Three in particular are all that is really necessary to schedule any project, from the simplest to the most complex: the work breakdown structure, the Gantt chart, and the schedule network.

## Work Breakdown Structure

The work breakdown structure (WBS) is a top-down view of the project that shows how the pieces of the project fit together. It comes in three varieties: task WBS, product WBS, and hybrid WBS.

TASK WORK BREAKDOWN STRUCTURE. When people begin scheduling a project, the first thing they often do is to generate a list of all the tasks that will be included. First, they take a big picture view of the project and list the major phases that must be addressed. Then they begin adding detail to each phase; they later add detail to the detail. Typically, then, the project schedule takes form in a top-down fashion, starting with the big picture and working down to the minutiae.

Most project workers I encounter have been organizing project tasks in this way for years without knowing that the approach they are taking has a fancy name: the task WBS. The task WBS is nothing more than a top-down formulation of how project tasks fit into the overall project structure. It is an important planning tool because it serves as the basis of the project schedule. The task WBS usually takes one of two possible forms: a table or a chart.

Let's say the project is to write a spy novel. Exhibit 6.1 shows a tabular task WBS created for the project. The hierarchy of tasks is plainly evident in this four-tier WBS. At the highest level is the overall project: to write a spy novel. At the next level down, there are four basic phases (for example, research background material, outline story). Each phase is broken down into tasks (for example, go to library), and each task is further broken down into subtasks (read up on U.S.-Kazakhani relations).

The number of levels needed for a WBS varies according to personal preference and project size. Clearly, very large projects demand more levels than small projects. Today's project scheduling software permits you to create WBSs with as many levels as you want. Planners beware! Each time you add another level, you are increasing data entry and maintenance requirements dramatically, because a subtask typically has three to five sub-subtasks hanging off it. If you are not careful, you will create a WBS that will consume enormous amounts of administrative effort to maintain. When trying to determine how many levels to add to the WBS, ask yourself: Do I really need to track my project at this level of detail? On software development projects, for example, it often does not make sense to have WBSs with more than three layers, because the degree of uncertainty these projects experience is so great that it is not possible to collect and track reliable data at a fine level of detail.

Figure 6.2 shows a pictorial version of the WBS for the same project. The WBS in this form looks something like an organization chart. With this format, we can see at a glance the hierarchical relationships of the different pieces of the project.

Sometimes it is useful to include cost estimates for each subtask. When we do this, we have something called a *costed* WBS. To find out the cost of a given level of the WBS, we add together the individual costs of the related items in the next level down. We can estimate the cost for the total project by summing the costs of all the items at the lowest level of the WBS. The lowest level is given the name *work package* level. Such a process is called *bottom-up cost estimating*.

10.0.0  Research background material
    10.1.0  Go to library
        10.1.1  Read up on U.S.-Kazakhani relations
        10.1.2  Read other spy novels
        10.1.3  Read current periodicals to identify hot topics of interest today
        10.1.4  Locate maps of relevant cities (for example, Balkh, Washington)
    10.2.0  Interview relevant government officials
        10.2.1  Visit intelligence agencies
        10.2.2  Visit military agencies
        10.2.3  Visit civilian agencies, including FBI and State Department
        10.2.4  Interview local police

11.0.0  Outline story
    11.1.0  Rough out plot
        11.1.1  Establish story theme
        11.1.2  Identify principal theme
        11.1.3  Link story events chronologically
    11.2.0  Refine plot
        11.2.1  Create detailed chart linking characters and events
        11.2.2  Identify chapters to be used in novel

12.0.0  Write story
    12.1.0  Chapter 1
        12.1.1  Kids discover body in the Potomac River
        12.1.2  Body identified as Kazakhani agent
        12.1.3  Frank Masters, FBI agent, put on case
        12.1.4  The Masters family
    12.2.0  Chapter 2
        12.2.1  [And so on, through all the chapters]

13.0.0  Contact publishers
    13.1.0  Identify likely publishers
        13.1.1  Examine *Writer's Guide* to learn of publisher requirements
        13.1.2  Talk to published authors experienced in dealing with publishers
        13.1.3  Contact four likely publishers and have preliminary discussion with editors
    13.2.0  Send three sample chapters to prospective publishers
        13.2.1  Select appropriate chapters
        13.2.2  Send chapters to target publishers
    13.2.3  Follow up with publishers

---

**Exhibit 6.1.    Tabular Work Breakdown Structure to Write a Spy Novel.**

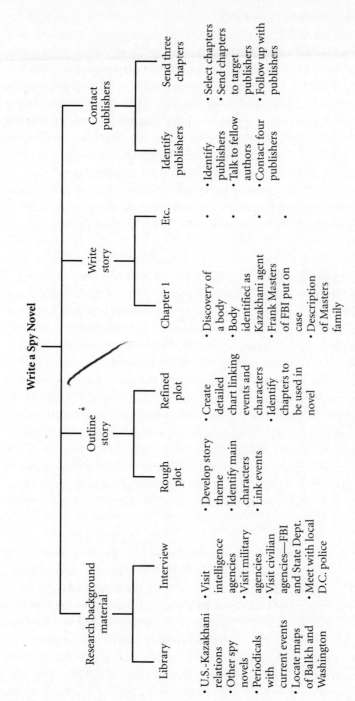

**Figure 6.2. Work Breakdown Structure in Chart Form.**

**PRODUCT WORK BREAKDOWN STRUCTURE.** When WBSs were first developed by the U.S. Department of Defense, they were intended to be product-oriented tools. As with the task WBS, we develop the product WBS from the top down. Let's say we are managing a project to build an aircraft. At the top level, we identify the aggregate product: an aircraft. At the next level down, we identify the components of the aircraft at a high level of aggregation, such as fuselage, wings, landing assembly, tail assembly, and avionics. At the next level, we list the subcomponents of the components. We proceed in this fashion until we have described the aircraft in as much detail as is necessary.

The physical structure of the product WBS is identical to that of the task WBS. It can be portrayed in tabular format or pictorial format. Similarly, the bottom level of the WBS is called the work package level.

**HYBRID WORK BREAKDOWN STRUCTURE.** In 2001, the Project Management Institute published *Practice Standard for Work Breakdown Structures,* which offers examples of actual WBSs developed in eleven industries. The majority of these follow a hybrid approach to WBS construction. At the highest levels, they depict the physical product to be developed. Then at lower levels, they describe the tasks that lead to the building of the defined subproducts. For example, in developing an accounting software package, "Accounting System" stands at the top of the WBS. At the next level, components of the accounting system are identified. They might include "Accounts Receivable Module," "Accounts Payable Module," "Financial Statements Module," and "Depreciation Schedules." At the next level, more detailed subcomponents can be identified. At some point, descriptions of the deliverable cease, and the tasks and subtasks needed to build the defined subcomponents are laid out.

**DETERMINING THE APPROACH.** Ultimately, the planning team must make a determination about what approach to take in building a WBS. The hybrid approach appears to be the dominant approach today. However, the team may not be given an option if their customers dictate a specific WBS format. For example, the U.S. Defense Department requires contractors to employ a product-oriented WBS format as described in the *Department of Defense Handbook: Work Breakdown Structure* (U.S. Department of Defense, 1998). If the customer requires a particular approach or if the project organization has a standard approach that all projects should follow, then that is the approach the team should take.

## Gantt Chart

The Gantt chart allows us to see easily when tasks should begin and when they should end. There are two dominant approaches to creating a Gantt chart, and these are pictured in Figure 6.3. In both approaches, tasks (taken from the WBS) are listed on the vertical axis, and time is measured along the horizontal axis.

Figure 6.3a is nothing more than a variant of a bar chart. By reading time data from the horizontal axis, we know the planned start and finish dates for different tasks. When actual start and finish times are added, the Gantt chart is also useful for project control. It then lets us visually compare our plan with the actuals, enabling us to determine the amount of schedule variance on projects.

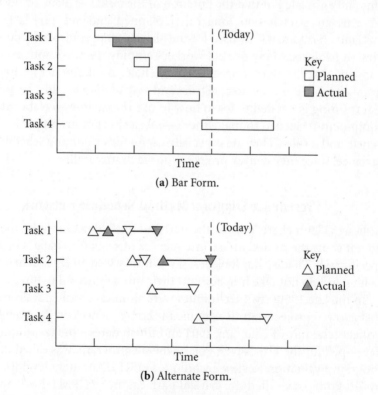

(a) Bar Form.

(b) Alternate Form.

Figure 6.3.  Gantt Chart.

In Figure 6.3a, for example, we see that our project is off schedule from the very beginning, when task 1 begins later than planned. Notice that the actual duration of task 1 is equal to the planned duration, so the schedule slippage for this task is entirely accounted for by the fact that it began late. With task 2, it is clear that the task not only began late but took longer to accomplish than planned. Schedule slippage here is caused by both a late start and sluggish performance that stretched out the task's planned duration.

Figure 6.3b presents a different approach to the Gantt chart. The basic facts are identical to those offered in the bar chart but presented in a different way. With this alternate approach, specific dates are pictured as triangles: upright for start dates, upside down for finish dates; planned dates are represented with hollow triangles, actual dates with solid triangles.

A comparison of the charts in Figure 6.3 shows that they both tell us the same thing. Once again, in Figure 6.3b, we see that task 1 begins and ends late but that the duration of the task is as planned. Task 2 begins late, stretches out longer than planned, and ends very late.

Gantt charts are widely used for the planning and control of schedules on projects. Many project workers employ them without even knowing that they have a special name. Their popularity lies in their simplicity. They are easy to construct and easy to understand. No special training is needed to learn how to use them, and no elaborate equipment is needed to make them—just a sheet of graph paper, a pencil, and a ruler. They are especially useful for examining schedule variance, since they convey project slippage dramatically.

## Precedence Diagram Method Schedule Network

Although Gantt charts portray the start and finish dates for tasks, they do not show the projectwide consequences of schedule changes on a specific task. That is, they look at tasks as if they were independent activities and do not take into account their interconnected nature.

In the late 1950s, two techniques were simultaneously developed that allowed project staff to examine the consequences on the overall project schedule of changing start and finish dates. One technique, developed for the U.S. Navy's Polaris missile program, was called the Program Evaluation Review Technique (PERT). Another, developed by Du Pont, was called the critical path method (CPM). Both approaches are based on flowcharts that look similar, but each has a different way of approaching schedule computations.

Over the years, countless hours have been spent debating the merits of one approach over the other. Today less and less distinction is being made between the two; in fact, in scheduling software, a generally accepted PERT/CPM hybrid has emerged that capitalizes on the finest features of each approach. This hybrid approach has been given the name *precedence diagram method* (PDM). I will make no distinction between PERT and CPM in this chapter and will describe the PDM approach.

**BUILDING A PDM NETWORK.** The first step in building a PDM network is to create a task WBS for the project. Exhibit 6.2 portrays a very simple task WBS for a project to prepare for a picnic.

The next step is to create a special kind of flowchart from the information contained in the WBS. PDM networks incorporate scheduling information into a basic flowchart diagram. This is illustrated in Figure 6.4a. Here, the tasks listed in the task WBS are placed into boxes, the boxes are laid out according to the sequence in which they should occur, and their relationships with each other are shown with lines. For example, the line connecting "Prepare sandwiches" and "Prepare fruit" shows that we begin preparing the fruit only after we have completed our sandwiches. The lines feeding into "Prepare basket" show that we cannot begin work on the picnic basket until we have made the iced tea and finished preparing the fruit. In each box that represents a task, the amount of time it takes to complete the task is

| | Task | Duration (minutes) | Worker |
|---|---|---|---|
| 1 | Start | 0 | |
| 2 | Make iced tea | 15 | George |
| 3 | Prepare sandwiches | 10 | Martha |
| 4 | Prepare fruit | 2 | Martha |
| 5 | Prepare basket | 2 | Martha |
| 6 | Gather blankets | 2 | George |
| 7 | Gather sports gear | 3 | Martha |
| 8 | Load car | 4 | George |
| 9 | Get gas | 6 | George |
| 10 | Drive to picnic site | 20 | Martha |
| 11 | End | 0 | |

Exhibit 6.2.  Work Breakdown Structure for a Picnic Project.

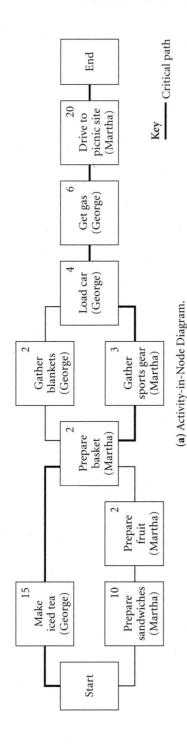

**(a)** Activity-in-Node Diagram.

Key ─── Critical path

| Task | Early Start | Late Start | Slack |
|---|---|---|---|
| Make iced tea | 0 | 0 | 0 |
| Prepare sandwiches | 0 | 3 | 3 |
| Prepare fruit | 10 | 13 | 3 |
| Prepare basket | 15 | 15 | 0 |
| Gather blankets | 17 | 18 | 1 |
| Gather sports gear | 17 | 17 | 0 |
| Load car | 20 | 20 | 0 |
| Get gas | 24 | 24 | 0 |
| Drive to picnic site | 30 | 30 | 0 |

**(b)** Calculating Slack.

**Figure 6.4. Activity-in-Node PERT/CPM Network.**

given in the upper-right-hand corner. Making iced tea, for example, takes fifteen minutes.

THE CRITICAL PATH. An important concept necessary for an understanding of PDM networks is that of the *critical path*. The critical path in a schedule network is the path that takes the longest time to complete. In Figure 6.4a, consider the two paths from "Start" to "Prepare basket." The upper path, "Make iced tea," takes fifteen minutes to complete, while the lower path, which is composed of two tasks ("Prepare sandwiches" and "Prepare fruit"), can be completed in twelve minutes. Given the way the network is drawn, the longest time that can elapse between "Start" and "Prepare basket" is fifteen minutes. Consequently, this segment of the overall network is part of the critical path. This also means that the lower path has three minutes of slack built into it.

Since the critical path is always the one that takes the longest to complete, the critical path has no slack at all. In fact, if there is schedule slippage along the critical path, the slippage will be reflected in the project as a whole. Thus, if as a project is being carried out, a task on the critical path takes three minutes longer to complete than anticipated, the overall project schedule will slip by three minutes. It is this feature of the critical path—its inflexibility with regard to slippage of schedule—that gives it its name. What makes it *critical* is that it defines project length. Slippages on the critical path translate into overall schedule slippages. By the same token, if the critical path is shortened, the project can be carried out more quickly than planned. Because activities off the critical path have some slack associated with them, they can tolerate some slippage in schedule.

In Figure 6.4a, the critical path for the project is portrayed by a thick line. To find out how long the project takes to complete, we add together the durations for each of the tasks on the critical path. In the example, the time needed to accomplish the whole project is fifty minutes ($15 + 2 + 3 + 4 + 6 + 20$ minutes).

NONCRITICAL TASKS AND SLACK TIME. Because noncritical tasks have slack associated with them, there is flexibility in scheduling their start times. As we have seen, the lower path, between "Start" and "Prepare basket," has three minutes of slack. Consequently, we need not begin to prepare the sandwiches until three minutes into the project. If we begin sandwich preparation at the three-minute mark and if nothing goes wrong, we can still complete the project in the allotted time. However, if we begin sandwich preparation at, say, the four-minute mark, we will cause the overall project schedule to slip by one minute.

In project management, the term *float* is often used in place of *slack*. Both terms mean the same thing. *Slack* was the term employed by inventors of PERT, while *float* was the term employed by inventors of CPM. In this book, I use *slack* to keep things simple. In real life, I use the terms interchangeably.

EARLIEST AND LATEST START TIME.  Calculating the earliest and latest start times for projects is easy to do. To calculate earliest start times, we begin at the left of the PDM network and work our way to the right. First, we calculate the earliest start times for tasks on the critical path. "Make iced tea" starts at time 0, "Prepare basket" at time 15, "Gather sports gear" at time 17, "Load car" at time 20, "Get gas" at time 24, and "Drive to picnic site" at time 30.

After earliest start times for critical tasks have been calculated, we turn to calculating earliest start times for noncritical tasks. Again we move from left to right. "Prepare sandwiches" can begin as early as time 0, "Prepare fruit" at time 10, and "Gather blankets" at time 17.

To calculate latest start times, we work from right to left. Once again, we first concentrate on the critical path. Since the project takes fifty minutes to complete, the latest time to start "Drive to picnic site" is at time 30 (that is, 50 − 20), to start "Get gas" is at time 24 (that is, 30 − 6), to start "Prepare basket" is at time 15, and to start "Make iced tea" is at time 0. Note that the latest start times are identical to the earliest start times. This is always the case with tasks on the critical path; there is no flexibility in when we start tasks.

To calculate latest start times for noncritical tasks, we also work leftward. Consider the noncritical task "Gather blankets." The activity that occurs after "Gather blankets" is the critical task "Load car," which we have determined should start no later than at time 20. Since "Gather blankets" consumes two minutes of time, its latest start time is at time 18 (that is, 20 − 2). With similar logic, the latest start time for "Prepare fruit" is at time 13; for "Prepare sandwiches," at time 3.

Slack for individual tasks is calculated by subtracting earliest start time from latest start time. For example, the latest start time for "Prepare fruit" is time 13, while its earliest start time is time 10. Slack for this task is 13 − 10, or 3. This means that we have three minutes of breathing space in carrying out the task.

As a project is carried out and slack time is consumed on individual tasks, the slack left over for the remaining tasks is reduced. If we do not finish preparing sandwiches until time 12, we have consumed two time units of slack, which means that the earliest time we can start "Prepare fruit" is time 12 and the latest start time is 13, leaving us with only one unit of slack (13 − 12) for "Prepare fruit."

Information on the earliest start time, latest start time, and slack for the picnic project is provided in tabular form in Figure 6.4b. Note that all critical path tasks have slack values of zero.

**RESOURCES AND NETWORK CONFIGURATION.** The actual configuration of a PDM network is heavily dependent on the amount of resources that can be devoted to the project. For example, the more people we have available, the more parallel activities we are capable of conducting. In preparing for a picnic, five activities could be conducted concurrently if George and Martha had three helpers. One person could be making the iced tea, another preparing the sandwiches, a third preparing the fruit, a fourth gathering blankets, and a fifth gathering the sports gear. Given these circumstances, we should have a different PDM network from the one portrayed in Figure 6.4.

**ACTIVITY-IN-NODE VERSUS ACTIVITY-ON-ARROW NETWORKS.** The kind of schedule network we built in Figure 6.4 using PDM is called an *activity-in-node network,* because each box portrays a node. Originally, in the 1950s, schedule networks were built as *activity-on-arrow networks,* an approach illustrated in Figure 6.5. Unlike the activity-in-node approach, which puts tasks into boxes, the activity-on-arrow approach places the tasks on the arrows that connect events (the circled numbers in Figure 6.5). Events represent either the beginning or the end of a task. Thus, in Figure 6.5, event 3 represents both the end of task 2➤3 ("Prepare

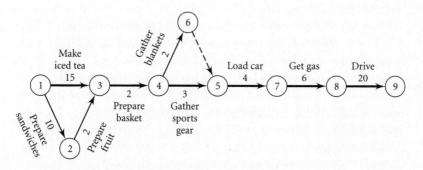

**Figure 6.5. Activity-on-Arrow PERT/CRM Network.**

fruit") and task 1➤3 ("Make iced tea") and the beginning of task 3➤4 ("Prepare basket").

With the activity-on-arrow approach, we sometimes have occasion to create *dummy task,* that is, tasks that consume no resources. Task 6➤5 in Figure 6.5 is such a dummy task, created because to get from event 4 to event 5 we wish to undertake two tasks: "Gather blankets" and "Gather sports gear." Both of these tasks cannot be described as 4➤5, since this would lead to confusion as to whether 4➤5 represents "Gather blankets" or "Gather sports gear." Consequently, one of the tasks ("Gather blankets") is arbitrarily given the assignation 4➤6, to distinguish it from 4➤5. To do so, however, requires the creation of dummy task 6➤5.

Today, only the PDM approach is used. All the new project scheduling software is PDM software.

**ADDITIONAL USEFUL CONCEPTS IN PDM NETWORKING.** The paragraphs immediately above provide the basic information needed to build and interpret PDM networks. In this section, we examine a number of additional concepts that can help schedulers devise more robust PDM networks: working time and elapsed time, hard logic versus soft logic, and full precedence diagram logic.

*Working Time Versus Elapsed Time.* When people are sitting at their desks writing software code, or working on a construction site laying brick, or setting up an experiment in a research laboratory, they are engaged in *working time* efforts. Working time refers to the active allocation of the effort of people or equipment to carry out a job. In contrast, paint drying and concrete curing reflect *elapsed time* efforts. Paint will continue drying after the painters have gone home. It will dry over weekends and holidays. It is a passive effort. With elapsed time, we are working with a 24/7 clock.

Most knowledge workers work according to a working time calendar. The moment they stop working—for example, during lunch break or after they leave the office—the work stops. People working on a wide range of physical efforts may encounter significant levels of elapsed time activities. This is especially true on construction projects, where a large number of tasks entail drying and curing.

If schedulers do not account for the differences between working time and elapsed time activities, this can result in faulty schedules. Consider, for example, a worker who paints chairs for a living. Let's say she finishes painting her last chair on Friday at 5:00 P.M. After she puts away her materials, she goes home for the weekend and does not return to the job until Monday morning at 8:00 A.M. She operates according to a working time calendar. The chair, however, is functioning on an elapsed time calendar. Although the painter is taking a break over the weekend, the paint on the chair is hard at work drying. If you were to create a task called "Paint dries" and entered into a scheduling package "two days" as the duration for this effort, the computer would report that drying commences on Monday morning at 8:00 A.M and finishes at 5:00 P.M Tuesday (a working time computation) unless you instruct the software to treat the drying activity as an elapsed time task! As an elapsed time task, the computer would recognize that the paint begins its two-day drying effort immediately at 5:00 P.M. Friday. It would correctly compute that drying would be completed by 5:00 P.M. Sunday night.

All scheduling software packages enable schedulers to stipulate whether a given task is a working time or elapsed time task. The default is always working time.

*Hard Versus Soft Logic.*  When reflecting on the logical links between tasks, it is obvious that some activities must be carried out in a prescribed order. For example, on a construction project, you must pour a concrete foundation before you begin framing a house. You don't frame the house and then slip a foundation under the framework retroactively. When task A must precede task B, the link between the two is called a *hard logic* link.

In the example just given, the rationale for having a hard logic link is based on physical factors. But hard logic links may be based on non-physical factors as well. For example, they may reflect legal requirements. Government regulations may stipulate that you fully test a new drug and get approvals before you distribute it to the public. Or they may reflect good practice ("Be sure to review project progress with customers before moving on to the next phase of the project"). The point is that for whatever reason, task A *must* proceed task B.

There is a practical reason for distinguishing between hard and soft logic links. Project managers often receive directives from their bosses or customers to speed up project work. One way to do this is to carry out tasks in parallel, so they review their project's PDM network to see what tasks that are currently scheduled to be implemented sequentially can instead be carried out in parallel. What they want to do is to cut the sequential links between tasks, thus enabling the tasks to be carried out concurrently. However, they need to be careful in cutting such links. Hard logic links cannot be cut, because they reflect the reality that task B must follow task A. Only soft logic links can be cut. Consequently, it becomes important to highlight which precedence links are hard logic links and which are soft logic links.

*Full Precedence Diagram Logic.* The discussion thus far has assumed that when creating a task A–task B link, task A must be completed before task B can begin. This link is called a finish-to-start (FS) link. More often than not, this assumption holds true: it often makes sense to get one chore done before launching yourself on another. But it is not universally valid. On occasion, we may want the launching of task B to be triggered by the initiation of task A—for example: "Two days after you begin painting room X, apply a second coat of paint." This represents a start-to-start (SS) link. Or your chief concern may be to finish two tasks by a given target date: "Make sure to complete tasks A and B by April 15." This represents a finish-to-finish (FF) link.

Scheduling software allows you to accommodate different approaches to dealing with start and finish linkages between tasks. While it is likely that more than 95 percent of the links you deal with are FS links, it is still possible to establish other links if appropriate.

USEFULNESS OF THE PDM NETWORK FOR PLANNING AND CONTROL. PDM networks are clearly useful for project planning, because they force project staff to identify carefully the tasks that need to be undertaken and to determine precisely the relationships of the tasks to each other. Given the tendency to rush into a project without giving much thought to what needs to be done, this is no small accomplishment.

PDM networks are also useful in planning because they allow planners to develop what-if scenarios, by which planners can determine the impact on the overall project schedule of slippages and speedups of individual tasks. This what-if feature also enables project planners to create more realistic estimates of project schedules. With computerized scheduling software, it is relatively easy to create worst-case, best-case, and most likely scenarios, and thus schedule estimates need not be based on only one set of assumptions.

Schedule networks are less useful as control tools. For one thing, continual updating of the network can be quite burdensome. For another, the networks do not graphically show schedule variances, as do

Gantt charts; to see variances, you cannot simply superimpose an updated PERT/CPM chart over the original.

## PLANNING AND CONTROL TOOLS: THE BUDGET

One major responsibility of many project managers is developing and adhering to a budget for the project. Often they will be rated a success or failure as project managers according to whether the project comes in under, on, or over budget.

Overshooting the budget can have serious consequences for project managers and the organizations in which they work. Consider a project that is funded through a contract: a cost overrun may lead to litigation, penalties, and financial losses for the performing organization. If the project is funded internally, an overrun may lead to a serious drain of scarce organizational resources.

In view of the importance of budgeting, it is not surprising that many organizations focus much of their management attention on that area. Consequently, many organizations have well-developed budgeting techniques that are custom-made for the organization's particular environment and operating style.

### Components of the Budget

Project costs are typically composed of four components: direct labor costs, overhead, fringe benefits, and auxiliary costs. *Direct labor costs* are determined by multiplying the workers' hourly (or monthly) wages by the amount of time that they are expected to spend on the project. In most service projects, which are not capital intensive, direct labor costs are the largest component of project costs.

*Overhead costs* are the typical expenses incurred in maintaining the environment in which the workers function. Included here are the costs of office supplies, the electric bill, rent, and, frequently, secretarial expenses. It should be noted that what is treated as an overhead expense in one organization may be given different treatment in another. In an organization that does not typically use secretarial service, for example, secretarial expenses might be included as a direct labor expense or even as an auxiliary expense. Overhead costs tend to be relatively fixed in relation to direct labor costs. For example, if over the long run labor costs increase by 50 percent, overhead costs similarly tend to increase by 50 percent.

*Fringe benefits* are nonsalary benefits that workers derive from the organization. They include the employer's contribution to the workers' social security payments. Depending on the organization, they may also include employer contributions to the workers' health insurance, life insurance, profit-sharing plan, stock options, pension plan, bonuses, and university tuition. Fringe benefit expenses are also directly proportional to direct labor costs.

*Auxiliary expenses* are project-specific expenses that the organization does not incur with any obvious regularity. Project travel expenses, purchases of special equipment and materials, computer time, consultant fees, and report reproduction costs are typical items in this category.

On many projects, if we know the labor costs, we can make good estimates of total project costs. For information age projects, on which knowledge worker salaries are often the most important component of the budget, estimating the budget is closely tied to estimating the amount of labor needed to carry out project tasks. Overhead costs and fringe benefit expenses are linked to direct labor costs. If we also know what auxiliary costs will be, we have a good estimate of total project costs.

Table 6.1 illustrates a typical project cost-estimating procedure for a company whose overhead averages 65 percent of direct labor costs and whose fringe benefits average 25 percent of direct labor costs plus overhead expenses. These overhead and fringe benefit figures are determined

| | | |
|---|---:|---:|
| Project manager (500 hours at $40 per hour) | $20,000 | |
| Analyst (1,000 hours at $25 per hour) | 25,000 | |
| Technicians (200 hours at $17 per hour) | 3,400 | |
| Total labor expenses | | 48,400 |
| Overhead (65 percent of labor) | 31,460 | |
| Total labor plus overhead expenses | | 79,860 |
| Fringes (25 percent of labor plus overhead) | 19,965 | |
| Subtotal | | 99,825 |
| Transportation (4 trips at $1,000 per trip) | 4,000 | |
| Microcomputers (2 at $3,500) | 7,000 | |
| Printing and reproduction | 2,000 | |
| Total auxiliary expenses | | 13,000 |
| Total project expenses | | 112,825 |

**Table 6.1.   Estimating Project Expenses.**

by accountants or auditors, who calculate them from data in the organization's accounting records.

Table 6.1 shows that in the case of our hypothetical company, direct labor, overhead, and fringe benefit expenses are $99,825. This figure turns out to be 2.06 times greater than direct labor costs alone ($48,400). Thus, in estimating project costs, a project manager in this company can reasonably guess that project costs (excluding auxiliary expenses) will be somewhat more than twice as great as direct labor costs. Of course, in making the final estimate of total costs, the project manager must include auxiliary costs, which may or may not be substantial, depending on the specific nature of the project. On construction projects, auxiliary costs, which include the costs of construction materials, may be significant.

This approach is called *parametric cost estimating*. It is an alternative to the bottom-up cost-estimating procedure that is derived from the WBS.

## Contingency Reserves

One unfortunate reality of project management is the ever-looming threat that project costs will be exceeded. To cope with this threat, project managers commonly build some "fat" into their cost estimates. One frequently used procedure is to make as realistic an estimate as possible of project costs and then multiply this estimate by some "fudge factor" to cover unanticipated problems. Building a contingency reserve of 5 or 10 percent is typical on projects with low levels of uncertainty; with high-risk projects, the percentage may be much greater.

Not everyone espouses the creation of a contingency reserve. Some project management experts are opposed to this concept, arguing that they encourage cost overruns and undermine the discipline of the tight purse.

An interesting variation on contingency reserves is *management reserve*. While contingency reserves are established to deal with untoward surprises that we know arise from time to time (called known-unknowns), management reserves are set-asides designed to handle the complete surprises (known as unknown-unknowns, or unk-unks). Contingency reserve levels can be established based on experience. For example, on routine projects, they may be set at 5 percent of the project budget, and for new-technology projects they may be set at 15 percent.

Management reserve levels, however, are usually set at a fixed value—say, 5 percent—because they deal with surprises we are not able to anticipate.

## Budget Control

Project staff can expect to encounter variances on their projects—that is, deviations of actual performance from the plan. The important thing is not whether a variance exists but what its dimensions are. If a deviation lies outside an acceptable range, the variance should be flagged and its causes investigated.

Table 6.2 gives an example of how variance analysis can be used in controlling the budget. This table portrays a monthly budget report for a small project. As the report states, we are in the sixteenth month of a twenty-month project.

A quick perusal of Table 6.2 suggests that things are going pretty well for this project. The total variance for the report month is positive ($116, or 3.7 percent), and the total variance for cumulative expenditures to date is also positive ($3,154, or 5.3 percent), indicating that the project is coming in slightly under budget.

A couple of items in the budget report warrant closer inspection. Why is the variance for supplies so large ($1,582, or 39.6 percent)? This positive variance might suggest that project staff have been able to procure supplies at a discount price, leading to cost savings for the project. However, it might also suggest that the project schedule is slipping—that is, supply costs might be low simply because supplies have not yet been purchased.

And why has only $99 been expended for consultants when $500 was budgeted? On the bright side, cost-conscious project staff may have been able to answer project questions through internal resources that otherwise would have required outside expertise. On the negative side, the positive variance could be a consequence of schedule slippage: consultants have not been paid because they have not yet been used.

Overall, this budget report suggests that the project is reasonably under control from the perspective of costs. As the project is nearing its end (only four months to go), we might have some concern about the 5.3 percent overall positive variance, because it might suggest that we have not yet accomplished all we planned to accomplish. A quick perusal of the project schedule (in particular, the Gantt chart) should allow us to see whether there is schedule slippage. If no slippage is revealed, we are in good shape and can expect to see some cost savings on the project.

| Expenditure Category | Amount Previously Claimed | Amount Budgeted | Amount Claimed This Period | Variance | Percentage Variance | Cumulative Total, Budgeted | Cumulative Total, Actual | Variance from Total | Percentage Variance |
|---|---|---|---|---|---|---|---|---|---|
| Salary | 28,716 | 1,500 | 1,716 | (216) | 14.4* | 30,000 | 30,432 | (432) | 1.4 |
| Transportation | 536 | 150 | 0 | 150 | 100.0* | 800 | 536 | 264 | 33.0 |
| Supplies | 2,418 | 300 | 0 | 300 | 100.0* | 4,000 | 2,418 | 1,582 | 39.6* |
| Consultants | 99 | 0 | 0 | 0 | 0.0 | 500 | 99 | 401 | 80.2* |
| Overhead | 17,804 | 975 | 1,115 | (140) | 14.4* | 19,500 | 18,919 | 581 | 3.0 |
| Fee | 3,965 | 248 | 226 | 22 | 8.9 | 4,950 | 4,192 | 758 | 15.3* |
| Total | 55,538 | 3,173 | 3,057 | 116 | 3.7 | 59,750 | 56,596 | 3,154 | 5.3 |

Table 6.2. Tracking the Budget: Month 16 of a Twenty-Month Project.

Note: Amounts in parentheses are negative variances.

*Variance > 10%.

## Cumulative Cost Curve

A common practice in project planning and control is to create a chart of cumulative expenditures for the project, called a *cost curve.* Cost curves for planned and actual expenditures are created by adding each month's expenditures to the previous reporting period's expenditures. In this way, smooth, climbing (or level) cost curves are generated, as illustrated in Figure 6.6. The height of a curve represents total costs to date for a given time. For example, the height of the curve of planned expenditures at the very end of the project represents total budgeted costs.

Cumulative cost curves (also called S-curves) are useful for monitoring cost variances at a glance. The difference in height between the curve for planned expenditures and the curve for actual expenditures represents the monetary value of variance at any given time. Ideally, the curve for actual expenditures looks very much like the curve for planned expenditures.

# PLANNING AND CONTROL TOOLS: HUMAN AND MATERIAL RESOURCES

The primary goal of human and material resource planning is the efficient and effective allocation of resources to a project. The fundamental problem that resource planners must deal with is resource scarcity; the need for resources usually outstrips their availability. In view of that reality, planners must carefully match available resources with project tasks. In matrix organizations, where many projects are

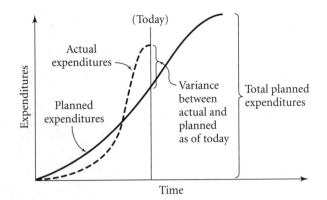

Figure 6.6. Cumulative Cost Curve.

carried out concurrently, this effort can become complex as planners try to assign resources to meet task needs in many different projects in such a way that the resources are being neither overcommitted nor undcrused.

A number of tools have been developed to assist resource planners to allocate resources effectively. Four common tools that will be discussed here are the resource matrix, the resource Gantt chart, the resource spreadsheet, and the resource loading chart.

## Resource Matrix

Exhibit 6.3 depicts a resource matrix. Its function is to link human and material resources to project tasks. It is constructed by listing the tasks found in the WBS along the vertical axis and listing available resources along the horizontal axis. Exhibit 6.3 shows resource allocations for a project to develop a science and math curriculum for a small school system. The WBS has been simplified for purposes of illustration.

Exhibit 6.3 shows who assumes primary responsibility for a task (P) and who assumes secondary responsibility (S). For example, in the task to design a preliminary curriculum, the chief responsibility lies with the curriculum specialists; methodologists, science specialists, and math specialists assume a supporting role.

The coding system used should reflect management requirements. In the example, we have coded the resource matrix with Ps and Ss. Other coding systems can be adopted. A popular approach to coding the resource matrix is using what I call the PAR approach, where P signifies who performs the work, A signifies who must approve the work before it can be carried out, and R signifies who reviews task efforts before the project team can proceed with their work.

Development of a resource matrix is a wise first step in determining how resources should be allocated. The matrix can be put together quickly and can serve as a guide for developing more sophisticated resource management tools.

## Resource Gantt Chart

The resource matrix shows only resource allocations for tasks; it does not show how these resources are allocated over time. This is achieved by means of a resource Gantt chart, as pictured for the curriculum development project in Exhibit 6.4.

Resources

| Tasks | Methodologists | Curriculum Specialists | Evaluators | Science Specialists | Math Specialists | Printing Facilities | Mainframe Computer |
|---|---|---|---|---|---|---|---|
| Identify needs | S | P | | | | | |
| Establish requirements | | P | | | | | |
| Design preliminary curriculum | S | P | | S | S | | |
| Evaluate design | S | S | P | | | | |
| Develop science curriculum | | S | | P | | | |
| Develop math curriculum | | S | | | P | | |
| Test integrated curriculum | S | S | P | | | | S |
| Print and distribute findings | | S | | | | P | |

Exhibit 6.3.  Resource Matrix.

P = primary responsibility; S = secondary responsibility.

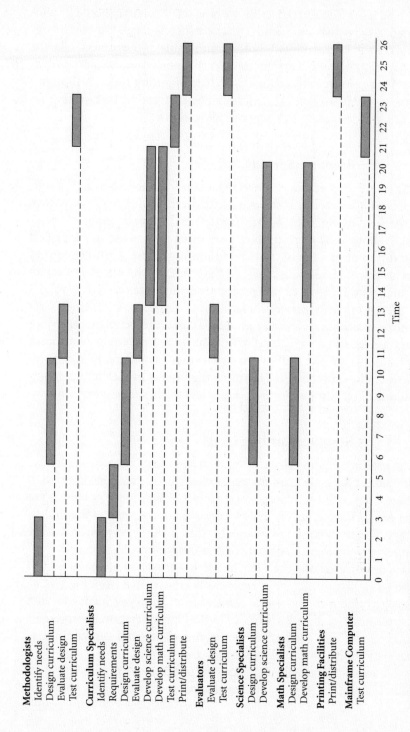

**Exhibit 6.4. Resource Gantt Chart.**

The resource Gantt chart shows how each resource should be allocated, task by task, over time. The chart shows at a glance how the resources will be distributed throughout the life of the project. Like the conventional Gantt chart discussed earlier, the resource Gantt enables tracking resource allocations as well as planning them. Although I have not done so here, variances can be pictured by juxtaposing actual allocations alongside planned allocations.

## Resource Spreadsheet

The resource spreadsheet shows in tabular form the information contained in the graphical resource Gantt chart. Exhibit 6.5 illustrates an aggregated resource spreadsheet for the curriculum development project. It shows how many units of a resource are needed on the project for different periods of time. By summing up the resource requirements across all resources for each time unit, we can calculate total resource requirements for the project over time (see the "Total" row).

Given the widespread proliferation of electronic spreadsheets, resource spreadsheets are very popular among project managers, since they are easy to develop and maintain. By computerizing a resource spreadsheet, project staff can easily create many different what-if scenarios, allowing them to determine the impact of different configurations of resource allocations and select the best configuration.

## Resource Loading Chart

The resource loading chart, also called a resource histogram, pictures the project life cycle from the perspective of resource consumption. It shows that at the early stages of a project, when we are gearing up to get under way, relatively few resources are employed; at the middle stage, we are moving full steam ahead in using resources; and at the end of the life cycle, our resource consumption winds down.

A resource loading chart for the curriculum development projects is shown in Figure 6.7. The chart is easily constructed from the "Total" data garnered from the resource spreadsheet. The area contained within the resource loading chart has a physical interpretation. It represents total person-days (or person-weeks, or person-hours, or computer-days) of effort consumed by the project.

Note that the resource loading chart in Figure 6.7 profiles actual resource allocations as well as planned, so that we can monitor variances.

Time

| | 1 | 2 | 3 | 4 | 5 | 6 | 7 | 8 | 9 | 10 | 11 | 12 | 13 | 14 | 15 | 16 | 17 | 18 | 19 | 20 | 21 | 22 | 23 | 24 | 25 | 26 |
|---|---|---|---|---|---|---|---|---|---|---|---|---|---|---|---|---|---|---|---|---|---|---|---|---|---|---|
| Methodologist | 1.5 | 1.5 | 1.5 | | | | | | | | | 2 | 2 | | | | | | | | | | | | | |
| Curriculum Specialists | 1 | 1 | 1 | 1 | 1 | 1 | 1 | 1 | 1 | 1 | 1 | 1 | 1 | | | | | | | | 1 | 1 | 1 | 1 | 1 | 1 |
| Evaluators | | | | | | 1 | 1 | 1 | 1 | 1 | 1 | 2 | 2 | 1 | 1 | 1 | 1 | 1 | 1 | 1 | 2 | 2 | 2 | | | |
| Science Specialists | | | | | | .75 | .75 | .75 | .75 | .75 | .75 | | | 2 | 2 | 2 | 2 | 2 | 2 | 2 | | | | | | |
| Math Specialists | | | | | | .75 | .75 | .75 | .75 | .75 | .75 | | | 2 | 2 | 2 | 2 | 2 | 2 | 2 | | | | | | |
| Printing Facilities | | | | | | | | | | | | | | | | | | | | | .1 | .1 | .1 | | | |
| Mainframe Computer | | | | | | | | | | | | | | | | | | | | | | | | .3 | .3 | .3 |
| Total | 2.5 | 2.5 | 2.5 | 1 | 1 | 3.5 | 3.5 | 3.5 | 3.5 | 3.5 | 3.5 | 5 | 5 | 5 | 5 | 5 | 5 | 5 | 5 | 5 | 3.1 | 3.1 | 3.1 | 1.3 | 1.3 | 1.3 |

**Exhibit 6.5.  Resource Spreadsheet.**

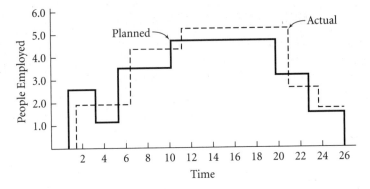

Figure 6.7.  Resource Loading Chart.

In general, if the area within the "actual" loading chart is much larger than the area within the "planned" chart, we have dedicated more person-days to the project than planned. If the area within the "actual" chart is smaller than the area within the "planned" chart, we have consumed fewer person-days of resources than planned. Resource variance is at a minimum when the area within the two charts is equal or nearly equal.

Resource loading charts are popular in managing projects because they simplify the resource control effort. To illustrate this, consider the "actual" versus "planned" portions in Figure 6.7. A comparison shows that we were somewhat delayed in beginning to use needed resources on our project. However, by using more resources than planned later on in the project, we are able to make up for some earlier deficiencies.

Note that the total number of person-days expended in carrying out the project is slightly more than originally planned. Does this mean a cost overrun on the project? Not necessarily. The principal deficiency of the resource loading chart is that it provides only highly aggregated information on resource consumption. It tells nothing about the quality or price of the individual resources. So although the actuals in Figure 6.7 suggest that more person-days were dedicated to the project than planned, this may not translate into higher project costs if the resources used to undertake the project had a lower unit cost than originally planned. In order to find out the impact of increases of person-days on the project budget, we would have to look directly at budget figures.

## RESOURCE LEVELING

The chief concern of resource planners is to allocate human and material resources efficiently and effectively, that is, to assign the right resources to the appropriate tasks in such a way that they are neither overcommitted nor underused. This is no easy accomplishment, particularly when a number of projects are being undertaken concurrently, each with its own resource requirements that developed independently of the resource requirements of sister projects.

For example, we may find that, by random chance, the staff artist is scheduled to work on four different projects on the same day. Unless the artist can be cut into four functioning pieces, he will not be able to meet the scheduled requirements for all the projects. Yet two weeks later, the artist may find no demand for his services. The artist faces a feast-or-famine situation common on projects.

Resource leveling applies to most project situations. With resource leveling, planners recognize that something has to give when there are dramatic ups and downs in the demand for limited resources—and that "something" is the project schedule. Resource leveling requires that task schedules be adjusted to create a smooth, consistent demand for resources. If it looks as though George will be overcommitted to project work in December, a project manager who wants to use him in December may have to reschedule her project so that she can obtain George in November, when he is available.

Resource leveling brings us face to face with the realization that there are trade-offs between schedules and resource utilization. If project planners plan a project purely on the basis of optimizing the schedule, it is likely that resources will not be employed efficiently. And planning a project in order to optimize resource utilization is likely to lead to suboptimization of the schedule.

On some projects—for example, projects to develop military hardware—it is often more important to optimize schedule performance than resource utilization. On most projects, however, resource constraints force us to engage in resource leveling, where scheduling must accommodate the availability of our precious human and material resources, not the other way around.

## GRAPHICAL CONTROL OF PROJECTS

So far we have covered the basic principles of project planning and control in this chapter and have discussed the most commonly used planning and control tools. At this point, let us examine how these principles and some of the most crucial tools can be brought together to provide project staff with a powerful methodology for controlling projects.

It should be obvious that if project managers focus all their attention on the project budget and ignore scheduling and resource utilization issues, they will have a seriously flawed image of what is happening on the project. They will be like the blind men in the old parable, each of whom had a limited and therefore distorted view of what an elephant looks like.

For example, when looking over the monthly budget progress reports, project managers may be delighted to see that budget variances are nearly zero. Nevertheless, they may be in serious trouble, because budget variance data tell them little or nothing about whether tasks are being completed on time. Similarly, if they look only at the schedule or only at resource utilization, they will have an incomplete image of project progress. In order to have a complete overview of the project, they must examine schedule, budget, and resource issues simultaneously.

An effective way of doing this is to place a graphical review of schedule performance (Gantt chart), budget performance (cumulative cost curve), and resource allocations (resource loading chart) on a single sheet of paper, so that project staff can easily compare schedule, budget, and resource information. This has been done in Figure 6.8, which portrays two different project scenarios, case A and case B.

In looking at the Gantt chart for case A, we see immediately that there is serious trouble. The project began according to schedule, but each task is taking longer to accomplish than originally estimated. That schedule delays are occurring because not enough workers are available is reflected in the personnel loading chart, which shows consistent underavailability of project staff. Because staff are not being employed in the numbers originally anticipated, the project is running under budget, a fact that is seen in the cumulative cost curve. The material resource loading chart, showing computer usage, reflects delays in the project: the computer is not being fully used because the system development task, which is computer intensive, has not yet begun.

In case B, we have a dramatically different situation. Here we see from the Gantt chart that the project is on schedule. If the project manager looks no further than the schedule, he will likely think that the project is doing just fine. However, we see from the budget data and the resource loading charts that the project is being kept on schedule at great cost. In fact, a particularly ominous piece of information emerging from the cumulative project budget chart is the knowledge that more has *already* been spent on the project than was budgeted for the project overall! This project is facing a serious cost overrun. The charts in case B illustrate a classic "crashing" scenario; extra resources are thrown into a project to keep it on schedule.

All project managers should use Gantt, cumulative cost, and resource loading charts in the way presented here for project control. When viewed individually, the charts offer easily understood information on schedule, budget, and resource utilization variances. When viewed collectively, they provide managers with immediate and full insight regarding their project's course.

With these valuable, comprehensive insights, project managers can make course correction decisions based on a full view of the project's status rather than on a keyhole glimpse provided by bits and pieces of scattered data. What makes this approach doubly attractive is that these charts are easy to put together. If the required planning and control data have been collected, the charts can be drawn freehand, or by means of a computer, in a matter of minutes.

## THE ACTION COMPONENT OF CONTROL

Project control has two components to it: analysis and action. Up until now, we have been talking only about the analytical aspect of control. We have seen that by using planning and control tools such as Gantt charts, cumulative cost curves, and resource histograms, we are able to determine the extent to which the project is achieving its schedule, budget, and resource targets. If the variances between what was planned and what is actually transpiring are small, then the project is seen to be under control. If the gaps are large, then planning targets are not being achieved and steps might need to be taken to bring the project under control.

The action aspect of control has us taking steps to handle unacceptable variances. If schedules are slipping, we need to figure out how to get the project back on schedule. Or if cost overruns are being incurred or insufficient resources are being employed, we need to take steps to get back on target.

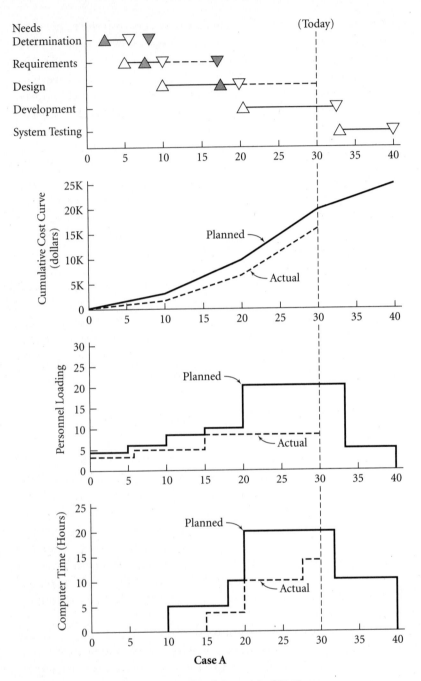

**Figure 6.8. Graphical Control of Projects.**

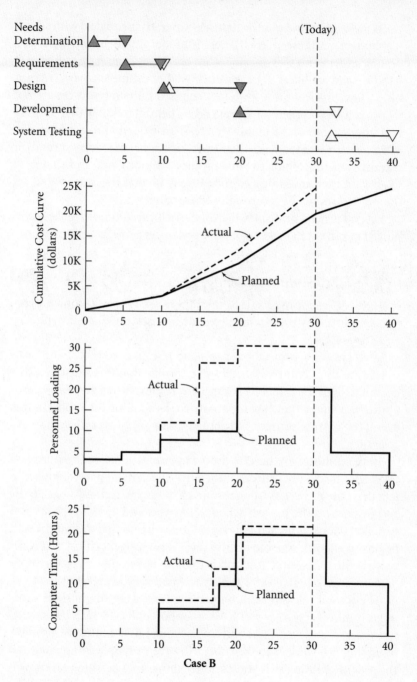

**Case B**

As a general principle, the first step when trying to deal with schedule, budget, and resource variances is to identify their sources. If you do not understand why variances are occurring, any steps you take to handle them are likely to be misdirected. For example, if you are running a low-priority project where promised human resources are not showing up to do their jobs, it would be helpful to know that they are tied up trying to save a highly visible, high-priority project from disaster. Demanding stridently that their functional managers meet their resource commitments to your project will not work. In fact, it will likely gain their unending enmity. It may be that the only way to get the needed resources is through outsourcing.

Beyond general principles, there are specific techniques regularly employed in project management designed to get projects back on track.

## Schedule Control

If a project is slipping its deadlines, there are two well-known practices employed by project managers to get back on schedule: *crashing* and *fast tracking*.

With crashing, project managers add resources to tasks in order to accelerate their completion. They recognize that this must be done carefully, since the mindless addition of resources to a task can lead to a situation where there are too many cooks spoiling the broth. In this event, the extra resources can actually slow progress rather than accelerate it.

With crashing, you need to follow two rules. First, add resources to tasks that lie on the critical path, since the critical path defines the length of the project. Adding resources to noncritical tasks has no direct impact on the project schedule. As you add tasks to the critical path and your actions achieve results, you will find that the critical path begins to change. The old critical path is no longer critical and is replaced with a new one. Your job is to focus constantly on accelerating performance of whatever is the critical path of the moment.

The second rule is to add resources to tasks where the cost of crashing is minimal. Let's say you have an opportunity to crash one of two tasks: task Y and task Z. In both cases, your project can save a month by adding two workers to the effort. However, a simple computation of the cost of crashing that you conduct shows that crashing task Y will add $5,000 to project costs, while crashing task Z will add $2,000. Clearly, you are better off crashing task Z, whose marginal cost of crashing is much lower than that of task Y.

Another way to get a project back on schedule is to engage in fast tracking. With fast tracking, you conduct work in parallel that normally you would carry out sequentially. For example, if you need to speed delivery of a refurbished hotel ballroom to a client, you may have the carpet laying crew and the ceiling tile crew work in the ballroom concurrently. Ideally, you would have the ceiling tile workers do their job first, so that debris that falls to the floor can be cleaned up before the carpets are laid. However, to speed performance, you instruct the two crews to carry out their chores concurrently.

By engaging in concurrent work efforts, you often increase project risk. In the example, debris from the ceiling tile may soil the newly installed carpet. In general, fast tracking increases project risk because work is not being executed in an optimal sequence. Why increase risk? The answer is that you have another risk to contend with that is more serious: if you deliver your product late, you may incur penalties and anger your client.

## Cost Control

A common feature of projects today is that they are underfunded. In order to receive support for projects, their champions often offer excessively optimistic estimates of what they will cost. The low-ball estimates make them appear attractive. But once the project is under way, it becomes obvious that it cannot be carried out within the approved budget. Cost overruns ensue, and the project team is pressured to get costs under control.

To the extent that this scenario reflects what is happening on projects, it suggests that the best way to control costs is to establish realistic cost estimates at the outset. If you promise to do a $1 million job for $700,000, then a serious cost overrun is built into the project before any work has begun.

Another common source of cost variance is *scope creep*, a project management term that describes what happens when project requirements are changed without the discipline of change control. Customers may insist on small adjustments to the deliverable to meet their changing needs, while the technical team may add sexy technical features that allow the deliverable to perform better than planned. As we saw in Chapter Five, changes to requirements are inevitable. The question is not, Will change occur? Rather, the question is, Do we have a formal change control process in place to handle the inevitable requests for change?

Cost variances rooted in scope creep can be controlled by establishing a good change control process and sticking to it. First, requests for project changes should be documented. The requests should describe the impact of the change on costs, the schedule, the technical integrity of the deliverable, and other work being carried out on the project. Once they are properly formulated, they should be reviewed by a panel of players who are charged with overseeing progress on the project. In many organizations, the panel goes by the name *change control board*. If the changes require additions to the budget and they are approved, then the budget should be adjusted accordingly.

Developing realistic cost estimates and implementing disciplined change control procedures are ways to avoid untoward cost variances. But what if good management procedures are not followed, or what if unanticipated change (such as a surprise recession) plays havoc with budget baselines? What should project managers do when they detect unacceptable cost variances?

When dealing with cost overruns, the answer is simple: they should do whatever they can to contain costs. The details of their actions will, of course, depend on the specific circumstances they face. They may tighten purchasing procedures to make sure that money is not wasted on frivolous or expensive items. Or they may have the project team work longer, unpaid hours to get the job done more cheaply. Or they may try to negotiate reduced scope of effort with their customers and managers. The point is that they must take active steps to contain costs.

## Resource Control

The optimistic cost estimates that plague so many projects have implications for the use of human and material resources. If a project budget is unrealistically low, this means that funds will not be available to hire adequate numbers of people and purchase needed materials. Consequently, when project managers detect cost overruns on their projects, they invariably encounter resource variances as well. To a large extent, handling resource variances, where insufficient resources are available to do the job, requires dealing with budget shortfalls. As we saw, this may require tightening purchasing procedures or rescoping the project effort.

Even well-funded projects may encounter resource variances. This often occurs when promised resources are diverted to put out fires elsewhere in the organization. For example, we may grow concerned that the software testing team has not shown up to perform their scheduled testing activities on our project. When we call the team's boss at the testing shop, we learn that the team is assigned indefinitely to an important and highly visible project that is experiencing serious technical glitches. Regrettably, their reassignment to a problem project means that they will not be able to meet their commitment to our project.

This type of situation is typically handled in one of two ways. In the first, the project manager who is facing a shortage of resources contacts the functional manager who controls them and tries to negotiate their release. If the resources are truly tied up working on a significant disaster, the project manager will have difficulty getting the resources she needs. In this case, she should ask the functional manager whether he has any suggestions for dealing with the problem. Perhaps he has a solution, or perhaps he is willing to negotiate the partial release of human resources to the project.

If the resources are not forthcoming, the project manager can handle the situation in a second way: obtain resources from outside contractors. The outsourcing of work to contractors grew explosively in the 1990s and early 2000s. An advantage of outsourcing is that it gives project managers great flexibility in getting their hands on a wide range of skilled personnel. There are a number of disadvantages, however. A serious one is that the contracted workers are usually unfamiliar with the technology and operating environment of the contracting organization. For them to function effectively, time must be set aside for them to grow familiar with the client organization.

## PROJECT MANAGEMENT SOFTWARE

The discipline of project management received a major boost in the early 1980s with the creation of project management software that ran on personal computers. In particular, the creation of Harvard Project Manager software in 1983 focused management interest on project budgeting, scheduling, and resource management methodologies. Harvard Project Manager generated PDM charts, Gantt charts, cumulative cost curves, resource loading charts, and a bevy of tables. It was, in effect, an integrated project planning and control package. What was particularly remarkable was that its list price was only $299 (soon to be discounted to $165) at a time when vastly inferior software was selling for $1,000.

Since then, project management software has evolved into truly sophisticated tools. By the mid-1990s, one of the most popular packages, Microsoft Project for Windows, even had Monte Carlo simulation capabilities added to it.

As the personal computer project management software became more sophisticated, however, it also became harder to learn and to use. A software package like Harvard Project Manager could be learned in a day. Comparable mastery of a contemporary software package might take five days. With the growing demands for training on project management software, the obvious question arose: *Who* should be trained? Initially, the assumption was that project managers should be the lead users of the software. But experience showed that if this path were followed, project managers would be spending most of their time working with the software and little time dealing with project needs.

Today, most organizations that employ project management software have established internal consultants or support groups who are the resident experts on the software. It is their responsibility to keep up to date on the most recent developments in scheduling, budgeting, and resource allocation software packages. It is also their responsibility to translate these developments into practical applications for use by project team members.

For the most part, the project management software seems to benefit project professionals. It imposes needed project management standards on organizations executing projects. If all employees use the same software across multiple projects, their planning and control data become comparable. It also sensitizes people to the value of project metrics. As they plan and maintain their project activities through project management software, they are accruing historical data that can be used to offer guidance on how to manage future projects. Now when someone asks, "How long does it take to test fifty lines of code?" team members can answer the question by looking back on past performances that have been captured by the project management software.

The software does have drawbacks. For one thing, it imposes an increased administrative burden on project staff, a burden not always offset by any benefits derived from using the software. For another, it is fairly rigid, so that many of the charts and tables it creates are only marginally relevant to any given organization. Finally, it perpetuates the view that project management is chiefly concerned with standard techniques, such as PDM charts and cumulative cost curves, when in reality project management should be focused on soft issues as well, such as project politics, managing borrowed resources, and making sure needs have been defined properly.

## CONCLUSION

Effective planning and control are necessary for project success. It is difficult to visualize how a project can achieve its goals if the project team has not done a good job planning schedules, budgets, resource requirements, and technical implementations and then does not carefully monitor the work effort as the project is actually executed. Although good planning and control will not ensure project success, their absence will certainly guarantee some degree of failure.

The good news is that a number of tools have emerged over the years to help project staff plan and control their efforts effectively. We have covered the key tools in this chapter. Of course, by themselves, tools sitting in a toolbox cannot get the job done. For planning and control tools to be useful, project staff must learn how to use them, and senior managers in organizations must create environments that support their use. That is, clearly stipulated planning and control procedures must be developed, staff must be trained on the use of key tools, access to updated tools must be ensured, and everyone must be committed to doing the best job possible in planning and controlling project efforts.

# CHAPTER SEVEN

# Managing Special Problems and Complex Projects

I n this chapter, we look closely at a number of specialized issues, topics that are crucial to many project managers but are often overlooked in project management texts: planning and control on large projects, project portfolios, contracted projects, and projects with bureaucratic milestones. We conclude the chapter with a brief overview of two additional topics that have gained importance in recent years: establishing a project support office and managing virtual teams.

## PLANNING AND CONTROL ON LARGE PROJECTS

Someone with a first-rate track record in managing small projects may be a failure at managing large ones. By the same token, someone who has demonstrated great skill in undertaking large projects may have difficulty in carrying out small ones. There are some fundamental differences in the requirements of large and small projects that translate into differences in how they should be managed.

There are no clear-cut boundaries separating small and large projects, and to a large extent, our notion of what is small and what is large is colored by what we are accustomed to. At one of my project management seminars, an Air Force major said to me, "You keep talking about $10 million projects as if they were a big deal. Where I come from, $10 million is pocket money."

One way to get a grasp of the differences between small and large projects is to look at obvious extremes and determine whether there are features in the two extremes that would distinguish their management requirements. A $5,000 project that occupies two workers for one month is an obvious example of a small project. The $20 billion project to build the new airport in Hong Kong clearly falls at the other end of the spectrum.

A small project employs few human and material resources, it is short term, and its focus is rather narrow, that is, it deals with a small piece of the whole range of activities an organization carries out. The operational details associated with such a project lie well within the grasp of most project managers, so the need to spell out these details formally is small. In fact, because of the administrative costs associated with formally spelling out and keeping track of the details, there is a danger that unnecessarily large sums will be spent on planning and tracking.

A multibillion-dollar project, in contrast, employs huge amounts of human and material resources, it is long term, and its focus is quite broad. In fact, a discrete organization, called a program office, is often set up to handle the project. With this large project, there is so much to keep track of that a formal, well-specified planning and tracking system must be established to keep on top of planned and unplanned developments. More than half of the project budget may be dedicated to administrative matters associated with formal planning and control.

## The Need for Formality in Planning and Controlling Large Projects

While the planning and control techniques discussed in Chapter Six work well on large projects as well as small ones, the discussion of these techniques assumed that they would be used rather flexibly, which is perfectly appropriate on smaller and midsized projects. For example, in answer to the question "How many levels should the WBS contain?" a reasonable answer is, "Whatever the project manager is comfortable with and whatever seems workable."

However, this degree of flexibility in defining the WBS is not viable on a large project, where there might be one hundred task leaders, each creating a piece of a super-WBS for the whole project. Each of these task leaders must be given specific, formal instructions on how the WBS should be constructed; otherwise, the results of their efforts will not fit together into a cohesive super-WBS. Let me illustrate this point by describing the requirements for building a WBS on a large government military project. (I have greatly simplified the procedure for purposes of illustration.)

On a large military project, the dimensions of WBS levels can be fairly regular. This is illustrated in Exhibit 7.1. At the bottom level of the WBS (called the *work package* here), formal instructions may require that each item be constructed in such a way as to represent about 100 person-hours (2.5 person-weeks) of effort. Ten of these items taken together constitute a subtask, the next level up in the WBS. Thus, a subtask, as portrayed here, reflects about 1,000 person-hours (0.5 person-years) of effort. Ten subtasks in turn constitute a task, which represents about 10,000 person-hours (5 person-years) of effort. Extending this logic to higher levels of the WBS, it can be seen that a five-level WBS represents a total of about 1 million person-hours (500 person-years) of effort.

Unfortunately, one side effect of the need for increased formality is a proliferation of paper on large projects in order to maintain communications among project staff. Consider, for example, that even a minor change on a small task may require that notices be sent to fifteen or twenty project workers affected by the change. On a typical large project, thousands of changes are made each year, necessitating the generation of countless pieces of paper, which further requires the creation of a mechanism to make sure that the paper arrives at its intended destination, the establishment of additional procedures for

| Level 1 | Program | 1 million person-hours |
| Level 2 | Project | 100,000 person-hours |
| Level 3 | Task | 10,000 person-hours |
| Level 4 | Subtask | 1,000 person-hours |
| Level 5 | Work package | 100 person-hours |

Exhibit 7.1.    Formal Work Breakdown Structure for a Large Military Project.

storage and retrieval of this information, and so forth. I have seen an estimate that the paperwork associated with the production of one F-16 aircraft would fill the trailer of a tractor-trailer truck. It should come as no surprise, then, that such a high proportion of the effort associated with large projects is dedicated to administration.

On very large projects, there is always a danger that project staff cannot separate the wheat from the chaff as they are bombarded with project information. This ability becomes especially crucial with respect to tracking budgets and schedules. Given the plethora of data that are spewed out of the project planning and tracking machine, how can project staff make sense of the barrage of project performance facts and figures directed at them? Increasingly, they are turning to an approach called the *earned-value management* to help them better manage budget and schedule information.

## Earned-Value Management

Earned-value management was developed by cost accountants and is designed to help project staff keep better track of what is happening on their projects. It recognizes that cost data alone or schedule data alone can lead to distorted perceptions of performance. The fact that a status report shows that a project is under budget does not mean that project is doing well. The reported budget performance may reflect the fact that work is not being done, hence money is not being spent. The purported cost savings is chimerical.

In Chapter Six, we saw that this problem can be handled by viewing Gantt charts, cumulative cost curves, and resource loading charts together, a combination that provides an instant overview of schedule, budget, and resource performance. However, applying this approach to very large projects, with their tens of thousands of activities, would overwhelm project staff. Gantt charts would be so massive and complex that it would be difficult to interpret them meaningfully.

The earned-value approach does numerically what the graphical approach in Figure 6.8 does through charts. It allows project professionals to examine cost and schedule variances concurrently, enabling them to take a holistic view of progress on the project. A number of high-level government program managers have told me that it is hard to imagine how very large projects could be controlled without this approach. (In the U.S. government, the earned-value approach is given various names, including DODR 5000.2, the Cost/Schedule Control

System Criteria, C/SCSC, CS-Squared, and C-Specs. The Department of Defense, the Department of Energy, the Department of Transportation, and NASA require that contractors use this approach on very large projects.)

The earned-value technique is based on three fundamental building blocks. One is called the *budgeted cost of work scheduled* (BCWS). That is equivalent to the conventional concept of planned budget—that is, BCWS states what we think a particular task (or subtask or work package) will cost. A second building block, the *actual cost of work performed* (ACWP), is equivalent to the conventional concept of actual costs—that is, ACWP states how much was actually spent to accomplish a given effort.

So far, there is nothing new here. Project staff regularly use planned costs and actual costs to calculate cost variance. The earned-value technique becomes interesting with the introduction of the concept of *budgeted cost of work performed* (BCWP), also known as *earned value.* A moment's reflection on the term *budgeted cost of work performed* offers an insight into BCWP's purpose. The "budgeted cost" component of this term means that we are concerned with our original plan, whereas the "work performed" component refers to what has actually been accomplished. Thus, BCWP—or earned value—is a hybrid measure, combining elements of the plan with elements of the actuals. With BCWP, we are evaluating how much work we have achieved in the context of what we were supposed to do.

An example will help to clarify the meaning of BCWP. Let us assume that at the outset of a project, we estimate that task T will cost $1,000 to carry out and that it will be completed by November 1. On November 1, a review of progress on the task shows that it is only 70 percent complete. Although we have planned to undertake $1,000 worth of work (BCWS), we have actually achieved only $700 worth of work (BCWP). BCWP is a measure, then, of the dollar value of the work we have actually accomplished (hence the term *earned value*).

These three building blocks—BCWS, ACWP, and BCWP—allow us to calculate budget and schedule variance in a new and powerful way. Budget variance and schedule variance are each captured in a single number. These two numbers, when encountered concurrently, allow us to determine where we stand on our project from the perspective of both budget and schedule.

Budget variance is defined in the earned-value approach as BCWP minus ACWP. To understand why, let's extend the example to include information on actual cost of work performed: $500. BCWP tells us that we have done $700 worth of work, and ACWP tells us that it has cost us $500 to do so. Clearly, we are $200 (BCWP minus ACWP) ahead of the game for that portion of the work already carried out. That is, we have a positive budget variance of $200. Does this mean the project is in good shape? We cannot be fully sure until we have examined schedule information.

In the earned-value approach, schedule variance is defined as BCWP minus BCWS. Note that schedule variance is here being interpreted in monetary terms. We are looking at the difference between the work we planned to do and what we have actually done, valued according to our original budget estimates. Let's look at the example again to clarify the concept of schedule variance. Because we budgeted $1,000 worth of work but performed only $700 worth of work, the dollar value of the schedule slippage is −$300 ($700 − $1,000). That is, we have yet to complete $300 worth of work that we were supposed to have completed.

Considering both budget and schedule variances together, we find ourselves in the following situation. We have slipped our schedule; although the task should have been completed by November 1, $300 worth of work remains to be carried out as of that date. Looking at the work we have completed ($700 worth), we find that it has cost us only $500 to undertake this work, suggesting a cost savings to date of $200. However, this savings is to a certain extent misleading, because the schedule has slipped substantially. Had we dedicated more resources to the task, perhaps we could have avoided the schedule slippage. In fact, to finish the job, we may have to spend more money than planned, leading ultimately to a cost overrun for the project.

The perceptive reader will have noted a fundamental weakness in the earned-value technique. In order to calculate BCWP, it is necessary to know what percentage of a task has been completed. If a task has not yet begun, we have no trouble saying that 0 percent of the task has been completed, and if the task is finished, it is obviously 100 percent completed. However, we walk on treacherous ground when we try to estimate how much of a task has been completed for anything between those two extremes.

To see the nature of the difficulty, consider Imhotep's problem in determining how much work he had completed on a pyramid that had used 900,000 stone blocks out of a total of 1 million needed to complete the project. (Imhotep was the builder of the pyramid. They didn't have engineers in those days, but that's the identifier we'd use today.) Looking at these statistics, we are tempted to say that 90 percent of the work has been completed, since 90 percent of the principal construction material has been used. The problem here is that the last 100,000 stone blocks have to be hauled higher than the first 900,000; furthermore, they have to be fitted into a point at the very top—a formidable task. Clearly, the pyramid project is somewhat less than 90 percent completed. If it is difficult to say how much of a project has been completed when we are dealing with a down-to-earth, tangible undertaking, consider the added difficulty of making such estimates on information age projects that operate largely in the realm of the intangible.

The earned-value approach has a means of dealing with this problem: the 50–50 rule. Project staff are not asked to make wild estimates of how much of their task has been completed. Rather, as soon as a task is begun, it is assumed that half the effort has been completed, and half of the BCWS value associated with the task is entered into the project accounts book. Only after the task has been completed is the remaining half of the BCWS value entered into the accounts. When many tasks are being considered, this approach provides a good statistical approximation of BCWP.

In Figure 7.1, the Gantt chart shows five tasks, each of which represents $100 worth of work. Four of the five tasks have been begun; three of those four have been completed (leaving one partially com-

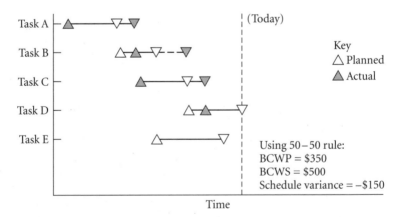

Figure 7.1. Application of the 50–50 Rule.

*Note:* In this example, each task has a planned cost of $100.

pleted task and one task not yet begun). Using the 50–50 approach, we enter into our accounts that we have completed $300 worth of effort with the three finished tasks, and we enter another $50 to take into account the task that has started but is not yet finished. Because we have not yet begun the fifth task, we enter nothing into the accounts for this task. What is earned value? Answer: $350. BCWS for the five tasks is, of course, $500, and we can now use this figure to calculate schedule slippage. That is, we have completed $350 worth of work, but we should have completed $500 worth of work, so the schedule has slipped to the tune of $150 worth of work (the slippage value is –$150). These data also enable us to calculate that we have completed only 70 percent (that is, 350/500 × 100) of the work scheduled on the five tasks.

Some prefer a more conservative approach than the 50–50 rule, and they may adopt a 10–90 rule. As soon as a task is begun, 10 percent of its value is entered into the project accounts. As soon as it is completed, the remaining 90 percent of its value is entered. Using this conservative rule to calculate BCWP, we find that BCWP on our above example is now $310. This suggests that we are only 62 percent (that is, 310/500 × 100) finished with the five tasks. An even more conservative rule is the 0–100 approach, which would indicate in this example that we had achieved only 60 percent of the target (that is, 300/500 × 100). Software development projects often employ the 0–100 rule under the premise that a half-finished software task has no value.

Many project management experts strongly believe that the earned-value approach is vital for the control of very large projects. I believe that it can be useful on small projects as well. On large U.S. Defense Department projects, the rules for implementing DODR 5000.2 are highly complex; for example, they require major contractors to overhaul their cost accounting systems completely to accommodate the earned-value approach. However, on small projects, there is no need to follow the complex rules. All we need to implement the earned-value system are estimates of planned task costs (BCWS), data on actual expenditures (ACWP), and a good guess on the percentage of work completed on the task (a risky approach) or employment of the 50–50 rule.

In the 1990s, an attempt was made to make earned-value management more user friendly. When people are introduced to the technique, many are overwhelmed with its unfamiliar terminology. Many feel that the difficulties they have in learning the process are tied as much to problems in understanding the vocabulary as in dealing with the concepts. Consequently, organizations are beginning to adopt friendlier terminology. Increasingly, organizations are adopting *planned value* (PV) as a replacement for BCWS, *actual cost* (AC) as a replacement for ACWP, and *earned value* (EV) as a replacement for BCWP. Thus, schedule variance would be reported as EV − PV and budget variance as EV − AC. Currently, both sets of terms are being employed in the earned-value management community.

## PLANNING AND CONTROL FOR PROJECT PORTFOLIOS

Projects are often organized into a portfolio, a collection of projects that must be co-managed. Whether these projects are interrelated or independent of each other, the important point is that they fall under a single management umbrella.

Project portfolios are found in many different situations. For example, they are common in data processing departments, where staff are busily working on a wide array of projects—some long term, some short term, some large, some small. Management consultant firms often are nothing more—from a functional perspective—than a conglomeration of individual projects. Similarly, multiple projects are the rule in R&D departments, auditing departments, and advertising agencies.

### The Project Portfolio

Project portfolios come in many different shapes and sizes. Figure 7.2 shows three different forms that portfolios can assume. The structural relations embedded in each of these forms present managers with different challenges and requirements.

Figure 7.2a pictures a portfolio of projects that deal with the same basic subject matter but are otherwise independent of each other; the outcome of one project has little or no bearing on work on the other projects. Research projects in an electronics laboratory have this characteristic. What ties the projects together is a strong project selection process, which filters out project possibilities that have nothing to do with, say, the mission of the electronics laboratory.

The principal management challenge associated with this kind of portfolio is selection of appropriate projects. Because the projects are

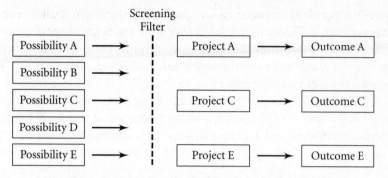

(a) Portfolio of Independent Projects That Have Much in Common.

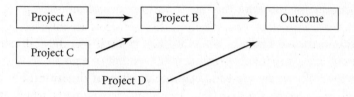

(b) Portfolio of Interdependent Projects (a Program).

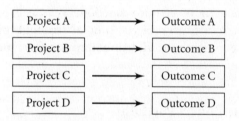

(c) Portfolio of Independent Projects.

**Figure 7.2.  Varieties of Project Portfolios.**

independent, the matter of coordinating their activities does not loom large. Planning and control issues are primarily the responsibility of the individual project managers.

In Figure 7.2b, the portfolio constitutes what is often referred to as a *program* (for example, the Apollo program, the space shuttle program). Its chief characteristic is the heavy interdependence of projects that constitute the portfolio. These assorted projects dovetail tightly and are directed toward a common outcome. If a project runs into trouble, the whole portfolio may be jeopardized. Consequently, this kind of portfolio requires vigilant portfolio-wide planning and control efforts. Typically, a program office is set up to carry out these efforts, and a powerful program manager holds sway over the entire portfolio. In the military, this approach to configuring a portfolio is called program management.

Figure 7.2c portrays a portfolio that is nothing more than a loose agglomeration of projects with little or nothing in common. Planning and control here are the responsibility of the individual project managers. These projects may have been put under the same roof simply because there is nowhere else to put them. The principal portfolio management concern here is administrative: making sure that projects get the funding they need according to their budgets and that they are producing the work they are supposed to accomplish.

SPECIAL CONSIDERATIONS IN MANAGING A PORTFOLIO. There is usually more complexity involved in the management of a portfolio of projects than of a single project. Let's look at some of the reasons:

• *Portfolios are administratively more complex than single projects.* To see this, consider the differences in managing a single $1 million project versus ten $100,000 projects. Although the $1 million project has one project manager, the portfolio of smaller projects will have several managers. With the $1 million project, there is only one project to plan and track; with the smaller projects in a portfolio, there are ten projects that must be followed. In general, the ten smaller projects will collectively have more administrative overhead associated with them—more forms to be filled out, more project review meetings—than will the one larger project.

• *Optimization of the portfolio's performance will require suboptimization of individual projects.* The portfolio manager's objective is to optimize portfolio performance, and this invariably requires making resource allocation and scheduling decisions that benefit high-priority projects at the expense of low-priority projects. While suboptimization of individual projects may be necessary to enhance the good of the portfolio, this is small consolation to the manager of the suboptimized project, whose credo is, "Get the job done—on time, within budget, and according to specifications!" Consequently, portfolio managers are likely to face unhappiness and resistance from some quarters of their portfolio staff.

• *Portfolios run the risk of falling victim to the tyranny of large projects.* It is difficult to maintain a balanced perspective on large and small projects that may coexist in a portfolio. Large projects, by definition, have a more pronounced profile than small projects; they are more visible. They tend to have access to the best of scarce resources. Furthermore, when large projects run into trouble, small projects in the portfolio often get lost in the shuffle. Their meager resources may even be diverted away from them and directed toward the large projects. When that occurs, we find not only the large projects in trouble but the small ones as well.

SEQUENCING PROJECTS IN THE PORTFOLIO. How projects are sequenced in the portfolio may have a strong bearing on the portfolio's performance. For example, in a program of heavily interrelated projects, considerable planning may be required to identify start and finish dates of projects that will improve program performance. If these dates have not been carefully chosen, scheduling bottlenecks may arise, and the overall program performance may deteriorate.

The way in which projects are sequenced in the portfolio also has an impact on the flow of benefits emerging from them (for example, profits, units of output produced, increased productivity). In Figure 7.3a, projects A and B, which have equal budgets, are carried out concurrently. Benefits do not emerge from them until both are finished. In Figure 7.3b, the budgets for projects A and B are the same size as in Figure 7.3a, and the budget period covered is of the same duration. However, the benefit streams emerging from the staggered projects are quite different. Benefits begin earlier here, emerging just as soon as A is completed. For the time period shown in the figure, the benefit stream for A is larger in the second case, while the benefit stream for B is equal in both cases. Consequently, from the perspective of benefit streams, the second scenario, picturing projects carried out one after the other, is better.

## Gap Analysis

Chapter Six discussed the difficulties in producing a budget for a single project. Budget allocations for a portfolio of multiple projects present even greater challenges. With a portfolio, we typically face the situation our grandmothers encountered when they had to divide up

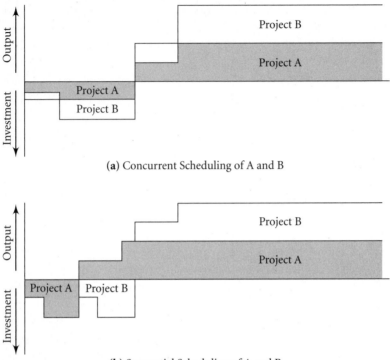

**(a)** Concurrent Scheduling of A and B

**(b)** Sequential Scheduling of A and B

**Figure 7.3.  Project Scheduling Sequences Affect Output Flows.**

an apple pie among a throng of grandchildren of different shapes and sizes—that is, we have a fixed budget to work with, and there are obvious practical limits on how we can carve it up. We may opt to spread funds over many small projects, or decide to concentrate them on one or two larger efforts, or take some position between these two extremes.

*Gap analysis,* illustrated in Figure 7.4, is a technique that can help project professionals visualize the practical budget options available to them in project portfolios. Gap analysis employs both exploratory and normative forecasting. With normative forecasting, we look at an anticipated future state of affairs and ask, "What will it take to get us there?" With exploratory forecasting, we extrapolate from past experience into the future. Gap analysis uses exploratory forecasting when it requires us to make estimates of the future budget demands of projects that are currently in our portfolio.

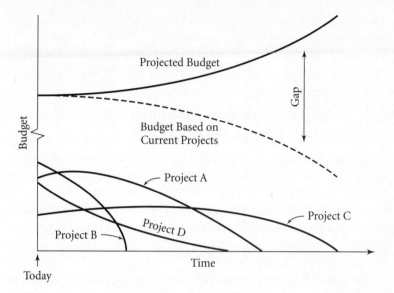

**Figure 7.4. Gap Analysis.**

In Figure 7.4, we have these estimates for projects A, B, C, and D. Note that these overlapping budget curves are a pictorial representation of the anticipated project life cycle for each of the four projects. After future budgets for individual projects have been made, these budgets are added together to create a total budget for projects currently in the portfolio (the top half of the figure). Because projects ultimately are completed and no longer consume resources, the long-term trend for this total budget is downward.

In gap analysis, the curve associated with the total budget requirements of existing projects is compared with a curve of the total anticipated budget for all projects, even those that have not yet been started. In Figure 7.4, this projected budget is rising, while the budget for existing projects is declining, leaving an ever-growing gap between the two over time.

It is at this point that normative forecasting enters the picture. We examine the anticipated gap and then ask, "What should the project portfolio look like in order to fill the gap?" At one extreme, we could try to fill the gap by initiating a single large project; its budget would take up the slack created by the winding down of existing projects. At the other extreme, we could plan to increase the number of projects in the portfolio by carrying out more and more small projects.

Gap analysis does not provide an automatic answer to this question of how portfolios should be constructed, but it can serve as a useful tool that helps planners conceptualize the future character of their portfolios.

## PLANNING AND CONTROL FOR CONTRACTED PROJECTS

A large number of projects are carried out under contractual arrangements. Construction projects, for example, are often based on a contractual agreement between a developer, who organizes project financing, and a contractor, who oversees the construction effort. The contractor, in turn, works with subcontractors, each of whom specializes in a particular area, such as plumbing, electrical wiring, heating and ventilation, and carpentry.

The largest funder of project contracts is government. In the United States, the federal government issues billions of dollars of contracts each year for projects ranging from the minor modification of software all the way up to the building of a space defense system. State and local governments carry out most of their project work through contractors. Everything from establishing an alcohol inventory system for the state liquor control board to redesigning a science curriculum for a municipal school system is fair game for contracts.

Contracted projects are also common in the private sector, where big and little companies alike employ outside expertise to help them address special needs that cannot be handled cost-effectively with internal resources. Private sector firms prefer to call the contracting effort outsourcing. During the corporate downsizing and reengineering of the 1980s and 1990s, companies decided that much of their work could be done more cost-effectively if it was carried out by outsiders. As a consequence, the payrolls of many corporate giants shrank dramatically, while there was a corresponding increase in employment in the smaller companies that served as outsourcers.

When we talk about project management in contracted projects, we add another layer of complexity to an already complex situation. The customers are now outside the performing organization. These customers, who are paying hard-earned cash for results, are going to be interested in getting their money's worth out of the project. Consequently, they may insist on playing an overactive role in overseeing progress and may, in fact, perceive themselves to be de facto project managers, the individuals calling the shots. Furthermore, the questions discussed in Chapters Four and Five on meeting customer needs and specifying project requirements take on an added urgency with contracted projects, since unhappy customers may now mean costly and painful litigation.

## Types of Contracts

A contract is a legally binding agreement specifying the rights and responsibilities of the contracting parties. Contracts can assume an endless variety of forms. Common contract forms found in project situations include the following:

- Firm fixed price
- Fixed price, economic price adjustment
- Fixed price, incentive
- Fixed price, award
- Fixed price, with provisions for redetermination
- Firm fixed price, level of effort term
- Cost reimbursable
- Cost sharing
- Cost plus incentive
- Cost plus award fee
- Cost plus fixed fee
- Time and materials

To understand the impact of contractual arrangements on the management of projects, we need not delve into the intricacies of all the different kinds of contracts that exist. Rather, we will focus on the two most common types of contracted projects: fixed price and cost plus.

FIXED-PRICE CONTRACTS. With a fixed-price contract, funder and performer negotiate a set price for understanding the project. The performer agrees to do what is described in the contract for a flat price. If the performer can carry out project work at a cost below the price, he or she will realize a profit. If it costs more to undertake the project than the negotiated contract price, the performer faces a loss.

With fixed-price contracts, project managers in performing organizations face enormous pressures to reduce project costs, because every cent saved is translated into an increase in profit margins. Many project organizations that regularly carry out fixed-price contracts offer incentives to their project managers to keep costs down. For example, project managers may be given bonuses tied to cost savings. On the surface, this may seem to be a worthy tactic that rewards project managers who can effectively promote efficiency on their projects. However, there is a danger that corner cutting is being encouraged and that cost savings will be realized at the expense of quality.

Theoretically, fixed-price contracts place project management responsibilities totally in the hands of the performer, since the performer has agreed to do certain things for a given price. If it costs the performer more—well, those are the breaks. The performer eats the loss. Theoretically, all the funder has to do is sit back and wait for the results to be delivered on the promised date. In practice, the funder must maintain vigilance in observing the performer's work.

A fixed-price contract is an agreement, not a guarantee that the deliverable will be turned over on time and as promised. Things have a way of turning out differently than anticipated. A delay may arise in shipping the deliverable, and this could seriously hurt the funder. A dispute may flare up as to whether the deliverable is what the funder ordered or whether the quality of the deliverable is acceptable. The unhappy funder can wave the fixed-price contract under the nose of the performer, but this contract reminder offers no assurance that the funder's desires will be satisfied. As a last resort, the funder can take the performer to court, a costly and painful procedure that may or may not work out to the advantage of the funder.

From the perspective of the project manager working in the performing organization, fixed-price projects can be stressful, especially when things start going wrong. If costs get out of hand, profits shrink; in the worst-case scenario, the project generates losses for the performing organization. Experienced performing organizations typically shy away from entering into fixed-price arrangements on unpredictable, nonroutine projects. If they do undertake a risky fixed-price project, they charge a high-risk premium, generously inflating estimates of project costs to account for unanticipated contingencies.

**COST-PLUS CONTRACTS.** With a cost-plus contract, the funder agrees to reimburse the performer for project work and offers an additional fee or bonus so that the performing organization can earn a profit on its efforts. These contracts are common on highly speculative projects, on which it is difficult or impossible to predict accurately what the project will cost. Most contracted R&D projects are cost-plus projects.

Project professionals in the performing organization face far fewer pressures on cost-plus contracts than on fixed-price contracts. If there are cost overruns, the additional cost is borne by the funder, not the performer. There is always a danger on cost-plus contracts that the performer will grow lax in monitoring progress. With poorly monitored cost-plus contracts, it is easy for spending to get out of hand, since there are no obvious penalties for profligacy. There may even be incentives for overspending, because spending creates work for staff who might otherwise be idle. Ultimately, profligacy can backfire, particularly if the performer develops a reputation for being a big-time spender.

Given the lack of obvious cost restraints facing the performer, the funder must actively monitor project efforts on cost-plus contracts. The performer may be required to submit twice-monthly progress reports to the funder, for example, and present monthly briefings. On significant projects, the funder may insist on having a company representative working on site in the performing organization in order to monitor project efforts continuously. Although it is crucial that the funding organization keep track of project developments, it should avoid meddling to the point that it contributes to project failure.

## Managing Changes to the Plan on Contracted Projects

Project managers can count on changes to the project plan. With contracted fixed-price projects, project managers must consciously employ an explicit methodology for dealing with change requests from the funder, since changes increase project costs more often than not. Building contractors are sensitive about this point and demand that their staff keep track of all changes requested by the funder, no matter how small, so that the funder can be billed for the changes. In the absence of such a policy, fragile profit margins can disappear quickly.

Without an explicit policy for dealing with change requests, naive project managers can get into serious trouble. In their eagerness to please the client, they may acquiesce to nickel-and-dime changes here and there. After a while, they realize that the nickels and dimes are adding up and putting a squeeze on profit margins. At this point, it is difficult to know what to do, because they have already established a pattern of compliance with client requests. They worry that any reluctance to meet future requests will be perceived as a sign of unresponsiveness to client needs. Yet they also recognize that they cannot go on eating the extra costs resulting from the changes.

It is far better for project performers to make it clear at the outset that any funder-requested changes to the plan will be noted and that the funder will be responsible for their cost. Each time that funders want a change, they should be required to fill out a change order. Before the change is actually implemented, the funder should be told what the cost of the request will be. If the funder still wants to proceed with the change, he or she should be asked to sign a statement to this effect, so that the cost consequences of the request are perfectly clear to the funder. This policy will force the funder to think carefully before requesting changes. It will also avoid putting the performing organization's project manager in a position of switching from compliance with to hard-nosed resistance to client requests. (Change orders are discussed in more detail in Chapter Five.)

## Government Versus Private Sector Contracted Projects

Several years ago, I did some work with a company that had recently established a Washington, D.C., operation. The company's Washington strategy was to grow 30 percent annually, with all new business coming from federal contracts. I met with over eighty corporate project managers, the majority of whom had been transferred to the new Washington facility from corporate headquarters out West. Most of these project managers were unhappy with their Washington contracts and were sour on doing business with government. They longed to return to private sector work.

This feeling was so common among the project managers that I decided to investigate the sources of unhappiness. I invited the project managers to describe to me their perceptions of government work and to contrast this with work in the private sector. The responses, quite uniform, boiled down to a handful of points.

Two points in particular stand out. First, there was a general perception that it is difficult to do business with government because government is slow and bureaucratic. A contract that may take a few days to work out in the private sector will likely take months or even years to negotiate in the government sector. Second, there was a sense that the government wants something for nothing in dealing with the contractor. This is particularly evident in fixed-price contracts, they claimed: government clients may request changes to the project and then, after the changes have been made, refuse to authorize payment for the changes (because they were not covered in the original contract).

Virtually all of the project managers believed that doing business with the private sector was more satisfying. They noted an emphasis on good faith and flexibility in the private sector. All parties recognize that it is in everyone's best interest to get the job done as effectively as possible. Contractors that do not perform satisfactorily do not get repeat business. (As the national news accounts attest, the situation is different with government: poor performance and corruption are no barrier to obtaining government work for the large government contractor!) If modifications to the project are requested, the requests are sealed with a handshake, and the funder recognizes that the contractor should not be expected to eat the additional costs incurred by the modification.

When asked *their* opinion about contractor performance on projects, *government* project officers held a different view. For the most part, they agreed that the government contracting procedure is cumbersome and difficult to deal with. However, they pointed out that there is ample evidence to show that many contractors take advantage of the government whenever they can, and plenty of major scandals attest to this fact. They also suggested that because government is so large, strong budget control procedures must be implemented on projects. For example, in order to avoid requests for costly changes on projects by overly enthusiastic government clients, only contract officers are authorized to approve change orders. Without such tight control, there would be few constraints keeping government customers in line.

In general, government-funded contracted projects are more difficult to manage than corresponding private sector projects. This is primarily a consequence of the fact that large pieces of the project management process are governed not by good sense but by rules and regulations that, in the context of a given project, may be arbitrary and unwise. An important key to minimizing problems in government projects is knowledge of the legal and administrative aspects of the contracting procedure. This is important for both the contractor and the government funder. To the extent that each side knows what is allowable under certain circumstances, many of the problems rampant in government-contracted projects can be dramatically reduced.

## PLANNING AND CONTROL WITH BUREAUCRATIC MILESTONES

Project management instructional material typically focuses on schedule optimization or resource optimization. Yet in many bureaucratic organizations, successful planning has less to do with schedule or resource optimization than with identifying key bureaucratic milestones of importance to the organization, and sequencing tasks in such a way that the milestones are achieved.

These milestones are often tied to the organization's budget cycle. For example, all project managers desiring funding in the fiscal year 2009 budget may be required to have preliminary budget requests filed by December 2006. Frequently, these milestones are unforgiving: if you miss, say, the December 2006 filing date, your project may not get funded in fiscal 2009. Given this bureaucratic reality found in many organizations, it would seem a wise policy for project staff to plan their projects around such milestones.

Technical people often pay little attention to bureaucratic milestones. They resent having their work governed by arbitrary requirements that have no logical bearing on their projects. Typically, they ignore the milestones or put off meeting the requirements of the milestones until the last possible moment. While the resentment of arbitrary milestones is understandable, resisting or ignoring them is often dangerous. By the same token, as we saw in Chapter One, project staff who become masters of bureaucratic intricacies can use their skills to develop bureaucratic authority that will help them negotiate their projects through the inscrutable maze of the bureaucracy.

Figure 7.5 pictures a planning and control tool developed a few years ago by U.S. Navy project managers who looked around their organization and saw projects failing right and left. They analyzed these failures and

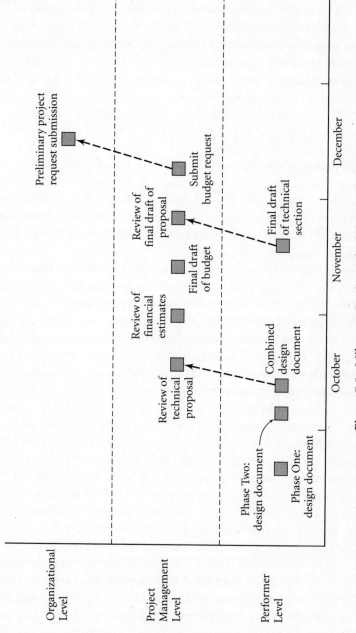

Figure 7.5. **Milestone Review Scheduling Technique.**

determined that the number one cause of failure was inattention to arbitrary, organizationally imposed milestone requirements. Project managers did not have budget requests, or progress reports, or test data submitted at bureaucratically crucial times; as a consequence, they often lost their funding.

The planning and control tool that they developed, the milestone review scheduling technique, consists of three tiers: organizational, project management, and performer. The top tier notes the crucial organizationally imposed milestones. To keep Figure 7.5 simple, only one milestone is portrayed: a requirement to submit a preliminary project budget request in December. In practice, there would be many milestones noted at this level.

The next level down represents the special requirements that project managers must concentrate on in order to address the organizationally imposed milestones. For example, as Figure 7.5 shows, management must review the technical and financial elements of the project that will be incorporated into the final draft of the budget request.

The bottom level represents milestones that project workers must achieve if the December budget request deadline is to be met. Much of the project manager's energy is devoted to making sure that project workers take these bottom-tier milestones seriously.

The construction of this planning chart starts from the top down. The first order of business is to fill the top tier with the nonnegotiable "drop dead" requirements of the organization. Once the relevant organizational milestones have been noted for this tier, the middle-tier milestones (project management level) are established. These milestones are created with a view to meeting the top-tier milestones. Finally, the bottom-tier milestones are determined. These milestones are sequenced in such a way as to enable project management to achieve its middle-tier milestones. Thus, if the milestone "Review of technical proposal" (at the project management level) is to be achieved by mid-October as planned, project workers will have to produce a Phase One design document, a Phase Two design document, and a combined design document on the appointed dates.

The bottom-tier milestones should be established after consultation with project workers. Otherwise, there is a danger that the project managers are imposing unrealistic, unattainable milestones. Furthermore, when project workers are involved in setting milestones, they are encouraged to buy into the project plan and to make a personal commitment to carrying it out as effectively as possible.

# ESTABLISHING AND RUNNING A PROJECT SUPPORT OFFICE

The 1990s witnessed an explosive growth in private sector interest in project management. Historically, it was seen as lying in the bailiwick of the government sector or the construction industry. However, as organizations began abandoning traditional functional business structures and sought more flexible ways of doing business, they started to adopt project management as an important way of doing their jobs. Suddenly, project management became important in nontraditional areas, such as telecommunications, pharmaceuticals, finance, training, and information technology. Everything was becoming "projectized."

The rapid introduction of this new way of doing business created organizational challenges. Even as senior managers were issuing directives for their departments to adopt project management methodologies, it was clear that a lack of experience was hampering attempts to establish project management in the enterprises. Few employees had any knowledge of project management perspectives, tools, and techniques. No project management standards existed (such as scheduling standards, change control standards, or software standards). Project management training curricula were nonexistent. Furthermore, project management was not yet a career track in the company and project management job descriptions often had not been written, so employees were wondering whether they wanted to commit emotional and intellectual energy to jumping on a project management bandwagon that might not be going anywhere.

This environment led to a situation where companies spontaneously set up a small office of one or two people who were designated the project management gurus for the enterprise. Their charter was to figure out how to introduce project management good practices into the company. Meanwhile, they were expected to serve as in-house consultants addressing the needs of senior managers desiring pointers on what project management can do, as well as addressing the needs of project teams requiring guidance on how to conduct a kickoff meeting, and the needs of project planners who were clueless about how to plan a project effort from the perspective of schedules, resource allocations, budgets, and specifications.

In many organizations, demand for the services of these internal project management consultants outstripped their availability. To meet the demand, many enterprises established formal project support offices that would "own" project management. Ultimately, these offices provided a number of services that have since become standard offerings:

• *They establish project management standards and procedures.* For project management to be implemented effectively in organizations, it is important that standard processes for handling projects be developed and followed. For example, all projects should adopt the same change control procedures. To establish standard change control procedures, project office personnel can begin by designing a change request form to be used throughout the organization. They would then develop a process for reviewing change requests that should be followed by anyone desiring a change. They would also establish procedures for dealing with change requests that are accepted and those that are rejected. And so on.

• *They offer project management consulting within the enterprise.* Few people know how to plan effectively. They may be excellent in designing software, or computing tax obligations, or laying brick, but they do not know how to lay out budgets, schedules, and resource requirements. Competent project support office professionals are expert planners. They know how to write a proposal. They know what steps to take to develop a schedule. They are familiar with project management software. They can develop both top-down and bottom-up cost estimates. They understand the pitfalls of defining requirements and can avoid them.

Because they possess important planning and implementation skills, project support office professionals can help their less knowledgeable colleagues function more effectively on their projects. By serving an internal consulting role, they provide valuable insights and skills. Beyond this, they teach project management skills to colleagues during the normal course of their consulting activities, helping to disseminate project management knowledge and skills throughout the organization.

• *They provide project management mentoring to senior managers.* For projects to be successful, it is helpful for them to receive strong support from senior managers. The larger and more visible a project is, the more this is true. For senior managers to be supportive in a productive way, it is important that they have an understanding of what project management is and what it can do. Yet it is unrealistic to think that they will sit in the classroom with corporate employees to study project management fundamentals in three day long courses.

One way for senior managers to get up to speed on project management is to assign project mentors to them. These mentors, coming from the project support office, can sit alongside the senior managers for several days, helping them to understand the connections between the business's activities and how project management bears on them. Through a process like this, senior managers can quickly gain valuable insights into project management in an efficient and palatable manner.

•   *They arrange for project management training.* There is more to the practice of project management than good sense. Over the years, a set of tools, perspectives, and methodologies has emerged that allow individuals in organizations to implement their projects more effectively. Employees assigned to carry out projects cannot simply intuit the good practice procedures they should employ. They need to learn them, and an effective way of doing this is through training.

Project support office employees can play an important role in defining the project management training curriculum for their organizations. What topics should be covered? In what sequence should courses be taken? Should the courses be organized into a cluster that, when completed, entitles employees to receive an executive certificate? They can also play the lead role in identifying providers of the training. Some instructors may come from within the organization. Others may be outsiders employed by training companies. In short, project support office personnel can play the lead role in defining the organization's training needs.

•   *They support project management professional development.* With the growing importance of project management, companies have begun developing career tracks for project professionals. For example, a number of companies have created cadres of what are called *black belts* or *top gun* project managers: men and women who have undergone extensive training in project management and have several years experience of running significant projects. They will be given assignments to run the enterprise's most significant projects.

To keep these people focused and motivated, project office employees need to develop career paths that encourage them to continue pursuing advanced work in the project management arena. For example, black belts may be offered support to prepare for and take the Project Management Institute project management certification examination. They may have their memberships paid at professional societies. They may be asked to attend courses that deal with advanced management issues—not just project management courses but others as well, including conflict resolution, team-building, and financial management courses.

Project support office personnel should also work with new employees who stand at the other end of the experience spectrum. They need to counsel them on steps they should take to strengthen their project management capabilities. They should serve as mentors and sounding boards, being accessible to inexperienced employees and addressing their concerns.

## VIRTUAL TEAMS

Today's technology makes it possible to have a project manager who is operating out of headquarters in Montreal, running a project whose design team is located in Vancouver, whose manufacturing expert is in Singapore, and whose sales team resides in New York City. Running a project in such a virtual fashion, reasonably rare at the outset of the 1990s, is commonplace today. What enables it to be commonplace is the availability and employment of low-cost telecommunication and computer technologies, including two-way telephone communication, teleconferencing, videoconferencing, facsimile transmissions, e-mail, access to informative Web sites, real-time on-line written dialogues in chatrooms, and asynchronous threaded discussions on discussion boards. Add to this the capacity to ship physical objects around the world overnight using services such as DHL, FedEx, and UPS, and it is clear that geography no longer presents a serious impediment to keeping scattered team members engaged in project activities, regardless of where they reside.

### Managing Virtual Teams

We have reached the point where in managing virtual teams, managers no longer need to be concerned about technological issues. The technology is here. It is cheap and universally employed. Their chief concerns address the soft side of managing virtual teams, and the challenges in this arena can be daunting. They include mundane matters, such as how to schedule a teleconference call when the attendees are scattered over twelve time zones. Somebody has got to get up at 4:00 A.M. local time. Who will it be?

They extend to much trickier issues, such as: How do you engage in team building among a group of people who have not seen each other and who, during the course of a typical workday, are distracted by many events that have no bearing on their project effort?

All managers need guidance on managing virtual teams, because they have become ubiquitous. While much of the discussion of virtual teams focuses on teams with members scattered across the country or globe, we should recognize that we even encounter them where team members work in the same building complex. A few years ago, I was engaged in work with a major American manufacturing company located in the Midwest, where winters are fearsome. One project I was monitoring was carried out by a team scattered among three buildings on a campus. Many of the meetings they held were teleconferences, because no one wanted to cross the campus quadrangle during subzero days to attend a physical meeting with colleagues.

## Team Building on Virtual Teams

The team-building challenge is obvious. On many virtual teams, team members have had little or no prior contact with each other. We have been told that team formation typically goes through a number of stages, poetically denoted as forming, storming, norming, and performing (Tuckman, 1965). This model presumes that team members physically interact with each other. When we conjure up an image of the players storming, we see them in a meeting room surrounded by white boards and sticky notes, with different groups vociferously arguing their points. On virtual teams, things don't play out this way. In the earliest stages of a virtual team project, colleagues may be viewed as nothing more than disembodied voices heard during teleconference sessions and senders of e-mail messages and documents.

Such circumstances do not lend themselves to promoting a sense of "teamness" that we encounter when dealing with traditional teams of men and women interacting with each other physically as a project is being executed. Achieving teamness is important so that we can get team members working together seamlessly to accomplish project goals. In *The Wisdom of Teams* (1993), Katzenbach and Smith remind us that teams are more than assemblages of people. With real teams, the team members must agree on mutually determined performance objectives and then set out to achieve them. They must develop a commitment to serving and supporting each other for the good of the team. This means that individual desires may have to be subordinated to the group's requirements. D'Artagnan and his musketeer compatriots got it right when they said: "All for one and one for all."

Creating team spirit is tough enough when the team members see each other regularly and work near each other. Creating it when the team is virtual is far tougher. However, it is not impossible, and as we gain more experience in working on virtual teams, we are getting better at learning how to build teams under new circumstances. Following are some steps often taken by team leaders who manage virtual teams effectively:

• *Attempt to get key team members together in a physical meeting, if possible.* SITA is the Paris-based telecommunications arm of the airlines industry. It operates in some 220 countries and territories and has projects being implemented in all corners of the globe. I have met with some of the company's top project managers, most of them based in Europe. They tell me that when a significant new project is launched, say, in a nation in the South Pacific, they immediately contact by telephone key players in the target country and introduce themselves. When possible, they arrange for a face-to-face meeting with the key players and take a flight to the local site. If appropriate, other team members attend the meeting also. For example, if the project entails heavy use of equipment, they may invite a pertinent player from SITA's manufacturing facility in Singapore to attend. Although holding these meetings is burdensome, these project managers assure me that they pay rich dividends in the long run. The important point, they say, is that through these meetings, they establish a personal relationship with team members whose cooperation they will need. When problems arise, and Murphy's Law assures us that they will, they find these team members are much more responsive to their requests than team members whom they have never met.

Of course, perhaps it is not possible or practical to have face-to-face encounters with team members. In this event, project manager should still do everything possible to make their relationships with team players "personal." This can be done by establishing cordial relations with them over the telephone, learning something about their personal interests and aspirations, and maintaining frequent telephone contact with them.

• *Make the virtual team as physical as possible.* Effective managers of virtual teams often ask team members to provide biographical information to the team as a whole. What work do they do? How long have they been with the company? What life did they have before joining the company? What are their nonwork interests and hobbies? What facts can they share about their family life? They may also have team members submit electronic pictures of themselves in order to make them more real to their colleagues.

As team members become less abstract and more real, there is a tendency of team colleagues to take more interest in them as working partners. This may contribute to creating an environment where team members walk the extra mile to help each other out. It is easier to feel loyalty to someone real than to an abstraction.

In personalizing team members, team leaders should be sensitive to the fact that they can go too far. Although most team members will cheerfully contribute bios and photos, some may be reticent to do so, viewing the exercise as an unwanted intrusion into their personal lives. If the team leader encounters such people, the smart policy is to back off and let these people maintain their sense of privacy.

• *Create a project Web site as a substitute for a project work space.* With traditional projects, team members were often colocated in a common work space. When they were not colocated, project war rooms would often be set up in order to provide the team with a physical space. Project documentation would be kept here. The walls might contain charts showing schedule progress. When team members assembled for a meeting, they would often gather in the war room.

A well-configured project Web site makes a good substitute for the war room. The Web site should be continually updated, so team members can learn the latest developments on their project no matter what time it is or where they are physically located. It should contain an electronic message board, allowing team members to communicate with each other asynchronously. It should also provide all the information that team members need, including important milestone dates, meeting dates, and information on rules and regulations that affect the project.

• *Create well-defined procedures.* People leading virtual teams have a special burden to make sure they are well organized when handling team affairs. In a face-to-face world, sloppy leaders can get away with a measure of disorganization. For example, if you suddenly decide to hold a meeting, you can walk down the hallway, drop by the offices of the team members, and tell them to assemble in the conference room in ten minutes. If at that meeting you do not have an agenda, the group can agree on an agenda on the spot. Team procedures are loose, but so what?

Virtual teams are unforgiving in this regard. Teleconference meetings must be scheduled and set up in advance. Everyone must be provided the telephone number for the conference site and possibly be given a conference access code number. They must call in to the teleconference site at the right time. It is especially important that the agenda for these meetings be well defined and distributed to participants before the meeting is held.

Well-defined procedures are, in a sense, the glue that holds the team together. If team processes are not developed, communicated to team members, and adhered to, the virtual team soon falls apart.

## CONCLUSION

This chapter has addressed a number of planning and control issues that many project managers face but that are not as widely discussed: earned-value management, managing project portfolios, working with contracted efforts, scheduling with bureaucratic milestones, organizing a project support office, and managing virtual teams.

I hope that the emphasis on tools in this chapter and the previous one does not obscure the important lesson that successful planning and control is more a function of attitude and commitment than the routine application of tools. A project whose team spends a good deal of time developing a thoughtful qualitative plan that team members agree is viable has a higher likelihood of success than a project where plans are developed by one or two people working alone with a sophisticated, computer-driven PDM network. Similarly, an attitude reflecting the view, "I've got to keep on top of project developments!" is far more important for project control than the routine generation of monthly progress reports.

Of course, it should not be an either-or proposition. The combination of strong commitment and good tools is the best possible situation, reducing dramatically the likelihood of all-too-frequent project failure caused by planning and control deficiencies.

# CHAPTER EIGHT

# Achieving Results

## Principles for Success as a Project Manager

—〰—

One common problem project professionals face is getting so caught up in the helter-skelter of putting out fires and focusing on minutiae that they lose the big-picture perspective. When things are popping all around them, it is difficult for them to step back and view their projects from a distance.

In this last chapter, we do precisely that: stand back and take a big-picture view of the project management process as it pertains to information age projects. What are the elements of good project management—the most rudimentary principles—that we should keep in mind to maximize the likelihood that we will bring our project to a successful conclusion?

## RUDIMENTARY PRINCIPLES

There are five basic principles that, if followed, will help project professionals immeasurably in their efforts:

1. *Be conscious of what you are doing; don't be an accidental manager.* Project management, as we have seen, has been called the accidental profession. Men and women stumble into project management

responsibilities accidentally, only vaguely aware of what projects are and how they should be managed. Their management approach is pure trial and error. They reinvent the wheel, and in most cases do a bad job of it.

The pity is that much of the grief they encounter and much of the waste they engender could be avoided if they made an effort to learn something about the theory and practice of project management. For example, if they learned that project staff are usually borrowed workers over whom they seldom have any direct control, they could direct their energies toward *influencing* these workers to do well rather than spend time sulking in a corner because of what they perceive as the insubordination and lack of commitment of these people.

In order to maintain consciousness of the fact that they are working on something over which they have the power to do a good job— *if only they knew what they were doing*—perhaps project professionals should say to themselves several times a day, "I am a project professional. I work on projects. Projects are undertakings that are goal oriented, complex, finite, and unique. They pass through a life cycle, which begins with project selection and ends with project termination." The purpose of this ritualistic litany is simply to remind the project professional that over the past several decades, many people have thought a lot about what projects are and what their management entails. Projects are hard to manage even when we know what we are doing. They are nearly impossible to manage by accident and happenstance.

2. *Invest heavily in the front-end spadework; get it right the first time.* Many of us have a tendency to rush in where angels fear to tread. We tend to leap before we look. We are results oriented and often overlook some rudimentary matters regarding the basic steps it takes to achieve these results. This characteristic serves some people well: by throwing caution to the wind, they achieve breakthroughs that more cautious people would never accomplish. Such people are trailblazers—bold, dynamic, and filled with exuberant energy.

This tendency to leap before we look also has its drawbacks. Where, for example, does one draw the line separating boldness from impetuosity? Fearlessness from foolishness? In many situations, a moment's reflection on what action to pursue is more important than boldness. For the most part, projects can use more forethought and less impetuosity.

By definition, projects are unique, goal-oriented systems; consequently, they are complex and cannot be managed effectively in an off-hand, ad hoc fashion. They must be carefully selected and carefully planned. A good deal of thought must be directed at determining how they should be structured. Great amounts of time must be spent hand holding with customers (internal or external) to ensure that the final deliverable is something they find useful.

Care taken at the outset of a project to do things right will generally pay for itself handsomely. Doing things right takes time and effort. For example, it takes time to find out what the real needs are on a project, specify requirements carefully, and plan out a course of action for accomplishing project objectives. For impetuous people, it is far more satisfying to rush into projects and begin solving problems than to identify precisely what those problems are.

Unfortunately, if the proper spadework is not done at the outset of a project, it is likely that various project tasks will not be done properly; those tasks will have to be redone again and again until project staff finally get them right. Rework is expensive. It is invariably more expensive to rework something than to take the time to do it right at the outset.

3. *Anticipate the problems that will inevitably arise.* This book has stressed repeatedly that many of the problems that project professionals face are predictable. For example, if project professionals are working in a matrix organization, we know that they will face the following people problems:

— anticipate problems

- They will have little or no direct control over the borrowed staff members.
- Their staff will have little commitment to the project.
- Their staff are not likely to be precisely the workers they want or need.

We can also count on the following additional realities:

- The goals of portfolio managers are often different from those of individual project managers, since maximization of portfolio performance will likely require suboptimization of the performance of individual projects.

- Schedule and budget variances will occur, since it is impossible to predict the future precisely. We should not ask, "Do we have variances?" but rather, "Are the variances we face acceptable?"
- Customer needs will shift.
- If project requirements are stated vaguely, they are likely to be misinterpreted. (They may also be misinterpreted even when they are stated precisely.)
- Overplanning and overcontrol will lead to project inefficiencies and may result in cost and schedule overruns, just as with underplanning and weak control.
- All projects have hidden agendas, which are usually more important than the stated agenda.

By reviewing these inevitable realities (and this is only a small sampling from a much larger list), we see that conflict and problems are built into projects and will arise. If we anticipate these problems, however, we can determine in advance how to cope with them. As we become more experienced project managers, we can even learn how to use them to our advantage.

4. *Go beneath surface illusions; dig deeply to find the real situation.* Project managers are continually getting into trouble because they accept things at face value. For example, customers usually have only the vaguest conception of what their needs are, even when they think they know exactly what they want. The project manager who blindly accepts a customer's needs statement is likely to encounter customer requests later for major changes in the project, or perhaps that manager will produce a deliverable that the customer rejects, saying, "This is neither what we asked for nor what we want."

As another example, a project manager, assuming that secretaries are *the* customer of a project to install a new document management system in the office, fails to determine the needs of such hidden customers as the secretaries' bosses, the office's clients, and the division's information resource manager. Consequently, while secretaries' needs are met, the needs of the other significant actors may be unsatisfied, possibly resulting in project failure.

To the extent that project professionals do not understand what is really happening on their projects, they are likely to be chasing after shadows. They will not make the right decisions.

Robert Block's approach to project politics, described in *The Politics of Projects* (1983), can greatly help project managers to be more realistic. Using his approach, they systematically go through a number of steps designed to let them penetrate surface illusions and identify what is really happening. First, they identify all the players, paying special attention to those who can have an impact on the project outcome. Then they try to determine the goals of the players and the organization, focusing particularly on hidden goals. Having done this, they assess their own strengths and weaknesses. It is only at this point that they should begin defining the problems facing them in their project.

It is crucial to the problem definition step that project managers root their efforts in reality—isolating the facts, identifying the real situation, and recognizing the assumptions underlying the whole project effort. Once the problem is defined adequately, they can develop solutions, test them, and fine-tune them. (See Chapter One for a more complete discussion of Block's approach.)

5. *Be as flexible as possible; don't get sucked into unnecessary rigidity and formality.* Project management can be viewed as a struggle to contend with the basic principle of the second law of thermodynamics, which states that things tend to dissolve into a state of random disorder. With project management, we try to reverse this sequence, creating order where the natural state seems to be chaos.

In our drive to create order, however, we run the risk of sacrificing reasonable flexibility on the altar of formal project requirements. The rationale for inflexibility is that order comes from structure: we convince ourselves that the more formal the structure is that we impose on projects, the less chaos we face. Thus, we may require all project changes to be approved by three levels of management, and we may require staff to fill out six-page progress reports every week. We may also put together very detailed plans for the project, so that nothing is left to chance. We may hold daily staff meetings to make sure that workers know what they are supposed to do. And so on. In this attempt to realize order, we may instead achieve stifling bureaucracy.

One of the hardest tasks facing policymakers in project organizations is striking a balance between the need for order and the contrary need for flexibility. Why is flexibility necessary? Because projects are full of surprises, and overly rigid systems cannot respond adequately to surprises, just as a rigid stick will snap after it has been bent only a little. This is especially true with information age projects, which deal with intangibles and tend to be amorphous. By their very nature, they are hard to plan in detail and defy attempts at tight controls.

Too often people do not understand that order can be attained without excessive formality. If we are conscious of what we are doing on projects and avoid being accidental project managers, invest in front-end spadework, anticipate inevitable problems, and penetrate beneath surface illusions, we will help establish order in our projects. If, in addition, we reject unnecessary formality and rigidity, we may be able to have our cake and eat it too—that is, we may be able to achieve order and flexibility simultaneously.

Strong degrees of formality are appropriate on some projects. For example, as projects get larger, the number of communication channels that must be maintained grows explosively, and formal protocols must be established to coordinate communication efforts. As a consequence, it is common in programs with budgets greater than $100 million to find from 50 to 65 percent of the total project budget dedicated to project administration.

Heavy formality may also be appropriate on low-risk projects when we know precisely what must be done to produce the desired deliverable. When we build a house in a development of nearly identical houses, for example, we specify in detail many formal requirements that project staff should meet; we leave nothing to chance. Such low-risk projects have a minimal need for flexibility, since they encounter fewer surprises than high-risk projects.

Information age projects typically do not fall into either of these two categories. First, because they deal with information rather than with bricks and mortar, they do not usually achieve the size of projects to construct buildings or build fighter aircraft. Second, because they deal with intangibles and are hard to get a handle on, they tend to be filled with uncertainty. Given the smaller size of typical information age projects and their high degree of uncertainty, the need for rigid formality in their management is generally low; therefore, in most such cases, heavy formality is undesirable. Nevertheless, this call for flexibility on information age projects should not be used as an excuse for poor planning and control.

## THE LAST WORD

As I stated in the Introduction, I envision this book as a travel guide. In part, it is a road map, showing readers the twists and turns, obstacles, and potholes they are likely to encounter on their journey into the realm of project management. In part, it is a repair guide, focusing primarily on preventive maintenance—avoiding breakdowns—but also offering instructions on fixing minor problems.

I suppose that my travel guide is a bit more cautionary in tone than the typical travel guide written for travelers to, say, the Greek isles or Scotland. In these typical travel guides, the writers usually engage in extravagant hyperbole, extolling the beauties of the countryside and offering fascinating historical detail that makes readers wish fervently that they had lived in the region during its heyday. My travel guide is more like a guide to some of the more trouble-plagued spots on the globe. Whereas the guide to Scotland may spend most of its time addressing the best restaurants to visit, the variety of local flora and fauna, historical tidbits, and the like, the guide to the trouble spot focuses on avoidance of land mines, how to make and apply a tourniquet, and the fifty-seven different ways to camouflage oneself against helicopter attack in rocky terrain.

I believe that the project management environment is more akin to the environment of the trouble spot than of Scotland. Wandering through project management terrain can be dangerous to the naive. In the land of project management, things can and will go awry.

It is also true that being a project manager can be an enormously rewarding experience. For many individuals, managing projects is their first foray into management. It allows them to develop the management skills they need for career advancement. In addition, it offers them an independence of action and a degree of responsibility they infrequently encounter in other areas. For people who thrive on challenges, like to solve problems creatively, and enjoy creating order out of chaos, the management of projects can be exhilarating.

# —⁓— References

Block, R. *The Politics of Projects*. Englewood Cliffs, N.J.: Yourdon Press, 1983.

Brooks, F. P. *The Mythical Man-Month: Essays in Software Engineering*. (2nd ed.) Reading, Mass.: Addison-Wesley, 1995.

Frame, J. D. *The New Project Management*. (2nd ed.) San Francisco: Jossey-Bass, 2002.

Hamel, G., and Pralahad, C. K. *Competing for the Future*. Boston: Harvard Business School Press, 1994.

Hammer, M., and Champy, J. *Reengineering the Corporation*. New York: HarperCollins, 1993.

Jung, C. *Psychological Types*. New York: Harcourt, 1923.

Katzenbach, J. R., and Smith, D. K. *The Wisdom of Teams: Creating the High-Performance Organization*. Boston: Harvard Business School Press, 1993.

Keirsey, D. *Please Understand Me II*. Del Mar, Calif.: Prometheus Nemesis, 1998.

Kidder, T. *The Soul of a New Machine*. New York: Little, Brown, 1981.

Morita, A. *Made in Japan: Akio Morita and Sony*. New York: Dutton, 1986.

Nadler, D. A., and others. *Organizational Architecture: Designs for Changing Organizations*. San Francisco: Jossey-Bass, 1992.

Project Management Institute. *A Guide to the Project Management Body of Knowledge*. Upper Darby, Pa.: PMI Publications, 1996.

Project Management Institute. *A Guide to the Project Management Body of Knowledge*. Newtown Square, Pa.: PMI Publications, 2000.

Project Management Institute. *PMI Practice Standard for Work Breakdown Structures*. Newtown Square, Pa.: PMI Publications, 2001.

Senge, P. M. *The Fifth Discipline: The Art and Practice of the Learning Organization*. New York: Doubleday, 1990.

Tuckman, B. W. "Development Sequence in Small Groups. *Psychological Bulletin*, 1965, *63*, 284–399.

U.S. Bureau of the Census. *Statistical Abstract of the United States: The National Data Book.* (120th ed.) Washington, D.C.: U.S. Bureau of the Census, 2001.

U.S. Department of Defense. *Department of Defense Handbook: Work Breakdown Structure.* Washington, D.C.: Department of Defense, 1998.

Weinberg, G. A. *The Psychology of Computer Programming.* New York: Van Nostrand Reinhold, 1971.

# ⟿ Index

Earned-value management, 213–218; applied to small projects, 217; calculating variances in, 214–215; components of, 214; 50–50 rule in, 216–217; 10–90 rule in, 217; terminology reform in, 217–218; 0–100 rule in, 217

Educating: customers, 144–145, 156–157; project staff, 156–157

Efficiency, project teams, 82–87

Egoless team structure, 90–93, 96

Elapsed time, PDM networks, 184–185

End-of-project evaluation, 13

Environment: business, and changing needs, 121; external to organization, 37, 42–44; full project, 36–44; politicians' assessment of, 45–46; within organization, 37, 38–42. *See also* Organizational context

Evaluation, 12–14; control vs., 12; end-of-project, 13; midproject, 12–13

Execution. *See* Implementation

**F**

Failure. *See* Project failure

Fast tracking, to control schedule, 205

Father-knows-best syndrome, needs articulation, 134–135

Feasibility studies, as preplans, 10

*The Fifth Discipline* (Senge), 5

50–50 Rule, earned-value management, 216–217

FIRO-B Awareness Scale, 61

Fixed-price contracts, 225–227

Flexibility: excessive, in specifications, 152–153; imprecise requirements for, 142; on large projects, 212; of project managers, 245–246

Flights of fancy, as requirement-related problem, 147–148, 149

Float time, in PDM networks, 180, 181–183

Forecasting, and needs recognition, 115

Formal authority, 33

Fringe benefits, in budgets, 188

Functional requirements, 118, 119, 138, 139. *See also* Requirements

**G**

Game playing, 76–78

Gantt charts: graphical review of, 200, 201, 202, 203; resource, 7, 193, 195–196; for scheduling, 177–178

Gap analysis, of project portfolio budgets, 221–224

GERT (Graphical Evaluation and Review Technique), 6

Goals: identification of, by politicians, 46–47; projects' orientation to, 3–4; setting realistic, 59–60

Gold-plating of needs, 133–134

Government: contracted projects funded by, 224, 228–230; as element of full project environment, 42–43; planning and control for bureaucratic milestones in, 230–232

Graphical control of projects, 6, 199–201, 202–203

**H**

Hammer, M., 114

Harvard Project Manager, 207, 208

Hierarchical structure: and customer satisfaction, 52–53; working within, 31–32

Human resources. *See* Resources

Hybrid work breakdown structures (WBSs), 176–177

**I**

Implementation of projects, as step in project life cycle, 10–11

Imprecise specifications, 141–145

Information age projects. *See* Information-based projects

Information-based projects: increasing number of, 15–16; as inherently nebulous, 143–144; rapid prototyping with, 144, 157–159; team structure for, 96–102; top-down management inappropriate for, 53; uncertainty in, 167; 0–100 rule in management of, 217

Insurmountable obstacles, as requirement-related problem, 147

Integration: with isomorphic team

Responsibility, given project managers,
    18–19, 29
Responsibility matrixes, 193, 194
Reward systems, for project teams,
    104–105
Rolling wave approach to planning, 166

**S**

Schedules: computer-assisted, 6–7;
    Gantt charts for, 177–178; methods
    of dealing with slippages in,
    204–205; as planning and control
    tools, 165, 172–187; playing games
    with, 77, 78; precedence diagram
    method (PDM) networks for,
    178–186; for projects in project
    portfolio, 221–222; variances in, in
    earned-value management, 215;
    work breakdown structures (WBSs)
    for, 172–177
Scope creep, 205–206
S-curves, 192
Seizing opportunities, as requirement-
    related problem, 148–149
Selection of projects, as step in project
    life cycle, 9–10
Senge, P., 5
SITA, 238
Size of project: and amount of planning
    and control, 170–171. *See also* Large
    projects; Small projects
Slack time, in PDM networks, 180,
    181–183
Small projects: earned-value manage-
    ment applied to, 217; large projects
    vs., 210–211; in project portfolios, 220
Smith, D. K., 237
Software: for computer-assisted sched-
    uling, 6–7; project management,
    207–209. *See also* Information-
    based projects
Software Handlers Inc. (fictitious
    name) (case study), 67–68
Solutions: premature identification of,
    123–124; steps for developing,
    45–49; testing and refining, 48
*The Soul of a New Machine* (Kidder), 78
Specialty team structure, 89–90, 96

Specifications: as constraint on project
    management, 7; detailed vs. flexible,
    150–153; guidelines for, 153–157;
    imprecise and ambiguous, reasons
    for, 141–145; inadequate, contribut-
    ing to project failure, 19–20,
    137–138; rapid prototyping ap-
    proach to, 144, 157–159. *See also*
    Requirements
Sponsors. *See* Project sponsors
Spreadsheets, resource, 196, 197
Staff: borrowed, 30, 31; changing, and
    changing needs, 121; characteristics
    of ideal member of, 56–58; commit-
    ment of, to project, 56, 57–58; devel-
    oping, 69–70; educating, 156–157;
    as element of full project environ-
    ment, 40–41; importance of good,
    51–52; improving relations with, 68;
    matrix management of, 40–41, 57,
    83, 89–90, 96; project managers as
    intermediaries between manage-
    ment and, 70; responsibilities of
    project managers toward, 69–70;
    selecting, 66–67; technical compe-
    tence of, 60–61; tips for improving
    quality of work by, 58–61
Stalin, J., 34
Status review meetings, project teams,
    103
Subcontractors, as element of full proj-
    ect environment, 42–43
Subject matter experts (SMEs), on in-
    formation-based project teams, 101
Suppliers, as element of full project en-
    vironment, 43–44
Surgical team structure, 93–95
Systems, projects as, 5, 30–31
Systems integration: with isomorphic
    team structure, 88–89, 96; poor, as
    source of team inefficiency, 86–87;
    and surgical team structure, 95

**T**

T-P (Task-People) Leadership Ques-
    tionnaire, 61
Task work breakdown structures
    (WBSs), 172–175